Praise For Rob

"I think I have just found myself a new crime thriller author and series that will be going straight on my "must read authors list"." **Lorraine Rugman – The Book Review Cafe**

* * *

"I really enjoyed this terrifying, clever thriller that is probably one of the best crime/ police thrillers that I have read." **Joanna Park – Over The Rainbow Book Blog**

* * *

"This is a very gripping psychological thriller that has the reader turning page after page." **Jill Burkinshaw – Books n All**

* * *

"Those That Remain is a blood curdling, terrifying rollercoaster ride that is just too damn good, I don't think any review I write would give it enough justice!!!" **Laura Turner – PageTurnersNook**

* * *

"The writing has such a natural style so you aren't thinking about what may happen in the story you just savour every moment as you read it." **Susan Hampson – Books From Dusk Till Dawn**

* * *

"In Your Name is full of non-stop twist and turns that I dare anyone to predict." **M.A. Comley – NY Times best-selling author**

* * *

"It is extremely gripping to witness the events in this spellbinding thriller with its occasional glint of dark humour – and I'm dying to get my hands on the next instalment!" **Caroline Vincent – Bits About Books**

* * *

"This is a brilliant follow on from the first book Those That Remain. I loved it!" **Gemma Myers – Between The Pages Book Club**

* * *

"This is storytelling that will stay with you...Chilled me to the core..Moran is one of the best characters ever...Love love loved this series..Brilliant.." **Livia Sbarbo – Goodreads**

* * *

"OMG. What a read. Absolutely fantastic with brilliant characters." **Susan Angela Wallace – Goodreads**

* * *

"For me the three Mechanic books have been some of the best that I have read so far in 2017 and I cannot recommend them highly enough!" **Donna Maguire – Donnas Book Blog**

* * *

"This has been an amazing trilogy and I am sad to see the end of it." **Dee Williams – Goodreads**

Also By Rob Ashman

Those That Remain (Book 1)

In Your Name (Book 2)

Pay The Penance (Book 3)

For Karen, who gave me the courage to write this book when the demons in my head told me to play it safe.

Preface

'Being psycho doesn't make you bad, being bad makes you bad. Being psycho and bad makes you dangerous. That's what my school report should have said but it didn't, and now the consequences of that oversight are everywhere.

'I killed for pleasure, now I kill out of a sense of duty. You understand that, right? Not sure which one I prefer more.

'No wait … I do know … killing family is best. You get to stick around and watch the fallout.

'This is not my fault.

'As the next few weeks play out, I want you to remember, it's not my fault.

'It's yours.'

Chapter 1

Detective Inspector Rosalind Kray lifted the flap of the letterbox and the stench of death hit her full in the face. The type of stench that lodges itself in your memory long after it has left your senses. The type of stench that lives with you forever.

She recoiled back into the cramped corridor and nodded to the young uniformed officer standing next to her. He removed his hat, donned a pair of heavy duty gloves and picked up the red thirty-five-pound steel bar with handles at either end. He steadied his stance and took a practice swing. The bar crunched into the moulded plastic surround of the lock. The frame flexed under the impact, holding the door stubbornly in place. The second blow shattered the screws from their mountings and the door shuddered open.

It struck the mound of unopened mail piled up on the hallway floor. As the door swung ajar they both stepped back with their hands covering their noses and mouths. Kray was sure she heard the officer gag as the smell of putrid flesh wafted around them. She glanced at the tall young man, the colour draining from his face. *That's all I need - a degree-qualified high flyer to compromise the scene with his own vomit.*

Kray pulled on a set of blue surgical gloves, threw a second pair for the officer and removed a perfumed handkerchief from her pocket. She stepped inside. The underside of the front door swept the larger letters into a heap against the wall as she edged it open.

'Hello!' she called out. 'Any one at home?'

Her voice echoed in the confines of the darkness. She tried the light switch – nothing.

Kray flicked on a torch and the beam cut shards of light across the inside of the flat. Her rubber-soled shoes squeaked against the laminate flooring as she made her way down the hallway. It was long and narrow with a door at the far end, the light from outside gradually faded as she made her way along. The walls were adorned with a collage of pictures and photographs, snapshots of happier times.

She could hear the officer behind her regain his composure and step across the threshold, his heavy boots crushing what was left of the paper under foot. Even through the scented fabric, the still air reeked of something bad. Kray guessed her fresh-faced colleague must be holding his breath. *Brilliant! Now he was going to vomit, then pass out.*

The door at the end was cracked open and she could hear a faint buzzing sound coming from the room beyond. The beam of light danced across the wood veneer and frosted glass. She eased it open onto a lounge and groped around the wall for a light switch – click – nothing. The room contained a three-seater sofa and an iron coffee table sitting in front of the TV. It was neat and tidy, and the curtains were closed. Kray motioned to the officer to take a look at the cups sitting on coasters on the table. Brown and green mould was cultivating nicely at the bottom of the mugs. The buzzing grew louder.

Off to the left was a kitchen filled with modern appliances and a stack of unwashed dishes lay in the sink, growing their own type of fungus. The officer put his hand on Kray's shoulder as his torch beam alighted on a closed door.

'Over here, ma'am,' he said, his words muffled against his hand pressed hard over his nose and mouth. He twisted the handle and it opened up onto a bathroom. But Kray wasn't looking. She was standing outside a closed door in the corner, her head tilted to one side, listening. The buzzing was coming from the other side.

She twisted the handle and the lock disengaged. As the door cracked open the buzzing grew louder, and the stench penetrated straight through her perfumed defences. She heard the officer gag.

The door glided across the carpet to reveal a bedroom. A Laura Ashley quilt and scatter cushions decorated the double bed and the blinds were pulled shut across the window. She scanned around the room and became aware of two things: the sound of retching as the officer bolted for the front door in search of breathable air and the feeling of flying insects touching her face and neck. In the glare of the torchlight she caught sight of a twisting swirl of flies, the air in the room seemed to come alive as waves of them fogged around her. Kray flapped her arms in an attempt to carve herself a gap to move forward, circled the foot of the bed and found the source of the buzzing. The body of a woman lay on the floor, she was naked apart from the seething mass of insects, white maggots and pupae that had invaded her bloated carcass.

The heady stench of rotting pork mixed with cheap perfume was overwhelming. Kray held the handkerchief tight to her face. The woman's flesh was marbled with blood vessels, and putrefied liquid pooled in the recesses of her body. More blow flies landed on Kray's face and she struggled to swat them away. They were persistent little bastards.

She tore her eyes away from the corpse and scoured the room. A chair lay on its side in front of a large dressing table and several items of make-up were scattered across the floor. The rest of the room looked untouched. Eventually the gut-wrenching stink proved too much for Kray, she hurried from the bedroom and down the corridor to the waiting uniformed officer whose face was the colour of magnolia paint.

'Sorry, I just couldn't—' Kray held up her hand to cut him off and inhaled deeply.

'Fuck, you never get used to that,' she said, gasping in air.

She fumbled around and pulled a phone from her pocket, hitting two keys.

'Hi, it's me. I'm at a flat seventeen, Dennison Heights, responding to a call from a neighbour who complained of a smell coming from the property.'

3

The metallic voice on the other end went into a monologue and Kray pulled the phone away from her head, cursing under her breath.

'Yes, I understand that, but you know how short staffed we are and I was with uniform when the call came through. Yes, I know—' The detached voice cut her off. 'Fuck!' She held the phone away from her and swore again, this time under her breath, spinning on the spot.

'I know it's not protocol but the officer was on his own, so I went along in support—'

The distant lecture continued.

'Okay, okay, I get it. Look, that's not why I called, we need a crime scene manager and SOCO down here, and if you can spare the time you should get here too.'

The voice protested.

'Yes, I'm well aware of—' Kray was interrupted again. 'But you need to see this.'

The distant voice got louder.

'With all due respect, sir, you have a choice: either you get in at the ground floor with this case or you can read it in my report and then be forced to get involved. Which do you want?'

Standing eight feet away the young officer could hear the bout of swearing taking place on the other end of the line.

It was Kray's turn to interrupt.

'There's a dead woman in the flat, she's been there for eight to ten days I reckon. The corpse has decayed badly and there are signs of a struggle.'

The voice on the other end sounded more reasonable.

'She's lying on the bedroom floor near an upturned chair and items of make-up have been knocked off the dressing table.'

The voice was calm and measured, putting forward an alternative view.

'I agree, that could have happened. She could have fallen, knocking over the chair and scattering the make-up. That might be a possibility. But it didn't happen that way.'

Kray cast her eyes up to the ceiling.

'No, there are no blood spatters that I could see. But this is definitely a homicide.'

The voice continued to wind her up. Kray finally had enough of appeasing her dickhead of a boss.

'You need to get here to see for yourself, and I can assure you I'm not overreacting. Whoever did this sliced off her face.'

Chapter 2

Roz Kray sat at her desk staring into space while nursing a coffee and contemplating a rather unexpected start to the week. She was in her mid-thirties with the body of a fourteen-year-old girl and the face of a woman ten years older. The ravages of cigarettes and excess alcohol had carved lines in her complexion that piled on the years. Still, she had no one to look good for now, so what was the point of trying?

It was late and the images of the past three hours played in her head like a low budget B movie. She smoothed the creases out of her freshly dry-cleaned trouser suit and cursed her lack of self-confidence. What the hell was she thinking asking her boss to take a look at the body? She knew what to do, she knew the correct procedures to follow - Christ she'd been a DI long enough. But the last eight months had taken their toll, it felt like she was cycling with stabilisers on.

Thankfully he hadn't shown up which had forced her to co-ordinate the crime scene herself. No doubt her moment of weakness would result in another pep talk from her fuckwit of a boss who was one rank her senior. Kray often wondered what it would be like to have him undermine her on purpose. Because since she'd returned to work he'd been making a damned good job of doing so under the guise of building her confidence. She'd been back in work a month and her working-muscles were still a little shaky. She didn't need him pulling the rug from under her at every opportunity. She logged out of her desktop and gathered her things together to head home. She could have done the paperwork in the morning, but where's the fun in sitting on your own, watching junk TV, next to a rapidly emptying wine bottle?

The phone rang.

Thirty minutes later Kray was kitted out in a blue mask, hairnet and over shoes, wearing a white coat made to fit someone twice her size. The mortuary was new, courtesy of an injection of funds into the Victoria Teaching Hospital. The place was bright and clinical with three stainless steel tables lined down the centre. Each table had a drain at one end and metal scales hung from the ceiling. Hoses and nozzles were connected to the frames and a set of shiny steel work surfaces and sinks ran around the walls. The room smelled of formaldehyde and rotting chicken.

The technician gestured for Kray to take a seat on a long bench that was bolted to the opposite wall, a precautionary installation for those medical students in danger of passing out. She held up her hand giving a 'no thanks' response.

Kray gazed at the sunken remains of the woman from the flat, lying face up on the middle table. The corpse had been washed clean of the infestation of white grubs, and the trademark Y-shaped scar that ran down the length of her torso told Kray the worst was over.

'Not seen one like this before.' A tall man with a shaved head and steel rimmed spectacles appeared out of nowhere. 'That's why I called. My name is Harry Aldridge by the way.' He looked every inch a Home Office Pathologist.

Kray snapped her thoughts away from the body. 'Sorry, I didn't hear you come in.'

'No worries, I thought it might be good for you to see this first hand.'

He moved over to the table.

'It must have been one sick son of a bitch to do this.' Kray shuffled over to the corpse and pointed to the faceless head.

'Yes, the flesh was cut away using a scalpel-like blade. Starting at the forehead and cleaving the flesh away from the bone down towards the chin.' He mimicked the action with his hands like a macabre game of charades.

'Got a name?' she asked.

'The vic's name is Madeline Eve, we linked her dental records to the name on the property lease and the personal effects at the flat. She's twenty-six years of age, single, worked in an advertising firm here in Blackpool. Time of death is difficult to tell; the body was already in the advanced stages of bloating and beginning the transition into active decay. And by the blow fly and house fly pupae found in the body, plus the quantity of insects present at the flat, I would estimate she'd been dead around nine days, putting the date of her death to be Sunday 1 May, give or take a day. There's no indication of her being restrained, no ligature marks on the wrists or ankles, no defensive bruising or evidence of a fight.'

'Any sign of sexual activity?'

'No.'

'Please tell me this happened post mortem.' Kray nodded towards the head.

'Probably but I can't be sure. The blade marks are clean which would suggest she was immobile when it happened.'

'Do you have anything to give me – skin under the finger nails, fibres on the body, anything?'

'No nothing. I've not fully completed my examination, but so far I've drawn a blank.'

'I don't get it. Whoever did this cut her face away from the bone, but I found no blood at the scene.'

'And that brings me to this …' Harry went over to one of the stainless steel workstations and returned with a glass jar. He handed it to Kray.

'What is it?' she asked, holding it up to the light.

'It's blood.'

'Blood? That doesn't look like any blood I've seen.'

'Nor me, but it's blood alright.'

The jar contained a thick, dark red, jelly-like substance. Kray tilted the jar one way then the other watching the congealed glob slop about.

'I don't get it?'

'Neither do I, which is why I'm reluctant to give you a cause of death. My guess is massive organ failure caused by the blood coagulating to the consistency of porridge. And there's something else ...' Harry went to the corpse and shone a pencil light onto the woman's neck. 'A single puncture wound consistent with a needle piercing the jugular vein. There is swelling and blistering around the entry wound.'

'So let me get this straight. The murderer killed her by injecting a substance capable of coagulating her blood, filling her veins with this stuff?' Kray once again examined the gelatinous blob. 'Is that what you're saying?'

'Yep, it effectively turned her into a human jelly mould. Until I do more tests I can't be sure, but judging by the organ degeneration and tissue damage, whatever it was acted like a hemotoxin and choked off the main arterial flow to the organs. The heart, kidneys, lungs are choked full of this stuff.' He took the jar from her hand.

'A hemo what? Where the hell do you lay your hands on that?'

'Snake venom.'

Chapter 3

My name is Jason. It's the name my mother gave me when I was barely a visible bump in her belly. I've always hated that name even more than I hated her. It's the name on my birth certificate and my passport, on my credit cards and my work pass - but I never use it. I should be named after an all-powerful God, that is, ever since I started to decide whether people should live or die.

For as long as I can remember I've always thought drowning would be fun, but the water here is too cold. Even in the summer months, when the diehard sun worshippers slap on chip fat to roast their parchment-coloured flesh, it's still too cold.

I live in a place where the grey of the town bleeds into the grey of the sea. Where children trudge along the Promenade with their parents in tow, all of them in search of *something* to make them happy.

But they seldom find it, even in summer.

I like watching the runners in the morning, in their budget trainers, dodging the rain and dog shit as they enrich their lives along the sea front. It is mid-June, in a holiday resort on the west coast of Britain, and the place is empty.

It's not as though I've not tried - drowning that is.

I remember my twelfth birthday, Mum did a beach BBQ. She thought it a good idea having watched it on TV. The fact that the programme depicted life in Brisbane and our miserable lives butted hard up against the Irish Sea seemed to pass her by. The party was all burnt meat, freezing skin and blown sand. In the years that followed, she paid for it dearly.

We played games in the biting wind. One involved running into the sea and back to win a prize. I remember thinking - *what would happen if I kept on running?*

I felt the water slapping against my legs, then my stomach, then my chest. I pushed on and the waves caught me full in the face washing my hair flat to my head. If I kept going, I'd be under.

Today I die. The words resonated deep inside my head. Driving me on. The force of the sea made it hard to stand. The whole world seemed to shift beneath my feet, my toes grasping at the sand for balance. The raw taste of salt in my mouth. And then, suddenly, with a swell of the tide, I was under. A dull silence washed through my head.

Even now when I drift off to sleep I can still feel the biting, lapping cold like it was yesterday. I remember thinking - *if I'm successful, there won't be any singing Happy Birthday. No, 'open your presents, Jason.' No, 'say thank you, Jason.'*

All I heard was the water coursing through my ears, the cold tightening a vice-like grip around my body. The chill tearing at my skin.

Today I die. What a perfect gift on my special day.

But the water was too cold and my mum had bought Iced Slice. And I love Iced Slice. I turned and fought my way back to the shore, fighting against the pull of the waves dragging me further out. Gasping, I reached the beach and looked at the faces of the children wrapped in towels. No one had missed me. I wasn't going to die today, even if it was my birthday. Besides, I would happily kill for an Iced Slice.

And two years later, I did just that.

Chapter 4

It was 7.30am and Kray was already on the rampage. Her commute into work was just long enough to bring herself to the boil nicely. That's the problem with being able to read your work emails while sitting in your pyjamas, drinking your first coffee of the day.

She marched up to DCI Jackson's office and barged right in.

'Morning,' he said, surprised with his early visitor.

'I got your email,' she replied ignoring the niceties of returning his greeting.

'Which one?'

'The one that said you had given the murder case to Colin Brownlow.'

'Ah yes, I was meaning to talk to you about that.'

'Bit bloody late now.'

'Come on, Roz let's go get a coffee.'

She stood her ground. 'That case was mine. It *is* mine. Why have you given it to him?'

Jackson retreated back behind his desk.

'Look, Roz, no one admires you more than I do for getting back in the saddle so quickly after …' he hesitated, 'well you know.' A silence hung between them that seemed to last a hundred years. Kray was not going to be the one to break it. 'God only knows I would not be back in work if that had been me. Everyone is on your side, we just need to be sure you're …' He hesitated again.

'Up to it!' This time she completed his sentence for him. 'Is that it? You need to be sure I'm up to it?' She spun the plain gold band on her finger, twisting it round and round.

'No, Roz it's not like that. I have a duty of care towards you and—'

'Or maybe you need to be sure I won't screw it up for everyone else. Is that it?'

'No, Roz you have this all wrong.'

'Well, excuse me, boss but I think I've got this all right. That case is mine and you know it. Brownlow already has his head firmly below water, he's struggling to cope with his current case load and now you've given him this murder on top. That makes no sense. I'm asking you to think again. This case is different. The woman had her face removed for Christ's sake, you need somebody who is able to be on point twenty-four seven.'

'We don't have the manpower for that level of commitment.'

'You do, you've got me!'

'DI Brownlow is an experienced officer who—'

'Oh come on, William, there are bodies in the morgue with more life in them than Brownbag.' A nickname that referred to the way he brought his lunch to work. 'He's biding his time until his golden handshake while desperately trying not to fuck things up. I want this case, it's—'

'That's enough, Kray.' Jackson banged the palm of his hand on the desk. 'I will not have you rubbish another office in my presence. I've cut you some slack but don't push it or you and me are going to fall out – big time. That's my decision, Brownlow is SIO on the murder, supported by you. Keep your head down, do a good job and wait your turn. Is that clear?'

Kray was visibly shaking. The ring spun round and round.

'I'll go see him, DI Brownlow, and get things moving.'

'You can't. He'll be in later, he's at the doctors this morning.'

Kray knew when it was time to shut up and leave. She skilfully avoided bumping into the door frame on the way out, which was no mean feat, as her eyes were cast towards the ceiling.

She sat at her desk trying to calm down, repeatedly rearranging the pens, post-its and mouse mat. No matter how she positioned them it was always wrong.

She had a healthy professional dislike for DCI William Jackson. He had transferred to Lancashire police from the Met to escape a torrid divorce and a toxic ex-wife. He was known as Jacko to his friends but no one in Lancashire ever called him that.

He'd moved up to Blackpool to start afresh and ended up starting a war. London to Blackpool is a journey of two hundred and forty-seven miles, however, in policing terms the two forces may as well be two hundred and forty-seven light years apart. Jackson's style and approach grated on everyone he came into contact with. Kray knew exactly why Jackson had given the case to Brownlow: he saw her as a threat. He was hell-bent on making a name for himself which for him meant he was the only one allowed to shine. While Brownlow drowned under his workload, Jackson would skim off any good news stories and feed them straight to the Chief. Old habits die hard.

Kray had clashed with him before she went off work. Now she was back it was only a matter of time before she clashed with him again.

She pulled on her jacket and headed out of the station, looking for something to take her mind off what she was going to do to Jackson's genitalia and where she was going to stick them. A fresh crime scene would do the trick.

The uniformed officer checked her badge as he pushed open the door to flat seventeen. Kray pulled on the white suit and overshoes and entered the hallway, immediately reminded of the smell of putrefied flesh. She put her hand to her face, an automatic reaction. Her fingers found the light switch on the lounge wall – click – nothing. She looked back at the front door and spotted the culprit; the main breaker was off in the distribution unit. It was mounted high on the wall, too high for her, but for a six-foot two-inch police officer it was well within reach.

Lights at last flooded through the flat.

Kray slipped into the bedroom, her mind running riot with the images from the night before. A brown stain on the carpet marked the outline where the body had been. Try as she might, she couldn't stop the sound of buzzing raging in her head.

She moved around the room touching objects with her gloved hand. She had a nagging sensation that something wasn't right. What was it? She patted the soft fabric of the quilt and pulled aside the curtains. She gazed at the make-up laying on the floor – something didn't add up.

What the hell was it?

Kray crept back into the lounge and repeated the process, touching each of the woman's possessions in turn. Tuning in to her surroundings, hoping they would speak to her. Tell her what had happened. But it was no use. She cursed herself for being off her game – she couldn't join the dots up. She glanced at her watch, it was mid-morning, time to knock on a few doors to see if the neighbours could shed any light on the victim. Kray was jolted from her thoughts by her phone ringing. It was Brownlow.

'Yes.'

'Hi Roz, can you get yourself over to Hounslow and Partners to gather statements from the people who worked with Madeline Eve. Then develop a known associates list and start knocking on doors. I'm meeting with the parents later today, they've been informed and have agreed to identify the body.'

'On my way.' Keeping the conversation brief was a conscious decision on her part. It prevented her from telling Brownlow to piss off.

In the car, on her way to the advertising agency, Kray's mind wandered around the flat, reminding herself of every detail – the mugs in the living room, a single toothbrush in the bathroom, the items left on the dressing table. There was something that didn't fit, something out of place.

The thirty-minute journey passed in an instant and she soon found herself edging the nose of her car through the gates of a large office block to the car park at the rear. She pulled into a spot marked 'visitors'.

Her phone rang on the hands-free. Brownlow again.

'Hey, Roz change of plan. Can you get yourself over to seventeen Dennison Heights? I got someone else covering the workplace and thought it would be good for you to go to the scene. You know, get a feel for the place, maybe talk to the neighbours.'

Kray wished she had spent more time chatting to Brownlow on the phone the first time he called, because then she could have told him to piss off.

Kray collapsed into bed at 11.25pm, the day had been long and frustrating. Brownlow had her running errands for him all over the place, it was less like an investigation and more like a badly organised treasure hunt. His style of management could loosely be described as command and control, although a more fitting description would be command and no fucking control whatsoever. That, coupled with his utter lack of time to devote to the case, made for slow, tedious progress. Kray stared blankly at the cracks in the ceiling, the sound of a million flies buzzing in her head.

She'd arrived home two hours ago, just enough time to watch some bollocks on the TV and down a cheeky bottle of Chardonnay. It was supposed to help her sleep, but the images of the day danced before her, ensuring that was not going to happen any time soon. She knew she should eat dinner, but the effects of the alcohol numbed her appetite. She couldn't remember the last time she had eaten food three times a day.

She threw back the duvet and strode into the living room, flicking on a side lamp. Her laptop was on the low coffee table. She pushed the mouse with her index finger and the screen ignited with a blue hew. She tapped at the keyboard, reached for a pen and a new notebook. Wikipedia pages opened and closed in a blur, to be replaced with another then another; the same with medical reports, research findings and YouTube videos. The scribbled notes spilled onto a second page and then a third.

Kray clicked away at the screen, gorging herself on the information. Hunched over her laptop, pictures and documents flashing before her eyes, she lost herself in her search.

Eventually she sunk back into the soft cushions, the photograph on the screen filling her vision. 'Gotcha,' she said to no one.

Kray looked across at the carriage clock on the mantelpiece, rubbing her eyes. It read 2.45am. She leaned forward and wrote two words in capital letters on the fourth page of the notebook and double underlined them. It was time for bed, three and a quarter hours' sleep was enough for anyone. Instead she curled up on the sofa and drifted off to the sound of buzzing flies.

Chapter 5

My alarm goes off at 3.30am. You'd think I'd be used to it by now. I hang last night's clothes in the wardrobe and pull on jeans and a T-shirt. It's so early no one gives a toss what I look like.

I hate my house. After fourteen years it still stinks of my mother. The lounge carries the stench of her slippers, the kitchen reeks of burnt shepherd's pie and the bedroom wraps you in a hundred wet carpets of fabric softener and rose water drawer liners. How does that happen?

I down a cup of strong coffee and stand watch at the bay window. The street is empty and quiet. The rubbish bins stand like sentries by the side of the road awaiting the arrival of the council lorry to take away the filth.

How can one household discard so much?

Take the people at number nineteen. They must have the cleanest hair in the UK, I once counted three bottles of shampoo in one week. What is that about? And the couple at fifty-one binge so much on ready meals they should each be the size of a house. Who the hell eats that much Moussaka in seven days? And the two new guys in the bungalow must be intent on shagging themselves into an early grave. Their bin is always crammed with more condoms and empty lube containers than the back of an Ann Summers shop.

I think about sex all the time, and for me it's a solitary practice to be enjoyed while something is dying. Nothing else comes close, excuse the pun.

I have never understood the pubescent riot that ensues over a torn copy of Readers' Wives or the adrenaline thrill of a late-night bar pickup. The prospect of the walk of shame has never entered my head and a furtive glance that says, 'fuck yes' has never darkened my face.

Whether it was blundering my way through my formative years only to drown in a sea of raging hormones, or careering through my catastrophic teenage development and into adulthood, I have never wanted any of it.

I class myself as sexually normal but not in the same way that normal people do. Give me my mother's clothes and something helpless, and I will give you a happy ending every time. I tell myself this every morning as I stare up the street, waiting for my ride.

'Train station please,' I direct, as I enter the taxi.

The driver nods. I don't know why I have to tell him. He's been to my house more times than I've sneaked into other people's.

After a coma-inducing one hundred minutes I enter a steel and glass building in Salford Quays and present my faded pass to the turnstile. My slender frame eases through the gap as it opens with a beep. The man standing duty in the ill-fitting uniform and fake leather shoes nods in my direction. With a yard of material bunching at his ankles and his hands disappearing into his sleeves, he looks like someone who's shrunk in the wash.

He has no idea who I am.

It's the same guy most days and I swear he looks at me every morning with all the recognition of a person seeing me for the very first time. I enter the lift and wait for the doors to release me. I step out into the frantic bustle of the corridor, it smells of make-up and hairspray.

My job is to make unattractive people look pretty. They turn up in their shit clothes, with their shit hair and their shit morning breath, and my role is to put them in front of the camera so they don't scare the nation. Some are nice, most are not.

The blokes are the worst. All happy plastic teeth and witty banter when the red light is on. Caffeine craving, nicotine smoking

7

idiots when it's not. The women chirp their early morning chorus to their latest luvvies, as I scrape and sculpt their faces into something decent.

They seldom acknowledge I'm there, apart from the occasional call of 'more cheek bones, more cheek bones'. I simply nod and wish them dead.

As soon as my final brush stroke glances their now flawless skin, I'm ushered out of the way to make room for the hair people. They are from a higher cast, always welcomed with the latest gossip, titbits of celebrity life not yet in the papers. Every morning I feel sick.

Still, soon they'll be gossiping about me.

Chapter 6

As predicted, on the stroke of 7am, Kray was keeping a seat warm in the smoking shed outside in the station car park. She puffed away on her second fag of the day and watched the uniformed bobbies hustle in and out of the modern four-storey building. She envied them, with their daily work orders, central control unit and strength in numbers. She drew hard on the dregs of her cigarette wondering what the hell the day had in store. Beside her sat a Costa coffee and a paper bag containing a cinnamon swirl. She had vowed before going to bed to eat a healthy breakfast when she woke in the morning – a cinnamon swirl was the best she could manage. Anyway, she'd only taken one bite out of it, so in her head that was technically healthy. She flicked the fag end onto the floor and, as she picked up her breakfast, her phone buzzed in her pocket.

'Hi, Mum,' she said.

'Hi, love, I just wanted to give you a quick call before your day started.'

'Oh that's nice, how are you?' Kray tried to deflect what she knew was coming.

'Never mind me, are you eating ok?'

'Yes, Mum, I'm eating ok.'

'Three meals a day is what you were told.'

'Yeah, Mum, it's three meals a day.' She looked down at the bag. *Well that's one down, two to go.*

'And how's work, have you settled in? It must be a month now.'

'Yes, Mum it's been about a month. Everyone is being really nice.' She lied.

'And everything in the house is ok? I could send your father round if things need fixing, you know that.'

'Yes, Mum, I know that.'

'And you've cut down on the booze and fags haven't you?'

'Yes, Mum,' Kray said, stomping on the glowing fag end on the floor.

'And—'

'Hey look, Mum, I have to dash, I've got work to do. You know how it is.'

'Oh yes love that's fine. Well, it's been lovely talking to you. Your father says hi.'

'Say hi from me. Bye, Mum.'

She pressed the red button on her mobile. It was the same conversation every time, the same questions and the same answers. It was as though her mum felt obligated to call every few days, and every time they went through the same routine. Her mother meant well but it wasn't helping. Her solution to everything was three square meals a day, plenty of sleep and live like a nun. Sage advice that came from watching too much day time TV, and while Kray appreciated her mother's concern, that was never going to happen.

Kray climbed the stairs to the office and elbowed the door open. The place was empty. She settled at her desk and logged onto the system. She could see somebody had made a half-hearted attempt at an incident board with a few photographs from the flat pinned to a cork board along with a couple of names she recognised. Her email box pinged at her.

'Fuck,' she said under her breath. 'You gotta be kidding.'

Her phone vibrated again, probably one last question from her mum. It was Brownlow.

'Hi, where are you?' she asked.

'On our way to Merseyside.' She cursed under her breath as Brownlow confirmed the content of the email.

'Have you all gone?'

'No just me and William. We are presenting at this National Police Chiefs' Council event, sorry forgot to tell you.'

'What about the others?'

And since when were you two promoted to the rank of Police Chief?

'That's what I wanted to talk to you about. They will be working on the other cases so if you can pick up where they left off, get hold of the witness statements and make a start on the house-to-house that would be great.'

'I started the house-to-house yesterday and left a partial report on your desk. What's the priorities for today? What came out of interviewing the work colleagues? Are there any leads to follow up from what they told us?' The line was silent. 'Colin are you there?'

'Err yes I'm here, the line is bad.'

'I can hear you fine. What are the priorities for today?'

'Continue with the witness statements, they should be on the system. If not, there's a list on Rebecca's desk.'

'Colin do we have anything from the post-mortem? There has to be a ton of leads to follow up on there?'

'Erm, not sure, maybe you could have a chat with them too.'

Kray lifted her eyes to the ceiling and ground her teeth together. 'So basically—'

Brownlow interrupted. 'I'm losing you, Roz and we are almost here anyway. Give me a call if you need to chat anything through, I will check my messages in the breaks. Gotta go.'

Kray shook her head in disbelief. *Who the fuck is Rebecca?*

Her worst fears materialised when she found there were no statements on the system and no update from the post-mortem. It was clear that Brownlow's strategy for running this case was to drag anyone in who could spare the time and give them a job to do. This had the dramatic downside of no one knowing what the hell was going on and no one had an overall picture. Kray surmised that was Brownlow's job to pull together, but how much of the 'overall picture' he was going to get by shining the arse of his suit trousers in a conference was beyond her.

She managed to find Rebecca's desk and sure enough there was a file with a list of names. Kray decided to start at the top but before she did there was somewhere she had to be.

Chapter 7

The young officer at the door, who seemed to be a permanent fixture, acknowledged Kray with a 'ma'am' and opened the door to flat seventeen. She donned her protective gear and glanced up at the distribution box, secure in the knowledge she would have the use of an electric light. She ground to a halt halfway down the hallway.

The fetid stench of rotting flesh erupted at the back of her throat and she gagged. It was just a memory, but the physical reaction was real enough. Kray gazed at the picture postcard views hanging on the wall, each one depicting a different time in the short life of Madeline Eve. Photos of her school friends, her family holidays, her time at university and nights out in Blackpool were lovingly arranged in chronological order. Kray touched the handle of the door at the end of the hallway and the sound of buzzing filled her head. It wasn't soft and melodic like the night she discovered the body, it was harsh and aggressive, demanding attention. It grated in her mind.

The place was exactly as she had left it. The crockery lay untouched in the sink, the cups continued to grow mouldy cultures at the bottom and the curtains were closed. She moved onto the bedroom touching items as she went. The buzzing in her head grew in intensity as she entered the room, stroking one hand across the duvet cover while fanning the fingers of her other through the folds of the drapes. The dark stain on the floor drew her like a magnet. She could see the dissolving corpse of Madeline Eve stretched out under a cocoon of insects and pupae larvae. She knelt at the side and placed both hands onto the carpet, her finger tips dug into the fibres. Her flesh crawled with the feeling of flies landing on her face. The insects moved, pricking at her skin.

What did you do?

Kray could feel the killer making his preparations for Madeline to arrive.

What did you bring?

He brought items with him, items to make it special.

Why are they special?

The items enabled him to—

Her phone buzzed in her pocket, wrenching her away from her thoughts.

'Hello.' Kray felt breathless and disorientated. 'Okay I'll be there in thirty minutes.'

Kray rocked back on her heels and forced herself to stand up. Her head felt woozy.

Shit!

She so nearly had it. That gnawing sensation at the back of her head was telling her something wasn't right. She had so nearly grasped it, but now she had to conduct an interview. The moment had gone. So had the fly.

Forty-five minutes later Kray was instructed to go to the fifth floor of Hounslow and Partners by a charming woman in reception. She was sat in a cramped-but-functional office with a great view of Pleasure Beach. A well-groomed young woman wearing a dark pencil skirt, high heels and enough make-up to keep L'Oréal in till receipts for a week, tapped on the door.

'Please come in and take a seat. Thank you for agreeing to see me at short notice,' Kray said wondering how the hell this woman walked around all day on those things. The woman perched herself on the edge of the chair and eyed Kray with an air of sartorial pity. 'My colleagues spoke to a number of staff yesterday, but you were missed off the list. Were you away?'

'No, I was here. A few people who knew Madeline were interviewed but your guys said they had run out of time.' Although her accent was bordering on eastern European, she spoke in perfect English. Her lanyard read 'Ania Sobotta'.

'What do you do here, Ania?'

'I'm accounts manager for our tier-two clients and have responsibility for our eastern European channels to market.'

That explains the accent.

'Did you know Madeline?'

'Not well, I have only been here six weeks. We worked together on a couple of proposals and had a few nights out with clients, but that was all. I cannot believe what's happened to her, no one can. She was so bright and lovely, and now she's gone. It is terrible, we are all in a state of shock.'

'Did she talk about a boyfriend or girlfriend?

'No, no one. She kept her private life and work life separate. She talked about having lots of friends of both sexes but never spoke of anyone special. I think she was a very sociable person, she often spoke about going out at the weekends. She loved live music and went away with activity clubs.'

'Did she have any disagreements with people? Or did anyone show up at the office asking for her?'

'No, she was lovely, everyone liked her. I cannot believe I was only talking to her at lunch on Thursday last week and she was telling me about—'

Kray interrupted. 'You were talking to her when?'

'Last Thursday, she was saying that—'

'Where were you talking to her? Was it here?'

'Yes it was here, where else would it be?'

'She was in work?'

'Yes.'

Kray nearly dropped through the floor.

Chapter 8

'Come on, come on,' Kray barked into her mobile. This was her third call since the revelation at the advertising agency. Brownlow was on answerphone, as was Jackson. She even tried to get a message to them via the Merseyside control room but was left frustrated. As soon as she mentioned that they were both at the NPCC conference the enthusiasm to track them down melted away to nothing.

She sat in her car drumming her fingers on the steering wheel. The phone continued to ring at the other end. It clicked through to voicemail and the monotone voice of DI Brownlow asked her to leave a message.

'Colin, can you get back to me asap. I'm sat outside Madeline Eve's place of work about to go back in. It's urgent.'

She banged her head back against the headrest and closed her eyes. The buzzing noise of a million flies ebbed and flowed in her ears. That annoying sound, pitched at the note of G and produced by the circular rotation of two sets of wings at two hundred cycles per second, resonated deep inside her.

In her mind, she roamed through the rooms of flat seventeen, Dennison Heights, recalling the stench of Madeline's insect ridden body and the feel of the stained carpet. Her fingers moved involuntarily as she remembered the touch and feel of the objects in the bedroom, the cold of the lipstick tube as she weighed it in her palm, the starched fabric of the curtains as they ran through her hands. She held her breath, sensing the tingling sensation of a fly as it landed on her face.

She fidgeted with the gold ring on her left hand, spinning it one way then the other.

Her mind raced, she felt the insect move across her cheek.

What the hell did you do?

The itching, scratching, tickling sensation of six tiny feet gripped onto her skin. She flinched.

What the hell did you do?

Then the answer went off in her head like a grenade.

Fuck, it's been staring me in the face all along. How could I have been so blind?

Kray snapped out of it when she heard the sound of her mobile buzzing on the dashboard.

'Hello, Roz.' It was Brownlow.

'Hey, Colin did you get my messages?'

'Err, no we've been in and out of workshops all day. Is there a problem?'

'Yes, I can't get hold of anyone who interviewed Madeline's co-workers yesterday and the notes are not on the system. I need to cross reference a vital piece of information. There are holes all over the place in this investigation.'

'Wow, now slow down. The rest of the team are out working the other cases. Have you called them?'

'Yes, but all I get is their voicemails. They missed something yesterday, something important. No one is pulling the information together.'

'They'll get back to you I'm sure.'

'Did they say anything to you about Madeline being in work last Thursday?'

There was a pause on the line.

'No nothing.'

'Do you know if anyone has checked her mobile phone records?'

'I think Derek was picking that one up.'

'Derek, Derek who?'

'Derek Croft.'

'Fine I'll talk to him.'

'I think he's off today. But he's due back in tomorrow.'

'Is Jackson there?'

'Err, yes but why do you want to speak to him?'

'Put him on the phone.'

'No I can't, we're being called back in.'

'For fuck's sake, Colin, we have inconsistencies everywhere in this investigation and I'm flying blind here. Can't you get back to the station?'

'Let's talk in the morning, Roz, we can iron things out then.'

'Colin, put Jackson on the ph—'

The line went dead.

'Shit!' Kray slapped both hands against the wheel.

After taking a minute to collect herself, she swung open the car door and headed back to the fifth floor of Hounslow and Partners to sit in a cramped office with a great view of Pleasure Beach, hoping that her swearing would stop by the time she reached the charming woman in reception.

Kray was sat in Jackson's office staring at the back wall. She'd been waiting over thirty minutes for him to return from Liverpool, but she didn't care. The buzzing in her head had gone. So had the fly.

The frustrations of the day were raging inside her and she was conscious of trying not to lose it. Her eyes were drawn to the scattering of pens and pencils at the one end of Jackson's desk and the empty pen tidy pot sat at the other. She tore her gaze away from the mess, steeling herself against the temptation. Each time she did, the desire ratcheted up a notch. The ring spun round and round on her finger.

Finally, she could take it no more. She grabbed the pens, squared them up by tapping them against the desk and shoved them into the pot. Then she moved the pencils across to the opposite side and lined them up like soldiers on parade.

She heard the sound of polished shoes on block wood flooring coming down the corridor and checked her watch, it was 4.30pm.

Jackson pushed opened the door.

'Oh hi, I wasn't expecting you. Don't tell me we had a meeting and I forgot?'

'No, boss this is a casual visit. Did you have a good conference?'

'The same shit as always. Big plans and big speeches, lots of top brass but precious little action.'

'Is Brownba—' Kray corrected herself. 'Is DI Brownlow with you?'

'No I dropped him off in the carpark, he had to head home. Do you want a coffee?'

'No, I'm fine, thanks. Did you get my voicemail messages?'

'No, I've been on the blower all the way here. So, what can I do for you?'

'It's more of what I can do for you.'

'I'm listening...'

'Firstly, can you tell me what DI Brownlow told you about the murder case? I mean, you had plenty of time together in the car, so he must have given you the low-down.'

'Yes we chatted about it a lot. He's dead impressed with you by the way, says you're keeping all the plates spinning and making great progress.'

Kray grimaced inside. 'That's good to hear.'

'What else did he say? He eh… he said certain aspects of the forensic pathology report were taking a little time to finalise and that the interviews with Madeline's work colleagues hadn't yielded much to go on. Neither had the house-to-house enquiries. He said it was slow going but was confident we are making good progress.'

'Did he say why the path report wasn't with us?'

'Eh… something about additional tox screens. Why do you ask? I'm really pleased that you've settled in with Brownlow, he's a good guy.'

'So, he didn't mention the inconsistencies or latest developments?'

'No. What do you mean, inconsistencies?'

'You know, inconsistencies, when things look like one way but they turn out to be another.'

Jackson dropped the 'let's play nicely' act.

'Spit it out, Kray. If you've come here to slag off Brownlow I'm warning you it won't wash.'

'No, sir I've come here to save your job.'

'What?'

'Because the way this investigation is being run, we are going to be caught in a shit-storm faster than you can say Independent Police Complaints Commission.'

'Now that's enough, Kray!'

'No, it isn't. You see if I had been in the car with you today we would have been discussing some pretty fucking major issues. Like, why do you think a young woman with a list of friends as long as my arm was not reported missing for the entire nine days that she was decomposing on her bedroom floor? And while you're getting your head around that - how do you think Madeline Eve managed to eat lunch with her co-workers last Thursday when according to the pathologist report she'd already been dead for five days? Did Brownlow happen to mention any of that on your way to Liverpool?'

Jackson looked like a landed carp, his mouth was moving but nothing came out.

'The reason why I ask is because we knew about that yesterday. And have done jack shit about it. No one has a grip on this case William and it's going to blow up in our faces. You want that to happen, fine, I'll keep my head down and do a good job, just as you asked, but don't say I didn't warn you.'

Jackson was still mute.

Kray slid a piece of paper in front of him and tapped it with her finger.

'When Brownlow finally gets his arse in gear and manages to track down the path report, it's going to say that. And when it does, ask yourself a question — where the fuck do you get one of those?'

Jackson looked down at the handwritten block capital letters scribbled on the paper, double underlined. It read 'Daboia Russelii'.

Chapter 9

I'm on parade. The taxi door swings wide as I step out onto the pavement. The sea breeze hits my face and cuts through my clothes, the dampness of dusk feels cold against my skin. I asked the driver to pull up short of the rank, so I can enjoy the walk. My heels clip against the concrete, announcing my presence.

A gang of guys tumble out of a pub, blocking my path.

'Wow!' A short fat man shouts as he sees me stop in my tracks. 'Ever so sorry, madam,' he says with a wicked grin painted across his face. 'Make way lads for the beautiful lady.'

He bows from the waist and waves his arm in a wide arc, removing an imaginary hat. The others part to form a guard of honour. The thin red material of my dress is clinging to the contours of my body.

'After you,' one of them says, his eyes giving everything away.

I lower my gaze in mock appreciation. 'Thank you, boys.'

I watch them feast their eyes as I sashay between them, each one getting a good eyeful. I walk away, the sway of my hips holding their attention as I go. One of them wolf whistles.

'If you fancy a lollypop later love, I've got something you could suck on,' he calls out as the others dissolve onto bawdy laughter. Just the reaction I wanted. I love being on Parade.

It's relatively early and the bouncers on the door of the Purple Parrot, with their bursting shirts and fluorescent armbands, see me coming. The tall one nudges the wide one with amateur tattoos inked around his neck.

'Evening,' he grunts as I approach.

'Hi.'

The wide one opens the door with a sweep of his arm. He stands his ground and I have to brush against him to enter the club.

'Have a good time,' he says as the door whooshes shut behind me.

The place is all purple and red, with flashing lights and thumping music. A few tables are occupied with pretty couples while the bar is a crush of stag parties and hen dos. I head over to the stag party where a man is dressed in a pink tutu and body suit with bright yellow wellies. He's wearing a red wig and pigtails and looks like he's been on the beer for a week. The men around him look happy and full of shots. I push my way between them and place my hand on the bar; a barmaid appears out of nowhere.'

'A large Sav Blanc please.' She nods. How the hell she can hear anything over this racket is beyond me. A couple of the guys pivot around and stare.

'Very nice.' I hear one of them say.

'Do you want to join us, love? My mate's getting married and we want to give him a good send off. You know, last meal for the condemned man and all that.'

I turn and smile as my bucket full of wine arrives on the bar. 'No thanks.'

A bloke pushes in beside me and slaps a tenner on the bar.

'Here, let me,' he says.

'No thank you.' I look up, he is tall and handsome with a stubble chin and blue eyes. I recognise him as the one who wolf whistled earlier.

'We all thought you looked like a girl who would know the best places to party, so we've taken your recommendation.' I glance over my shoulder to see the short fat one doing his Walter Raleigh act again, with a deep theatrical bow.

'Hey watch it mate!' The stag party must have taken offence to the new boy muscling in. He ignores them.

I hear the door whoosh open and a gaggle of girls fall into the club dressed in smart business attire. Thursday is the new Friday as far as after work drinks is concerned.

'Well?' The barmaid has her hand out poised to take the money. The tall good-looking man beside me smiles.

'Well?' He flashes his white teeth and the lines around his eyes crease.

'Thank you,' I say picking up the glass and taking a sip.

'Make it two, can you love?' he says to the bored barmaid who's seen this happen a hundred times a night.

'My name's Josh.' He holds out his hand.

'Hi,' I say placing my hand in his. He wraps his strong fingers around mine and gently squeezes. His skin is soft and cool. His aftershave has faded but the remnants of the musky smell wrap around me.

'Get in there Joshua my son!' A voice behind bellows out above the beat of the music, followed by gales of laughter.

'I think your friends are missing you.' I look up, taking another sip.

'Nah, they're just jealous that's all.'

'One of them has an interesting line of chat.'

'Pete is a bit of a dick when it comes to women, that's why he's never had one.'

Josh is still holding onto my hand, I make no attempt to pull it away.

'Do you buy drinks for every girl you meet on the street, Josh?'

'No, just the pretty ones.' His eyes crease again and his face lights up. He finally releases his grip and my hand falls away. The other drink is slid in front of us on a paper placemat. He picks it up and we chink glasses.

'Cheers,' he says.

'Cheers.'

'Here's to pretty girls and noisy clubs.'

I smile and bat my long eyelashes. The wine is cold against my lips.

There is a commotion to the side and Josh is shoved into me. In the collision I spill my drink down his shirt.

'What the fuck.' Josh holds me tight as the fracas continues. The man in the pink tutu clatters to the floor along with a tray of drinks. A star burst of glass erupts into the air showering my feet with beer. The doors fly open and within seconds the bouncers step in.

'Come on boys, he's had enough.' The tall one lifts the man to his feet and escorts him out, surrounded by his so-called friends.

'You okay?' Josh still has me in his arms.

'I'm fine, just got wet feet that's all.'

We part and he looks down and laughs. 'You have as well.' We are both stood in a puddle, my stockings are discoloured from the liquid. I place my hand against the wet patch on his chest.

'I spilled my wine.' I can feel the muscles in his chest harden against my touch. He places his hand on top of mine.

'That's fine.'

I gaze into his eyes. He is beautiful, with his gelled hair and groomed features. He presses my hand into his body. I look down and can see a faint white band circling the third finger on his left hand. Perfect.

'I didn't catch your name,' he says.

'I didn't give it.'

'My mum told me it was rude to drink with girls when you don't know their name.'

'Your mum was right.'

'So, we've not been properly introduced?' Josh offers his other hand. I take it and once again feel his cool skin against mine. 'So?'

'So what?'

'What's your name?'

'You can call me Madeline.'

Chapter 10

K ray was lounging at home with her feet up. She had figured she'd done enough damage for one day and had headed off after her showdown with Jackson. When she left his office he was already on the phone to Brownlow telling him to get his arse to the station, and no he wasn't interested that he had some 'personal matters to attend to'. He was not a happy DCI.

She poured herself a generous glug of white wine and surfed through the TV channels. For someone who didn't eat enough food to keep a five-year-old child alive she watched a shit load of cooking programmes.

They reminded her of her husband. With his selection of knives, heavy wooden chopping boards and white aprons, he would cook up his latest inventions, serving them to her with his usual 'well what do you think?' look on his face. She never had the heart to tell him they all tasted the same. It always struck her as ironic that somebody with an unhealthy relationship with food should marry a chef. But sometimes life sends you what you need when you least expect it.

A plastic container of half eaten curry and rice lay on a tray on the floor. Calorific content adequate, nutritional value questionable. She had no use for chef's knives, chopping boards or aprons. So long as the microwave went ding, that was all she cared about.

The revelations of the day played out before her as the Hairy Bikers knocked up a lamb tagine. Their humour and enthusiasm washed over her, only occasionally breaking her train of thought. She was glad the buzzing was gone, the reason for her intuition going into overdrive had been staring her in the face all along. She savoured the prospect of dropping that bombshell on Jackson when the time was right, but for now, she had given him enough to get on with.

She tore herself away from the TV and decided a hot shower would help wash away her frustrations. It would also allow her extra time in bed in the morning.

Kray sat at her dressing table with her fish bowl full of wine. The make-up pad felt soft against her face as it removed the grime of the day. Then it removed the extortionately expensive foundation cream which masked the scar running across her right cheek. She stared at her reflection as it slowly revealed itself. Her hands dropped into her lap, spinning the gold band around on her finger. The past rushed up on her and she shuddered.

Kray snapped herself away from her thoughts, shuffled off her bathrobe and stepped into the en suite. She stood in the shower, the steam rising from the cubicle to cloud the spotlights above. The half-bottle of shower gel she poured into her hands quickly produced a mountain of lather which Kray rubbed across her shoulders. Her fingers touched the raised flesh of a deep purple scar that ran from her left shoulder to midway down her back - the puckered uneven skin the result of fifty-six stitches. She washed her belly; her hands glided over a second scar that started to the left of her navel, traversed her stomach and bisected her right breast slicing through the nipple. This one was flat and faded, the result of forty-eight stitches.

The foaming suds covered her body, she liked the security they brought when she showered. The thick foam hid the slashes in her skin. It meant that if she was quick, and covered herself all over, she didn't have to look at them. The inch-long stab wounds that peppered her back and shoulders could only be seen if she looked in the mirror, a practice that she tried to avoid these days.

The last of the water washed away the suds and she wrapped herself in a towel the size of a bedspread. She padded out to the bedroom to reclaim her wine and gazed at her reflection in the dressing table mirror. It was like looking at someone else, someone she used to know. She downed the remainder of the wine in one and took a seat. The glass top was adorned with a rich collection of skin products and make-up all sitting in regimented order, most of which had not been used in months.

The phone rang.

Chapter 11

Josh and I fall out of the fourth bar of the night and zig-zag our way along the Promenade. His friends have long since gone. They got bored of taking the piss and were last seen disappearing into a dodgy-looking club, chasing a hen party. Pete was leading the charge and still performing like a dick.

I have my arm wrapped tightly around his waist to keep him upright. His arm is draped across my shoulders more for balance than in a show of affection. His body feels cold as the night sea air chills his skin through his shirt. I feel my own skin prickle with goosebumps, not a reaction to the cold, but in anticipation. I'm trying hard to keep my excitement under control. Josh is so beautiful.

'Where are weees going?' he slurs.

'Back to my place.'

'Thaas fuckin' brilliant.' He squeezes me into him and we teeter around falling off the kerb.

Josh proved to have a remarkable tolerance to alcohol, taking two drinks to my one. He alternated between wine and beer, wine on my round and beer on his. I needed to keep a reign on my natural tendency to match him drink for drink, after all it would be no use if both of us were incapable.

He veers off to one side and sits down hard on a low wall outside a hotel guest house. The momentum pulls me with him.

'Where are weees going?'

'Back to my place.' I lean in and plant a kiss on his cheek. He turns his head and our lips touch. I feel the wet warmth of his tongue as it darts into my mouth. The kiss lingers for a lifetime.

He even tastes beautiful. My heart is thumping.

'Thaas fuckin' brilliant,' he says as we pull away. I take his arm and pull him upright, once more gripping him tight.

'It's not far, a few more minutes.'

The tranquillising effect of the Rohypnol is taking its toll. The crushed white powder has been coursing through his system since I got the drinks at the last bar and he went to the gents. A large glass of dry white wine makes an ideal dissolving agent. The effects started to kick in after thirty minutes. I look at my watch. It's now been an hour since it first entered his system. He'll soon be approaching the peak and I need to get him to the right place before he collapses.

He is getting heavy and difficult to manoeuvre along the pavement. My heart thumps hard against my chest.

'It's here,' I say. 'Down this alleyway.'

'Doooes you live here?'

'Yes, I have a small flat in the building at the end.'

'Thass fuckin' brilliant.'

I guide him away to the right and we lurch into the gap between two high-rise brick buildings. The alley is about ten feet wide and the night sky disappears into a thin slit at the top as we make our way along. It stinks of piss.

'I live at the end.' My voice trembles with excitement.

We bounce off the left-hand wall, staggering up the alley, kicking cans and bottles as we go. The orange glow from the street lighting fades away against the deepening darkness. After twenty faltering steps, we reach a dead end. I feel his legs give way and he stumbles forward, landing on his knees.

'It's fuckin' dark,' he says.

'Wait here, Josh and I'll open the door.'

'Wheers the fucks are wez?' His words are melding into one.

'My place Josh, let me get my keys and open the door.' I lean forward cradling his face in my hands and kiss his forehead. He is totally gorgeous.

'I caaan't see mush, wheres yous gone?

'Just getting my keys, Josh,' I say, stepping to one side.

'Can we have a little kiss?'

'In a minute Josh, just finding my keys.'

'Can wees—'

The sound of his skull cracking resonates against the high walls as I slam the hammer into the side of his head. Josh keels over sideways without uttering a sound. The next blow follows quickly, connecting with a squelch on the back of his neck. His face skids into the concrete, he's dead before he hits the ground. I look down, allowing my eyes to adjust to the darkness. The outline of his body lies white against the grey slab paving, a dark stain growing around his head.

And one for luck ...

The lump hammer punches a square hole in the side of his head where his temple used to be.

That will teach you to take your wedding ring off. You won't do that again.

I love being on Parade.

Chapter 12

It was 7.15am and Kray was already regretting only puffing on one cigarette on her way to work. A plastic cup of something black and sweet from the staff vending machine sat in front of her on the desk, it was difficult to describe it as coffee. She flipped open a small round mirrored compact from her bag and checked her face, turning one way then the next to catch the light. She tutted to herself dabbing her index finger into the foundation cream and applying it to the purple line running across her cheek, smoothing and patting her skin until it was gone.

Note to self: don't rush the morning routine.

Kray snapped the compact closed and pushed it into her bag knowing only too well that when she took her make-up off at night, the mirror would once again serve as a painful reminder.

Jackson had been very specific in his instruction over the phone the previous night; she was to get into work early and wait until he called for her. She had replied with a faltering response of, 'Okay, I'll see you there' - it would have been foolish to engage in further conversation. The effects of the bottle of wine were beginning to tell. And besides, from the tone of his voice she had pictured him standing behind his desk and snarling down the phone with a red face, even she didn't think it wise to put up a challenge.

She could hear snippets of a discussion booming out from behind the closed door of Jackson's office. She thought she recognised Brownlow's voice but it was definitely playing a secondary role in the heated debate. It was not going well. She pushed the half-full plastic cup away from her to join the others lined up at the side of her desk.

The raised voices stopped, replaced with an onerous silence. She heard Jackson's door snap open and the sound of shuffling feet making their way towards her. Brownlow stuck his head into the office.

'He wants to see you.' His face was grey with a map of crimson blotches around cheeks and neck.

Kray rose from her chair and crossed the empty office.

'Look, Colin, I felt I had no option. You were so—'

'Leave it Roz, you got what you wanted. You could have come to me first.'

'I tried. We owe it to that poor woman to catch the sick bastard who—'

'Stick it up your arse, Roz.' And with that he walked away.

Kray was stunned, not because of the abruptness of the comment but because that was the most interesting thing Brownlow had ever said to her. She watched him skulk off towards the stairs then headed in the opposite direction to Jackson's office with a knot of tension in the pit of her stomach the size of the Tower Ballroom.

She pushed open the door. Jackson was sat behind his desk looking flushed. He slid a buff-coloured file across the desk.

'The Russell's Viper, or to give it its Latin name Daboia Russelii. The path report says it's the most likely source of the snake venom found in Madeline Eve's blood.' Kray took a seat and flipped open the file. She glanced through the densely written text and replaced it on the desk. 'So why don't you start by telling me what you know about this murder, rather than asking me a series of damned convoluted questions this time.'

'William, I need you to know that—'

'Save it, Roz. What I need to know now is what the hell is going on?'

'Okay first let's look at the chronology. The post-mortem puts the time of death around Sunday the first of May. This is based on the blown condition of the body, the quantity of flies at the premises, along with the development of pupae and grubs found in the corpse. That level of decomposition takes eight to ten days, maybe more. I found the body on Tuesday tenth of May after a neighbour had called to report the smell coming from the flat. So, on the face of it, that fits. But when I interviewed one of the work colleagues she told me that she had lunch with Madeline on the Thursday before I found her. That's also been confirmed by the interviews conducted the day before and by checking her records with HR. But we missed it, no one picked that up.

'I did more digging when I was at Madeline's place of work and she apparently called in sick on the Friday morning. One of Brownlow's team pulled her phone records and I got a message saying the call came from her handset.'

'Jesus H Christ! This keeps getting worse. I suppose we missed that too, did we?'

'I'm afraid so, sir. It was in one of the statements but no one joined the dots up.'

'Go on.' Jackson's face was turning a light shade of pink.

'I believe Madeline was killed on the night of Thursday, fifth of May. And the killer staged the scene to look like she'd been murdered much earlier to cover his tracks.'

'How did he do that?'

'Sir, I could not get the vast quantity of flies in the bedroom out of my head. You expect them to multiply because of their life cycle, but there were hundreds of them. I've been to houses before where a body has been undiscovered and, yes, there is a certain amount of insect activity but nothing like this. I went back to the flat a number of times and I kept thinking something wasn't right. It's been gnawing away at me then it hit me – how the hell do you get that many flies when the doors and windows were shut tight? There is no other access to outside that I could see. So how do you explain an infestation of flies that's on a biblical scale?'

Jackson shook his head but kept his mouth shut.

'I think the killer brought them with him.'

'Shit that's a new one.'

'I know but I can't explain it any other way. The flies accelerated the purification process and hence the post-mortem indicated an earlier date.'

'Why would the perp want to do that?'

'So the body is degraded, less opportunity for forensics to find evidence linking him to the victim.'

'And where does the snake fit into all this? Does he bring that with him as well?'

'Not sure, sir. There are a ton of unanswered questions.'

'Well you need to get started Roz because we are well and truly behind the curve on this one.'

'What about Brownlow?'

'He will not be playing any further role in this case. I want you to be SIO and let me know the resources you need. I have approval from the top for a complete news blackout on this until we get some traction.'

Kray felt a shiver run through her.

'How did you know?' Jackson asked.

'How did I know what?'

'The Russell's Viper. How did you know which snake produced the venom?'

'From a wonderful invention called the Internet.'

'You what?'

'I researched the types of venom that could cause the same degree of coagulation that we saw with Madeline and there were a handful of candidates. The Russell's Viper is very aggressive. Most snakes dry bite, which means they don't waste their venom on animals they don't think they can kill. The Russell's Viper injects venom every time it strikes. It thinks it can kill anything.'

Jackson shook his head. 'Okay but how did you know it would be this particular snake.'

'It's like the idiots we get around here, sir. You know the ones who walk about with an attack dog on a lead. They own big Staffs or Alsatians, they don't go walkies with a poodle. Same for our guy, he's a complete psychopath. If he's going to have a snake then it's going to be bad.'

'Okay, Sherlock, save it with the snake-ology lessons and amateur psychology. There must be plenty of snakes that fit the bill. How did you know it was that one?'

'Firstly sir, the correct term is Ophiology and secondly - I just knew.'

Chapter 13

The day was turning out to be full of surprises.

'I got a couple of bodies to help you out,' Jackson announced as he introduced Kray to two rookie officers.

Bloody hell. Jackson must be really panicking.

Kray shook their hands and welcomed them to CID, truth be told, any support at this stage was welcome.

Lucy Frost and Duncan Tavener were both fast-track graduates and exhaustingly keen. He had a face that wouldn't look out of place in any boy band, all clean lines and a ready smile, but with the build of a second row forward. She had a pretty face with angular features, crowned with a mass of auburn locks pulled back into a tight ponytail. She bore the sinewy physique of a long-distance runner. Kray wondered if this was finally a woman with a body fat index lower than hers.

Kray spent the morning briefing her new team and setting out a comprehensive investigation plan, meticulously ensuring every angle was covered. She had also commandeered one half of the office so they could all sit together and set up evidence boards. In doing so, she had moved a couple of people working with Brownlow. She had left him voicemail messages, and sent an email, but had received no response. If Brownlow wanted to make trouble she was ready for it, but she doubted he had the balls.

She focussed their attention on developing a profile of Madeline Eve, identifying who the people were in the photographs at the flat, which bars and clubs she attended, current or previous relationships, what she did for kicks - the full works. Also, there was the whole social media scene to dig around in, along with phone records and bank accounts.

Her new helpers were bright and enthusiastic. There was a lot of ground to cover and a mountain of statements to process, not to mention new lines of inquiry to chase down.

'Whoever killed her chose her for a reason,' Kray said to them as they hung on her every word. 'Part of our job is to work out what that is.'

'Yes, ma'am,' they responded in unison.

That is going to get right on my tits.

'Please call me Roz.'

'Yes, ma'am,' replied Tavener.

He was spared from being told a second time by Kray's phone bursting into life. She gave him a scowl and answered it.

'DI Kray.'

The voice on the other end was brief and to the point.

'Okay I'll be there in thirty minutes.' She replaced the receiver, picked up her jacket and strode out of the room. 'You know what you're doing, call me if you need to.'

'Yes, ma'am.'

Kray stepped into an enormous white coverall, tugged on a hairnet and overshoes and entered the mortuary. The now familiar smell invaded her senses, bringing with it images of the fetid corpse lying on the bedroom floor of flat seventeen, Dennison Heights.

Aldridge was hunched over a body on the stainless steel table at the far end of the room, speaking softly into a hand-held recorder.

'You called the station,' Kray said, interrupting him.

Harry looked up and pressed the stop button.

'Ah, DI Kray, I didn't hear you come in.'

Kray smiled beneath her mop cap. 'Sorry I didn't think to call ahead. I made my own way to the lab, picked up a pantomime costume and someone was kind enough to let me in. And please call me Roz.' She pulled at the acres of material to emphasise the point. 'Don't you cater for normal-sized people?'

'We do,' he replied without dropping a beat. 'I thought you might be interested in my latest findings and, rather than wait for the report, you'd prefer to get it first hand.'

Kray smarted at his 'we do' comment, making a mental note not to lead with her chin with this guy again. 'What have you got?'

'You know what it feels like when you have an itch you can't quite reach?' he said making his way over to her.

'Yeah.'

'I had three of the little bastards where your case was concerned.'

'How come?'

'Do you recall when you asked me if I had found anything under her fingernails? And I told you there was nothing.'

'Yes, I remember.'

'Well that's the first itch. I took a closer look and there was absolutely nothing. It's as if the attacker cleaned out her fingernails. I would expect to find something, maybe specs of dirt, clothes fibres, make-up or traces of her own skin. But there's nothing. Now why would the killer do that?'

'To be sure there was no residue to be found.'

'And why would that be important?'

'If there had been a struggle.'

'Correct. Now for itch number two.' He leaned over and picked up a printout from the desk and handed it to Kray. 'Our attacker administers snake venom which eventually causes massive organ failure. But we know it can take hours for that to occur, even with a large dose. However, there are no marks on the body, suggesting the victim was not restrained in any way while the venom curdled her blood.'

'She must have been knocked unconscious during the fight.'

'But there is no bruising or abrasions that would support her being struck.'

'So he used Chloroform on her,' Kray said flippantly.

'Very good, Detective Inspector. I found residues of dissolved ether in her lungs and throat. I've sent samples into the lab and we should receive the results any time now.'

'Well that's it then. They fight and the attacker smothers her with Chloroform to knock her out?'

'Not quite. This chemical doesn't work like you see in the movies. Holding a handkerchief over a person's mouth and them falling down in a matter of seconds is poetic licence. It would take several minutes to render someone unconscious.'

'But that would mean Madeline would have fought with her attacker for a prolonged period of time and that doesn't stack up. She doesn't have any defensive marks.'

'Correct again and that leads me to itch number three. Why is there no evidence of a struggle that potentially could have lasted many minutes?'

Kray had run out of answers this time. Harry reached over to a computer and pushed the mouse. The machine switched on to show a close-up photograph of a surgical wound. 'You might not be able to see this but there is a slight discolouration under the skin on the side of the victim's neck.' He left clicked on the mouse and a second picture came onto the screen. 'Same on both sides.'

'Injuries she sustained in the struggle?'

'Yes. I believe the attacker choked out the victim first, then applied the Chloroform to keep her unconscious.'

'He strangled her? But that makes no sense either. We would be able to see that from the damage to the trachea, the larynx and neck cartilage, not to mention external bruising. I've seen enough strangulations in my time to know that wasn't it.'

'No, not strangulation. I think the attacker used a technique called a rear naked choke hold where the carotid arteries are compressed, cutting off the flow of blood to the brain. The victim is able to breathe but is out cold within seconds.'

'How do you mean?'

'Let me show you. Do you mind?' Kray shrugged her shoulders as Harry positioned himself behind her wrapping his left arm around her neck so her windpipe was in the crook of his elbow. 'I reckon the attacker grabbed her from the back like this. The idea is the bicep and the forearm crush the carotid arteries in the neck, severely depleting the brain of oxygen. Your heart rate spikes in a frantic attempt to pump blood to the brain. This induces panic and in a matter of seconds the brain shuts down, rendering the victim unconscious.'

'So the attacker would need to be pretty strong to pull that off.'

'Not at all. It only takes ten pounds of pressure to compress the arteries. If the hold is applied correctly you need no more strength than it takes to break an egg between your fingers.' Harry released Kray and returned to the monitor.

'It's like something from an MMA fight. So ... let me get this straight ... our attacker chokes her out using this naked whatever-it-is hold and covers her nose and mouth with a piece of material soaked in Chloroform.'

'Yes. I think he kept choking her out until the anaesthetic did its job. When she was out cold, he released his hold.'

'Then the killer injects her with the venom from the Russell's Viper and watches her die as her blood turns to jelly. And to cap it all, he removes her face and infests the body with a million flies.'

'Yup, our killer went to a lot of trouble to murder Madeline Eve.'

An alert came up on the computer screen, Aldridge clicked on an email.

'What is it?' she asked.

'The results are back from the lab.' He opened the attachment and scanned the details. Kray read over his shoulder.

'What does it say?'

'It says it wasn't Chloroform.'

'Suprane? What's Suprane?'

Aldridge closed down the document. 'The sample tested positive for Servoflurane or Suprane as it is known in the trade.'

'What's that?'

'It's a powerful anaesthetic that works by suppressing activity in the central nervous system, leading to loss of consciousness.'

'So it acts like Chloroform?'

'Yes, but it is more powerful and faster acting.'

'Where would someone get their hands on that?'

Aldridge checked his watch. 'I'm sorry, I need to dash to a meeting. Can we pick this up another time?'

'Yeah, I suppose so. I have most of what I need.'

'If you call the lab they have my diary we can talk again if you think it will help?' Aldridge switched off the computer, gathered his things together and left.

The lab technician looked over. 'Something you said?'

'All I said was Suprane.'

Chapter 14

Kray made slow progress back to the station. The stop-start line of traffic crawled along the Promenade past the Tower - an inconvenience which normally would have her raging but, on this occasion, it gave her time to think. The discussion with Aldridge rattled around in her head and, try as she might, the pieces refused to glue together.

It was late afternoon by the time she marched into the station, taking the stairs two at a time up to the office. There waiting, as instructed, were her team of eager beavers. What she was not expecting was the place looking like a tip.

'Have you been having fun?' she said, eyeing the mounds of paper, empty box files and morass of post-it notes. The evidence board was festooned with new pieces of paper, notes scribbled across them in fat marker pen. The silhouette of a blacked-out face was pinned to the board with the name 'Gorgon' written underneath.

'What the hell is this?' Kray asked.

'DCI Jackson said that in the Met murder suspects are always given nicknames.'

'Did he now? That's helpful of him.'

'Our killer is now called Gorgon after—'

'A monster from the underworld in Greek mythology. Gorgon is the name given to three sisters who had snakes for hair and the power to turn anyone who looked at them into stone. He should have called him Medusa.'

Tavener eventually regained control of his bottom jaw. 'Why is that?'

'Because two of the sisters were immortal and Medusa was not. Let's hope our killer isn't one of the other two.'

'How do you know—'

'Don't they teach you people anything in school these days? Okay, apart from giving you both a history lesson what else do we have?' Kray was pissed off with Jacko interfering with his Met-related bollocks.

'Err, we were working through the statements and phone records,' replied Frost, immediately feeling the emotional temperature in the room increase a few degrees.

'We found something interesting, ma'am—' Tavener got no further.

'Okay, firstly you can call me ma'am when the Chief or the Dep are around, if you can't see either of them then my name is Roz. Secondly, I'm surprised you can find jack shit amongst this mess. This …' she waved her arms at the mound of stationery, 'is how information gets lost. This is how important details are not picked up. How the hell do you expect to conduct a thorough investigation when you're working in what looks like the customer returns bay at Staples? This is what you should be focussing on, not giving bloody nicknames to killers. Get this shit cleaned up and put in order by the time I get back. I need to see Jackson and we will do the debrief after that. Is that clear?'

'Yes m—, Roz.'

Kray stomped out of the room in the direction of the staff canteen. She didn't have a meeting with Jackson but she needed a cup of coffee and time to cool down.

She sat with the frothy drink in front of her and fidgeted with her wedding ring. She had overreacted but she could not stand working in a mess. Christ, when she thought about it, she couldn't stand working in a place where the pens and pencils were on the same side of the desk. Everyone knows that pens sit on one side, pencils on the other.

Kray felt her anxiety subsiding as the sugar and caffeine soothed it away.

I might have gone a little over the top but I may as well start as I mean to go on.

After twenty minutes, she made her way back to the office. Her new recruits were seated at two tidy desks.

'That's more like it,' she said nodding her head as she joined them. 'It's Friday and the sooner we get this done, the sooner you two can hit the town, or whatever it is you intend to do. Let me start.'

Kray ran through the latest findings. At times it looked like she was holding a story time session in a junior school rather than a briefing. They looked at her goggle-eyed as she relayed the gory details.

'What do you have?' she said ending her monologue.

'Let's start with Madeline Eve.' Lucy Frost was keen to get off the mark. 'She was twenty-six years of age, her parents still live at the family home in Selly Oak, Birmingham. She graduated from Manchester Uni with a two-one in Computer Science and took a gap year where she travelled extensively.' She pointed at the photographs taken from the hall and pinned to the notice board. 'Madeline came back to the UK in 2014 to start a law conversion course, again in Manchester. She worked part time for the university in a role where she promoted and advertised the Uni to colleges and schools. She got the bug for it and dropped out of her course to take up a position at Hounslow and Partners eighteen months ago.'

'She had no steady boyfriend.' Tavener wanted in on the act. 'But her friends said she had a couple of flings in the last six months. Nothing serious, we are checking out the men involved. She was a popular girl with a wide circle of friends. Her Facebook page is full of parties and social gatherings with her last post being on the day she was killed.' He consulted his notes. 'Something about after work drinks.'

'Anything unusual?' Kray asked.

'Yes, the phone call that she supposedly made into work on the Friday morning saying she was sick was not made from her mobile,' said Tavener.

'I thought Brownlow said …' Kray stopped herself, knowing to continue would only show her frustration and contempt.

'We checked the phone records and it definitely didn't come from her mobile.' Frost slid a printout in front of Kray. She didn't pick it up. Instead, she took a deep breath and balled her fists under the desk.

'The call was made from a public telephone box in Lytham St Annes.'

'Good work. Any more details about the call?'

Frost consulted a ream of paper. 'There are one hundred and sixty-five payphones in the Blackpool area and according to BT, apart from our call, this particular payphone hasn't been used in the last twelve months. It is due to be decommissioned. They were really surprised someone had used it. It's located on Albany Road.'

'We thought the best course of action was to get it cordoned off and let forensics have a crack at it,' Tavener said. 'What do you think, Roz?'

Kray sat motionless, staring into space.

'Roz? What do you think? Is it worth a crack?'

Kray had a one thousand-yard stare plastered over her face.

'We have a precise location. Here's the postcode and address.' Frost pulled a single piece of paper from a folder and handed it to her across the desk.

Kray left the paper hanging in mid-air.

'I know where it is,' she said, pushing Frost's hand away. 'It's right outside my house.'

Chapter 15

This is my third attempt and it is beginning to piss me off. The clock is ticking.

It's the same routine every Friday evening. While most people are out on the beer blowing away the effects of a hard week or relaxing with a takeaway and Netflix, she goes grocery shopping. Maybe it's because the place is quiet, maybe it's because she can park her car in her favourite space or, maybe it's because she has nothing better to do.

She buys the same items every week. Pouches of ground coffee, a ton of wine, a selection of snacks and the occasional ready meal. How anyone can get through that much alcohol in a week and still function is beyond me, especially when she eats so little. The whole trip should last no longer than ten minutes, but she insists on wandering up and down the aisles, gazing at the food but never placing it in the trolley. It is like she slips into a trance, blindly going through the motions of a ritual which used to have meaning but now no longer has relevance.

I've lost count of the number of times I've watched her go through the same drill. She arrives at eight o'clock, parking in the same spot each time. It's the bay nearest the trolley return and closest to the supermarket entrance. She gets out of the car, pulling the shoulder strap of her bag over her head so it crosses her body, and slips her phone into it. She zips it closed. Then she moves to the back of the car to retrieve a handful of shopping bags, banging the boot lid shut as the indicator lights flash orange and the car locks. She walks fifteen yards across the car park clutching the plastic bags in one hand and her keys in the other and struggles to pull an interlocking trolley free. The keys and plastic bags make it difficult, so she unzips her shoulder-bag and shoves the keys inside. The trolley finally disengages from the others and she walks away on autopilot.

If it's raining, she has the added complication of fighting with an unruly umbrella, but the routine is always the same. She saunters into the shop with her bag undone and the keys on the top.

I watch her disappear inside the supermarket. Then I get out of my car, collect a trolley and follow her inside. She browses along the display of fruit and veg that is spilling off the shelves on either side of the aisle. I do the same, except I place items into my trolley whereas hers remains empty.

She turns past the ready meals and heads down the raw meat section. The pre-packed items always hold a fascination for her as she picks them off the shelf, examines them, only to return them. My heart is banging hard against my chest and my mouth is dry. Twice before I've been this close and, on each occasion, I came away with nothing.

It *has* to work this time.

She breezes past the tinned section. I quicken my pace to get into position. The next aisle contains the breakfast bars. My stomach churns as she stops and goes through the weekly ceremony of picking boxes off the shelf.

I step backwards and bump into her. My left shoulder collides with her right and the trolleys clang angrily together.

The impact shoves her sideways.

'Oh, please excuse me,' I say in mock apology. 'I wasn't looking where I was going.'

She jumps a mile, like I've woken her from a deep sleep.

'That's okay.'

'I'm really sorry.' Our eyes lock. She has no idea.

'No, it's fine, I'm fine.'

'I'm so sorry.' I smile and move away, disappearing around the corner with my trolley. I abandon my shopping and head for the customer toilets, her keys tucked away in my pocket.

The cubicle door slams shut behind me and I slide the lock across. I put the toilet seat down and fish a leather rolled-up mat from my inside pocket. I lay it on the seat, undo the ties and unravel it to reveal a small pair of pliers, a cheap plastic lighter, a reel of Sellotape, scissors, a white plastic loyalty card from a coffee shop and a make-up wipe. Each item held in place with Velcro straps sewn into the leather.

I take out the bunch of keys and flick through them, the silver Yale key is the one I want. I slide it off the ring and grip the round end with the pliers. The lighter takes a couple of strikes before the orange and blue flame ignites from the end. I hold the serrated part of the key in the flame, running it along its length. After a few seconds, I place the key down onto the leather, with the hot side facing up, and cut a two-inch length of Sellotape off the roll. I carefully stick the Sellotape along the length of the key and apply gentle pressure. I can feel the heat from the metal passing through into my thumb as I smooth it flat. Once it has cooled I peel away the tape and stick it onto the face of the loyalty card.

One side of the Yale key is burnt black from the flame, so I clean it with the make-up wipe and slip it back onto the ring, taking care to replace it in the correct sequence of keys. I fix the items back in place onto the leather mat and roll it up, stuffing it into my inside pocket. Now for the tricky part.

I walk out of the toilets, find my trolley and scan around the shop. *Where is she?* I hurry between the aisles, but she's nowhere to be seen. By this point she should be mulling over her choice of wine, but when I get there I notice that particular aisle is deserted. I rush to the front of the store.

Fuck, she's at the till!

Why the hell isn't she picking bottles off the shelves looking for the best bargains, like she does every week? Why not today?

My mind races. How the hell do I get the keys back into her bag before she notices? Then an awful thought strikes me. *When she reaches for her purse she'll realise they're missing. Shit!*

The taste of panic floods into my mouth. My breathing is erratic.

Think, think.

I watch helplessly as she pulls her purse from her bag and pushes the credit card into the machine, casually chatting to the woman behind the till. She loads the bags into the trolley, stuffs the receipt into her bag and ambles away towards the exit.

I leave my trolley and follow her. Just as she is about to leave, I collar a member of staff.

'I think that lady has dropped her keys.'

'Are you sure they're hers?'

'Yeah, pretty sure. Can you run after her and give them to her? I'm afraid I can't walk that fast since my operation. Would you mind?'

'No not at all.'

I hand her the keys and she scurries off after the woman while I duck out of sight. I can hear her voice over the sound of the piped music.

'Excuse me, excuse me. I think you dropped your keys.'

I hide away at the back of the bread aisle and watch the minute hand on my watch sweep away the time. Ten minutes should do it.

I pay for my groceries and load them into the car. A thrilling wave of satisfaction rushes through me as I pat the leather roll-up concealed inside my coat. The blackened outline of her front door key imprinted onto the surface of a coffee shop loyalty card.

Chapter 16

The phone lying on the bedside table vibrated and the screen lit up, cutting through the darkness. Kray didn't stir, the bottle and a half of wine that was lodged in her head ensured she remained in a deep slumber. The call clicked through to voicemail. Seconds later it vibrated again.

Who the fuck? Kray reached out a hand and pulled the handset under the covers.

'Yeah.'

The voice on the other end spoke quickly, the words tumbling together in a rush.

'Okay, send me the details. I'll be there as soon as I can.'

Kray threw back the quilt, moaned out loud and made her way to the bathroom. The digits on her clock glowed green against the gloom - 3.53am.

Forty-five minutes later Kray flashed her badge to the officer standing at the mouth of an alleyway. She pulled on a pair of plastic overshoes, a coverall and gloves, and ducked under the yellow tape. The sun was up, casting a pink glow across the sky, a poetic sight that was totally at odds with what Kray was staring at.

'Morning. What have we got?' she said picking her way across the metal checker plates on the floor.

'Morning, Roz. Christ, you don't look good first thing, do you?'

'No and you don't look like your diet's working. What have we got?'

Mitch was her favourite Coroner's Office doctor. He was approaching fifty with a bald head and straining waistline, he was old school and well respected. Very business-like and to the point, just the way Kray liked it.

He was holding a wallet in his gloved hand. 'Joshua Steven Wilson, twenty-eight years of age from Preston. His friends reported him missing yesterday at around 2pm. He was in town celebrating a thirtieth birthday party and was last seen disappearing with a woman in the early hours of Friday morning. He never returned to his hotel and his mates raised the alarm when they couldn't get him on his phone.'

'How the hell can you tell all that from looking at his wallet?'

'The wallet gave me his name and the circumstances made me call the station.'

Kray was aware of a grotty-looking man sitting with his back against the wall, staring at the floor. She pointed a finger his way and cocked her head.

'That's the guy who found him. He said he could hear a phone going off and went to investigate, found Joshua here and called the police. He says he's homeless and was just passing by.'

Kray looked down at the vagrant. He raised his head and smiled, showing off a set of crooked teeth.

'How did you make the call?' she asked.

'I used the emergency function on his phone.'

She took the wallet, thumbed through the contents and lifted out a wad of notes.

'Well he wasn't robbed,' she said.

'I may not have a home but I'm not a thief,' the homeless man bristled.

Kray pursed her lips and moved further into the alleyway. A figure wearing a white shirt splashed with red lay face down against the back wall. His head cracked wide open.

'Ouch,' Kray said wrinkling up her nose.

'He's suffered massive blunt force trauma to the head. Three blows I reckon. One to the left side, another to the back of the neck and the third to the right-hand temple. With that amount of damage, it's unlikely it needed all three blows to cause death. We will know more once we do a post-mortem.'

'Was it a fight?'

'Doesn't look that way, I can't see any defensive wounds and his knuckles are clear.'

'Any sign of sexual activity?'

'Fucking loads of it, the locals call this blow job alley. There is more semen splashed about in here than in the back of a sperm donor van.'

'There is a fair amount of blood spatter. Will we be able to piece together the sequence of blows?'

'I would think so. There's a lot of forensics here to go on.'

Kray looked around and could see condoms scattered amongst the cans, bottles and food wrappers. She lifted her feet to check she wasn't carrying any unwanted guests.

'May I?' Kray ushered Mitch to step aside and squatted down near to the body. She checked Joshua's hands and his wristwatch, it was still going. His head was a bloody pulp with brain matter and bone spilled onto the floor.

'Is there any CCTV on the stretch of road?'

'No none, that's why the pros use it so much.'

'Time of death?'

'Can't be sure, he was seen out on the town at around midnight on Thursday.'

'So, that would make it between twenty-four and thirty-six hours ago.'

A man sporting the same white Teletubby outfit bustled in with a high-resolution camera and began snapping away. The staccato flash made the scene look a thousand times worse.

Kray took out a pen and poked around at the rubbish laying on the floor. 'No sign of a murder weapon I suppose?'

'You're not that lucky Roz, not even on a Saturday morning.'

'Ha. I can't remember the last time I was lucky on any day of the fucking week.'

'You're working the Madeline Eve case, aren't you?'

'Yup, Jackson re-assigned it to me.'

'Mmm, nasty shit from what I heard.'

Kray was silent, gazing down at the young man lying bludgeoned to death at her feet.

'What is it, Roz?'

'Oh nothing, just ...'

'What?'

'I wonder if this is linked to the Eve case.'

'Unlikely. This is a completely different MO. There are no similarities between the two.'

'That's true. But when was the last time we had two brutal murders in the same week?'

Mitch scratched at the stubble on his chin. 'As far as I know, never.'

'And that's the link.'

'Yeah, you might be right. Anyway that's your job, mine is to give you facts and opinion.' He changed his tone and lowered his voice, 'how have you been?'

'Oh, you know, up and down.'

'It's good to see you back.' Mitch placed his pudgy hand on her shoulder and smiled.

'Yeah,' she straightened up, replacing the pen in her inside pocket. 'I'm taking one day at a time.'

Kray spent the next fifteen minutes picking through the rotten debris around the body, placing items into evidence bags. The camera flash continued to illuminate the scene with its blinding light and an officer was making notes while talking to the homeless guy. Mitch was stood out on the kerb tapping away on his phone, waiting for the vehicle to transport the body to the morgue.

'That's me done. If you would like to follow me out, sir,' announced the officer as he replaced his notebook in his pocket and strolled out of the alleyway. Kray walked past the homeless guy and dangled a twenty-pound note in front of him.

'Take it,' she said.

He hesitated, not sure what to make of the offer. Kray stuffed the note in his hand.

'No, you're not a thief. Make sure you spend this putting food in your belly, not shit up your nose.'

Chapter 17

Kray was drinking coffee and ploughing through a mound of paperwork while she casually separated the pens to one side of her desk, the pencils to the other. She heard the sound of footsteps coming down the corridor, and she knew they belonged to Lucy Frost and Duncan Tavener. The clock on the wall read 11.43am.

'Christ, don't you two have anything better to do on a Saturday morning?' she said to them as they bustled in carrying a pizza box and enough cans of coke to start a children's party.

'We got your message about getting in early on Monday so we figured it must be something important,' said Tavener.

'And if it's that important, we thought getting a head start for a few hours would not be a bad thing,' Frost added as she eased into the corner seat flipping open the box and flooding the office with the smell of marinara sauce.

'Roz?' She offered her the box. Kray held up her hand in polite refusal.

'Well I appreciate the help even though I pity the pair of you if joining me in the office has been your best offer of the day.' They both laughed and munched at the food. 'DCI Jackson wants us to run with the latest murder as well as the Madeline Eve case. He said it would be good experience for you.'

Actually, his precise words were, 'you can take this case as well Roz because you are the one with the crèche' but she thought it best to paraphrase.

'Okay, we have Joshua Stephen Wilson, twenty-eight years of age from Preston.' Frost and Tavener scrabbled to locate their notebooks and snatched at the pens and pencils, disrupting their regimental setting. Kray winced as they scattered across the desk, she tore her gaze away and continued. 'He has suffered major blunt force trauma to the head with what looks like a lump hammer, we're hoping that the precise nature of the murder weapon will be confirmed during the post-mortem. He was struck three times with considerable force and his body dumped in an alleyway just off Richmond Street. There was no attempt to conceal the body and we have no CCTV footage. Time of death estimated to be the early hours of Friday morning. He was in town with his mates celebrating a birthday and was last seen on Thursday night when he went off with a woman. His friends raised the alarm when he failed to return to the hotel and they couldn't find him. The body was discovered around 3.20am this morning by a vagrant who heard his phone ringing. The motive does not appear to be robbery as he had a wallet stuffed full of cash. Forensics have his clothes, so we might get lucky, who knows? The body is at the morgue, the family have been informed and are on their way to identify the remains.'

The two members of the crèche scribbled away.

Tavener looked up. 'I'll get onto the clubs and bars to secure the CCTV from Thursday night, Friday morning. And if we have a current photograph of the vic I can take that with me, see if it jolts anyone's memory.'

'Yes that would be good,' Kray replied.

'I'll follow up with his friends and take statements,' said Frost.

'On a different topic, I will talk to forensics, see if they turned up any fingerprints from the phone box in the Madeline Eve case,' Kray said. 'Oh, and by the way, I appreciate you guys coming in.'

'That's fine, Roz.'

Kray was expecting them to get up and leave but they both sat there fidgeting. There was a pregnant pause which soured the atmosphere. Frost and Tavener stared at each other as if they were drawing mental lots as to who would speak first. Tavener obviously lost.

'Talking of the Eve case, there are a number of things which don't add up,' he said.

Kray nodded. 'I agree. A young woman is half strangled, dies from a massive injection of snake venom and has her body infested with a plague of flies, then has her face removed. I'd say that was an under-statement.'

Tavener and Frost glanced at each other again, drawing mental lots.

'We,' he gestured with his hand between the two of them, 'don't want to overstep the mark Roz, but what you've just told us doesn't make sense.'

Frost took up the challenge. 'The killer renders Madeline unconscious in a rear naked choke hold, or whatever it's called, and in a matter of seconds she's out cold. That would suggest that if the killer maintained the hold she'd be dead, right?'

Kray nodded her head.

'So the snake venom has to have another role in the attack other than a mechanism to kill Madeline. If the killer wanted to do that all he or she had to do was hang on a bit longer and that would be it. No more Madeline.'

'Okay I'll go along with that,' replied Kray.

'And the addition of the flies cannot be to throw us off the scent by giving us an incorrect time of death. The killer must have been aware that Madeline was in work on the Thursday. That doesn't fit either.'

'The flies were added to frustrate the collection of forensic evidence.' Kray made a bold statement, feeling uncomfortable with the line of discussion.

Tavener butted in. 'But what if it wasn't that, Roz? What if the flies were added for a different reason?'

Kray knew what was coming and was kicking herself.

'It's as though the killer didn't simply want to kill Madeline Eve, he wanted to obliterate her. The snake venom destroyed her body from the inside and the flies destroyed her body from the outside.'

'What are you saying?'

'I don't know Roz, it's as though the killer wanted to eradicate her as a person. Like he wanted to take away her very existence.'

Kray spun the ring around on her finger trying to control the urge to slap herself full in the face. She paused allowing her calm resolve to return. Frost and Tavener held their breath waiting for her to explode.

Why the fuck am I not the one telling them? Kray berated herself as the demons of self-doubt burst into her head. *Why did I not see that?* She was so far off her game it was unreal.

'Thanks for sharing that with me. You have some good points for us to consider as we move forward. Shall we get cracking?' Kray suggested.

'Sure, Roz.'

They both rose from the table still stuffing their faces with pizza.

Kray remained seated. 'I have some tasks to finish here first,' she said as the two of them marched out. One of the tasks was to give herself a thorough bollocking for not seeing what was right in front of her, or at least she would do, right after she put the pens and pencils back in order.

Chapter 18

I t's a short day at work today and I'm absolutely buzzing. My shift consisted of attending to a motley parade of B-list celebrities who were about to 'tell their story' to a brain-dead public, along with a bunch of current affairs experts who trotted out the same recycled drivel I had read in the papers the day before. Critical insight journalism it is not.

I made them look pretty and they spouted off in front of the cameras. Even the usual cascade of bitchy comments and snide remarks washed over me. I was too busy re-living every detail from the night before. The taxi pulls up to the kerb and I pile into my house not waiting for my change.

I pause in the hallway and drop my bag. I've got to collect myself, this is not something to be rushed.

I strip off my clothes, my heartbeat thumps out a marching rhythm in my head as I open the door under the stairs and remove the vacuum cleaner and coats. The wooden door at the back has a heavy duty dead bolt, secured with a padlock. I remove the piece of loose skirting board and retrieve the key. It fits snugly and the lock snaps open. I tug at the bar and as the dead bolt slides across, the door opens towards me.

I place my foot onto the top step and stare into the darkness. My left hand brushes against the cold plaster of the wall as I descend inside. The steps are steep, maintaining contact with the wall is crucial.

At the fifth step I can hear the sound of the refrigeration units humming in unison and by the eighth step my eyes become accustomed to the pale orange light pooling at the bottom of the steps. The grain of the wood feels sharp and gritty beneath

70

my bare feet as I feel my way deeper into the gloom. I reach the concrete floor at the bottom.

The green and red LEDs on the fridges illuminate the left-hand side of the room and the orange glow from the heat lamp gives the illusion that the right-hand side is on fire. The ceiling is low and flaky, where the paint of forty years ago has crumbled away. The walls are bare brick.

Solomon is eyeing me from the corner, tightly coiled with his tongue flicking at the air. He was fed five days ago so he's not excited to see me. A litter of three unwanted rabbits, Flopsey, Mopsey and Cotton Tail, bought from a lovely family who had advertised in the local paper, made a sumptuous dinner. I smiled sweetly at the children as they waved their pet's offspring goodbye with the promise of a life full of lush grass and veg peelings. I put Cotton Tail into Solomon's tank alive. He watched it jump around for a good twenty minutes before adopting his trademark S-shape and striking with a force that lifted the poor bunny into the air. Flopsey and Mopsey are stored as convenient ready meals in the freezer. I didn't kill them first, simply popped them in as they were. I reckon they taste fresher that way.

Propped against the wall is a shadow board, a six-feet wide and four-feet high piece of framed plywood upon which the tools of my trade sit. To be precise, they are the tools of my late father's trade, each one carefully selected and lovingly maintained to ensure a perfect execution every time. But they are mine now and I like to know that at any moment I have everything I need, a quick glance at the board tells me I'm ready to go. The black outline of the one-and-a-half-pound lump hammer drawn onto the board sticks out like a sore thumb. It is the only gap in the inventory. The hammer will be returned to its rightful place after it has finished soaking in a bucket of diluted bleach.

To the right is a self-standing clothes rail, racked out with garments and empty hangers. There are less empty hangers these days; I might need to think about getting a new rail for my latest acquisitions.

I walk across to the tall upright freezer holding my breath. I've been thinking about this all day. I yank at the handle and the suction on the door gives way with a whoosh, a wedge of clinical white light fills the room. The cold air tumbles out, pinching at my skin, making me shiver. My cock hardens.

The words flood into my head and I whisper them out loud, my breath condensing to white fog in front of my face.

'To chill her blood, how so divine,
Walk in her shoes, her face is mine,
With evil dripping from your pores,
The next face I need to take
… is yours.'

I mutter the lines over and over.

Standing on a glass shelf at eye level is a frosted black manikin head, covered with what looks like uncooked chicken skin. It is stretched around the contours of the head like a mask and held in place with pins. Dark ragged eye holes stare out at me and the slit for a mouth has a crooked smile. The eyebrows are perfectly aligned, but the nose is slightly off to one side, the cheeks tight and flawless.

I'm hoping my knife skills will improve with practice, because despite my best efforts this does not do the pretty face of Madeline Eve any justice at all.

The freezer contains two other glass shelves, each one supporting a frosted black manikin head. Their smooth crystallised surfaces waiting for their prize.

Chapter 19

The time Kray spent with the forensic team had been a complete waste of effort. What was it with these scientific types that they felt the need to drip-feed their findings like a bloody three-part BBC drama? The whole performance was like pulling teeth.

It should have taken a few minutes to tell her that there were no fingerprints on the handset or the buttons. The pound coin reclaimed from the cash box inside the machine was also clean. And apart from the phone box being home to three different sets of urine samples, it was also clear as a bell. They still had it cordoned off just in case there might be other leads to follow.

It should have taken a matter of minutes, not the hour and a quarter they made her sit through their long-winded proclamations.

Kray stepped out of her car, pulling a bag from the passenger seat. It was late afternoon and the cool breeze chilled her face as the sun struggled to warm the air. Puffy white clouds scudded fast across the sky, driven by the wind off the Irish Sea. She crossed the car park and headed up the hill. The grass, that had recently been cut, stuck to her shoes, shrouding them in green. Twenty yards further on, she joined a pebbled path. Roz stamped her feet, dislodging the unwanted greenery.

She crested the brow of the hill and a vibrant expanse of beautiful gardens opened up in front of her. It was a riot of colour. Flowers of every description carpeted the ground with wooden park benches dotted about for people to enjoy the beauty. Expertly tendered lawns and manicured pathways criss-crossed the scene stretching out in front of her. It was stunning, peaceful and serene. Kray fucking hated the place with a passion.

She left the path and circled around in an arc, heading for the fourth row from the far left. There was a time when this was the first row on the far left, then it became the second and then the third. At some point in the future she will not remember how many rows it was from the left.

The grass cuttings returned to her shoes as she trudged her way between the carnival of blooms. She stopped halfway along and knelt down, removing a handful of wilted foliage from a vase and emptying the dirty water out onto the soil.

'Hey, how have you been?' She rummaged around in the bag and brought out a water bottle, twisted off the cap and refilled the container. A fresh bouquet of flowers was stripped of its cellophane and arranged in the urn. Her eyes began to sting, she rubbed them with the back of her hand.

'I had a bust up with Wacko-Jacko the other day,' she said, as tears pooled against her lower eyelids. She set the vase back on the ground and gazed up to the sky, her bottom lip shaking.

'I got this new case ...' The words choked in her throat. She coughed into the crook of her arm and tried again. 'I got this new case. Wacko gave it to Brownbag to start with.' Her shoulders shook as sobbing overcame her.

'It's ... it's ...' She wiped her nose on her sleeve and cleared her throat. 'It's a murder case where a young woman ...' Raw grief dried her words in her mouth. Her head fell forward into her hands. Tears ran through her fingers.

'Fuck!' she cried in anguish, staring up at the clouds escaping into the distance. She straightened her shoulders and removed a card wrapped in cling film from the bag. It depicted a cartoon figure in a chef's hat standing in a kitchen. Around him in speech bubbles were innuendo jokes about the size of his chopper and what he was going to do with it.

'See, I didn't forget.' She inserted the card amongst the spray of cut flowers, her hands trembling. The lettering across the top read, 'Happy Birthday'.

'Anyway, I get this murder case …' Taking a ball of cloth from her pocket she soaked it in the last of the water from the bottle. 'I get this murder case and then like buses another one comes along. And I end up with that one as well.' Kray diligently wiped away four weeks of grime from the top of the stone like she was rubbing away the past. Every sinew in her body had told her not to come today, but she had to. The damp material kissed over the white lettering as dried tears stained her blotchy face.

'So now I have two fucking cases to manage. Fancy that, eh? Only been back a month.'

The cloth slipped from her grasp and her fingers came into contact with the cold black marble, sending a jolt of memories shuddering through her. Her fingers turned white as she gripped the top of the stone. In her mind she could see herself leaping from a car before it had even come to a halt and running up the street shouting through the open window as the vehicle cruised beside her.

'What the fuck do you know?' she yelled.

'I know fucking plenty, now get in the car.'

'Fuck off.'

She could see the people around her scurrying away as she skirted around the back of the moving car, dodging through the traffic to the opposite side of the road. She could hear the voice behind her calling out.

'Roz come back.'

But she had no intention of coming back.

It was the only thing they ever rowed about, it was the open wound in their life that refused to heal. Like clockwork, when things were going well, her poor eating habits would rise up and bite their happy relationship on the arse. The worse thing about these rows was that she knew he only had her best interests at heart. He loved her. Worst of all, she knew he was right.

As she clutched onto the stone with both hands, Kray could see herself stomping up the Promenade towards the Tower, crashing through the huddles of holiday-makers and day-trippers. She crossed a side road and once more joined the throngs of people out enjoying the thin sunshine.

Then Kray saw the flash of the blade. But it was too late.

His intention was to 'split her like a kipper' with a vicious upwards slash from groin to chin. She dodged to the side and the blade of the Stanley knife missed its intended target but cut a deep diagonal gash across her front. Starting at her belly, a glistening red line traversed her body slicing through her right breast. Her T-shirt erupted in blood as she spun away from the blow, hunching herself forward. The second blow ripped down her back, scything a yawning groove into her flesh. She arched her back, searing white pain tore through her.

In a sideways glance, Kray could see the attacker raise his arm and plunge the knife into her shoulder. He raised his arm again and blood spurted into the air as the short triangular blade exited her body. His clenched fist came crashing down, burying the blade deep into her back. Kray screamed in agony as she stumbled away, twisting and weaving to avoid the blows. Again and again the razor-sharp edge cleaved her open as the attacker stabbed and slashed her. Plumes of blood streaked across the pavement like some performance artist's painting. Parents grabbed their children and ran in all directions.

She could see herself whirling around, trying to dodge the flailing arm, then her legs gave way and she hit the concrete face first. She lay there staring at her attacker's feet. She could see flecks of blood imprinted on the white material of his trainers.

The sound of Joe's voice boomed inside her head. She could not make out if it was a throwback to their row or if he was actually there.

Then there was the crunching sound of two bodies heavily colliding and she saw her attacker's feet lift into the air as he was propelled backwards. She tried to move but her limbs refused to work. She felt wet and warm as the blood soaked through her clothes and pooled around her.

The two men landed with a spat on the ground - Joe on top, the man with the knife sprawled beneath him. They struggled briefly and her attacker rolled from under Joe and legged it. Joe lay motionless face down on the floor.

She could feel hands pulling at her as people arrived at her side.

'Call an ambulance!' someone shouted. 'Call 999!'

The cold pavement pressed into her cheek as she stared across at Joe. A middle-aged man appeared out of nowhere and rolled him over onto his back. A shower of arterial blood spewed into the air, covering the man's face and chest. He recoiled in horror wiping away the fluid.

From her position, Kray could see the Stanley knife sticking out of Joe's neck. His body was in spasm, his hands and feet twitching. She tried to get up to help but all she did was claw at the concrete. Kray watched the blood-soaked man strip off his shirt, roll it into a ball and clamp it to the side of Joe's throat.

'Get an ambulance!' he cried at the onlookers. 'Call an ambulance.'

Joe struggled to right himself but only succeeded in tilting his head forward, his body shaking and convulsing with the effort. Even as his life leaked out of him, Joe's only thoughts were of saving her.

Their eyes locked.

The six years they had spent together flashed between them in an instant. She could hear the sound of sirens whirling around as her world dissolved into darkness.

Kray was suddenly ripped from her thoughts by her phone ringing loudly in her pocket. She pulled her hands away from the polished marble as if it was red hot to the touch and staggered to her feet, wiping her eyes with her sleeve. She pulled the mobile from her pocket, her hand trembling.

'Yeah.' Her voice was coarse and breathless.

'Roz it's Lucy Frost. Where are you?'

'Can this wait, Lucy?'

'No, Roz, I don't think it can.'

'I'm in the middle of something.'

The voice on the other end paused. 'It's urgent Roz, how quickly can you get here?'

Kray put both hands on the phone to stop it shaking. 'What is it? What's so urgent?'

'We've trawled through the CCTV footage from the bars and have a positive ID on the woman who was with Joshua Wilson the night he was murdered.'

'That's good work. Put a face to the name and pull her in for questioning.'

'Roz, you need to come and see this.'

'I need to finish off here, then I'll join you later.'

'But Roz, we know who she is.'

'Even better. Drag her arse down to the station.'

'Not sure it will be that easy Roz, the woman in the picture is Madeline Eve.'

Chapter 20

The swing door to the station bounced back off its hinges as Kray battered her way through. Her car was parked in a disabled bay as it was the closest one to the entrance - she would deal with the snotty email from the facilities when it arrived.

Bounding up the stairs, she hurtled down the second-floor corridor and found the Imaging Suite on the left, a welcome addition to the forensic capabilities of the force since their third-party suppliers of imaging expertise developed a lead time of eight weeks to process a piece of CCTV. Sometimes effective policing and cost-cutting make unhappy bed fellows. Both members of her crèche were sat in front of an oversized flat screen.

'Hey,' she said, breathing heavily 'I got here as fast as I could.'

Frost's fingers flitted across the key board and a blur of images rolled back and forth.

'Hi Roz,' Tavener said, 'we thought it best for you to see this straight away.'

'I can't increase the resolution more than that. It's still not good enough.' Frost's eyes were glued to the pixelated figures in front of her.

'You know how to use this kit?' Roz asked.

'I did a six-week placement here when I was on rotation. It's state of the art gear, very cool.' Frost sped through the CCTV footage, occasionally stopping and zooming in.

'What have you got?' Kray asked, pulling up a chair.

Frost pressed a key and the image on the screen disappeared to be replaced by a menu of files. Three more clicks and the screen was once more filled with black and white pictures of grainy people.

'Okay, these are taken from the CCTV footage in town. We have fleeting screen grabs of Joshua Wilson and a young woman, but this is the best so far. This is him at half past midnight.' The image showed him standing in a crowded bar. The shot was taken from above by a camera located in the corner of the room. His face was caught in profile, it was definitely him.

'Wind forward a couple of minutes and we have this.' The pictures whizzed around like a Charlie Chaplin movie, then slowed down. 'Here, he is joined by a woman.' Frost froze the screen.

Kray leaned forward and scrutinised the image. It showed a woman with a dark bob sidling up to Josh and slipping her arm around his waist. They manoeuvred their way through the knot of people and out of shot.

'But that's only the back of her head.' Kray said.

'Yes, but then ...'

The image scrolled forward and the couple came back into shot. Josh was nearest to the camera, shielding the woman from view. They were heading towards a group of guys who were vacating a high table. Josh had his arm around her shoulder guiding her through the mass of people. He reached the table and put his pint down marking his territory. He seemed to exchange words with the men leaving and they laughed. Every now and then tantalising glimpses of the woman could be seen as they jostled position.

Kray was on the edge of her seat with her elbows on the desk, as if getting her face closer to the screen was going to help.

'Get out the way,' she said to herself as a tall man dressed in a sharp suit crossed in front of the couple.

The group of men parted and Josh pulled a bar stool up to the table for his companion. All that could be seen was the top of her head. She put her glass on the table and bent down, disappearing from view.

'What the fuck is she doing now?' Kray asked.

'We think she's sorting out her bag,' said Tavener.

The woman emerged, stood up and flicked her hair behind her ears. Josh steadied the stool and she slid herself onto it. She turned and lifted her wine, he chinked his glass against hers and they drank their toast.

Then the woman looked up, straight down the lens of the camera. Frost hit pause.

Kray's jaw dropped as she gazed at the face staring up at her.

It *was* Madeline Eve.

'Fucking hell,' Kray uttered, her face so close to the screen she looked in danger of toppling off her chair.

'That's what we said,' chipped in Tavener, looking over Frost's shoulder.

'That is the best image we have so far, Roz. There may well be others, but it takes time to trawl through the footage,' Frost said, pushing herself away from the desk.

'That's her alright,' Kray confirmed, pointing a finger at the image on the screen.

'How the hell does that happen? She doesn't have a bloody twin,' said Tavener.

'No, she doesn't, but from this angle, and from this distance, that *is* Madeline Eve,' said Frost.

'And she's laid up in the morgue with a decomposed body and no face. This is someone impersonating her,' said Kray.

'Are we sure of the identity of the body?'

'Yes. The dental records match and she had some scarring on her left knee following a childhood injury. Her parents positively identified the scar. It's definitely her,' Kray replied.

'Then who the hell are you?' Tavener asked, it was his turn to point a finger.

'A woman who dresses up as dead people,' said Kray.

'Maybe not. Have you ever seen the Lady Boys of Bangkok? I saw them in Manchester and they were the most beautiful women I've ever seen,' said Frost.

'You saw the ...' Kray left the sentence hanging.

'It was a hen party.'

'Oh.'

'What I mean is, it could be a man.'

Kray touched the face of the woman on the screen. 'I know this place,' she said in a whisper.

'Pardon, Roz.'

'This is the Purple Parrot, off Matlock Lane.'

'That's right,' said Tavener. 'You know it?'

'I used to know it, I don't go there any more,' Kray said, and a shiver ran through her. She traced the outline of the couple on the screen with her finger.

'Too many bad memories?'

'No, exactly the opposite. Too many good ones,' Kray mused to herself as she scrutinised the image. 'Shit! Did you see that?

'What? What is it?'

'Run it back and then forward again.'

'Okay.' Frost drew herself back into position and operated the keyboard.

The image of Madeline Eve ducked down beneath the table, stood up, sat herself on the bar stool, chinked glasses with Josh and looked up. Then she lowered her gaze and continued her conversation.

'Rewind,' said Kray.

Frost made the images go into reverse then pressed play.

The sequence repeated itself.

'And again,' Kray said.

Frost did it again.

'And again.'

The footage rewound and played.

'And again.'

'What is it, Roz?' asked Tavener. 'What can you see?'

'Stop! Stop it right there,' Kray said suddenly. 'Look.'

They both peered at the screen, then at Kray.

'Look at what, Roz?' he asked.

'She isn't simply looking up. This woman is staring straight into the camera, and if I'm not mistaken, she lifts her glass slightly when she does it.'

Frost played and rewound the images.

'See there, she lifts her glass as she looks into the lens.'

'Shit you're right.'

'This isn't someone who's been caught on CCTV. This person is posing for the camera saying, 'Cheers'.'

Chapter 21

I never laughed much as a kid, father saw to that. Whether it was the cut of his belt or the back of his hand, childish joy was something I encountered at the homes of others. And while he was busy thinking up different ways to inflict pain on my body, my mother was equally occupied screwing with my head.

She had always wanted a girl; I was a crushing disappointment from the second my life clock started ticking. To the outside world I was Jason - the socially awkward, scrawny boy with the over-excitable mother and a scary father. But when the front door closed I ceased to have a name. I was 'runt' or 'little shit', but never Jason.

At every opportunity my mother would whisper in my ear telling me how we would both be better off without Father. How our lives would be transformed if he should one day disappear. She even did it when he was in the house, she'd wait until he left the room then sidle up to me.

'You and I would be so much happier without him, don't you think? We'd be fine you and me and you wouldn't have to dodge his anger.' For years she bombarded my malleable brain with the poison that my father was nothing but a septic sore that lay at the centre of our lives, poisoning everything around it. A sore that needed to be lanced.

I later came to realise that it was my mother who had her finger poised above my father's anger switch. And when she pushed the button, she ensured it always exploded in my direction. But as much as I hated the beatings, as much as I hated feeling sick when I heard his key turn in the lock, what I feared most was when Father went out of the house and it was just me and her.

On those occasions my name was 'Pretty Girl'. My mum made me wear patterned skirts and dresses with satin slips. I had open-toed patent shoes and lace-topped socks. She spent hours teaching me how to apply make-up and how to fit a wig correctly.

'That's it Pretty Girl, be gentle, you don't want it to clump on your eyelashes.' Or, 'not too much red, you don't want the boys to get the wrong idea.'

The voice training was tough. I was not allowed to speak as a boy. I had to adopt the soft tones of a girl. I learned about chest resonance, timbre and pitch. I had to speak with my head voice, forcing the words to the front of my mouth to increase the pitch. The exercises were relentless - practice, practice, practice, until it was second nature. When my father was at home I spoke normally, but the second he was out of the door I had to transition to 'Pretty Girl'.

At first I fought against it, but if I defied her, or purposefully did it wrong, she would fly into an incandescent rage. She would shriek like an animal, screaming about how I should have been a girl and she would make me one, even if she had to kill both of us in the process. Once the rage had taken hold, nothing I did could bring her down. With her fury squarely in the red zone she would storm into the kitchen and return with a pair of drapery pinking shears and make me pull down my feminine underwear, forcing me to expose myself.

'Do you want me to cut it off?' she would hiss, grabbing my ear to hold me in place, while she snapped the shears open and closed. I would struggle against her hold, looking down as she brought them closer and closer to my genitals - the blades snapping open and closed. 'Do you want me to get rid of that thing?' I remember my body trembling with terror and feeling the warm flow of piss on my legs as I lost control. It always ended the same way, I would be thrown into the cellar under the stairs and left there in the pitch black. To this day, the sound of metal shearing against metal makes me want to piss myself.

My mother was pure evil in a floral dress and pearls.

Life improved when Father left, or it would be more accurate to say, when he didn't come back. He was never found.

A neighbour constructing an extension and the back of a shovel was all the encouragement a damaged fourteen-year-old boy needed. I had no idea about finger prints or dental records. No idea about shoe imprints or blood spatter patterns. All I knew was when I held the shovel in my hand I thought … *this will do the job nicely*.

I split his skull wide open. I was shocked by the amount of blood. It poured out and absorbed into the grass. I was worried that someone would see it, but it washed away to nothing and the swirl of the concrete mixer coupled with the close attention of a rake did the rest. He was gone.

The bastard had it coming to him, that was for sure. But not because of what Mother said, nor as the result of a slap to the face, or a dig in the ribs, or the slash of his belt buckle across my back, no it was something much simpler.

That Iced Slice in the fridge was mine.

He knew it was mine. He saw Mother buy it for me and he fucking took it. I watched him scoff his face with my treat right in front of me. Pushing his thick fingers into his mouth to lick away the last of the custard. Goading me, taunting me.

I never told Mother what I'd done, she just kind of knew.

I must admit, I laughed a lot that day.

Chapter 22

'Here's one to keep you awake at night.' Kray pushed the screen grab of Madeline Eve staring up into the CCTV camera across the desk. 'Joshua Wilson disappeared with her on the night he was killed.'

Jackson picked it up. 'And this is …'

'Madeline Eve, or at least someone posing as her.'

'It's a good likeness.'

'It's an exact likeness. I had a feeling the killings were linked.'

'Oh, how come?'

'Two murders in the same week, there's got to be a connection. This is Blackpool, not bloody Baltimore.'

Jackson snorted and nodded his head. 'So what's the next steps?'

'I got the crèche out pounding the streets with this picture, knocking on doors trying to find someone who saw them together on the night. The forensics report might give us more to go on.'

'Do you think Gorgon killed Joshua?'

Kray winced at the mention of the killer's new pet name. 'I think it's highly likely this person murdered Madeline Eve, impersonated her, and killed Joshua Wilson. It's too much of a coincidence.'

Neither of them said a word, both absorbing the size of the task ahead.

'I've been thinking about why Gorgon removes the victim's face—'

Kray cut him off.

'Obliterate,' Kray said under her breath.

'What?'

'Obliterate. That's what Tavener said the killer had done to Madeline. He said she wasn't just murdered, it was as though whoever carried it out wanted to obliterate her. Like they wanted to take away her very existence.'

'I don't follow—'

'Shit! See you when I get back.' And with that Kray hurtled out of his office, snatched the photographs of Madeline Eve from the notice board and wheel spun her way out of the station car park.

Forty minutes later she was standing in the bedroom of flat seventeen, Dennison Heights. Kray fished the photos from her bag and laid them out on the bed along with the screen shot from the CCTV. She moved the pictures around, laying one on top of the other.

Kray opened the wardrobe and flicked through the array of hangers. She opened up a chest of drawers, rooting through jumpers and tops. She went to the bathroom and rummaged through the laundry basket.

There was a noise in the hallway and Tavener appeared.

'Got your message, Lucy is on her way.'

'Good. I wanted you to see this first hand. How is the door knocking going?'

'Slow. They look like any other couple on a night out, or that's the most popular response.'

'Okay, keep at it.'

'What is this about, Roz?'

'It's what you said about the killer wanting to obliterate the body.'

'Yeah, what of it?'

'I think you're right. Look at this photo taken from her rogue's gallery in the hallway.' The picture showed Madeline Eve amongst a gaggle of young women smiling wildly for the camera. The woman in the centre was holding up a cut-glass trophy. 'The one on the far right is Ania Sobotta. She worked with Madeline. I suspect this was taken at a company awards ceremony. Ania has only been with the firm for six weeks, so it's pretty recent.'

'Okay.'

'Madeline is wearing a red dress with a distinctive neckline, scalloped with a V in the front.'

'Okay.'

'Now take a look at the screen grab taken from the pub. I reckon that's the same dress. It's a black and white image so you can't tell the colour, but it could be red.'

Tavener studied the two images. He was used to staring at women in dresses but not from the perspective of identifying material design elements.

'It could be,' he muttered.

Lucy Frost could be heard bustling through the front door, seconds later she appeared in the bedroom.

'What is it? It sounded important.'

'Ah, right on cue,' said Kray. 'If a girl is going on a posh works night out what does she need.'

'What?'

'Go with it Lucy, what does she need to wear?'

'Oh err, a new dress, a glitzy clutch bag to match and a pair of killer heels,' Lucy said.

'Excellent, that's the benefit of gender equality in the workplace right there. So, where is it?' Kray opened her arms wide.

'Where's what?' asked Tavener.

'Where is the red dress in the photograph? It's not here. I've looked everywhere and can't find it.'

'Do you—'

'Also, I've checked and there are plenty of bags and shoes but nothing that says, 'big night out'. I think the killer took Madeline's dress on the night she was murdered, along with her bag and shoes. I think the person in this photograph is wearing her clothes. I think the killer wants to become Madeline Eve.'

'Gorgon doesn't just want to take her life, he wants to take her identity,' Frost muttered.

'Yes, and that's why he removed her face.'

Kray's phone went off, breaking the moment.

'DI Kray.'

'I just seen her.' It was a woman's voice.

'Who is this?'

'Bóg mnie uratuje.'

'I'm sorry? Please speak English.'

'I just seen her. Walking about. I tell you, I saw her.' Her voice was breaking with panic and she was crying.

'Calm down. Can you tell me who this is and how you have my number.'

'You are DI Kray right?' Kray tuned in and detected an eastern European accent.

'Yes this is Kray. Is this Ania?'

'Yes, it is, we met when you came to the office. You gave me your card.'

'Ania, yes I remember. What is it? Are you in trouble? Are you in danger?'

'No, I am fine but I've just seen her. Pieprzone piekło.' Her words were tumbling together.

'Slow down, Ania? Who have you seen?'

'Widziałem ducha.'

'Who? Please Ania, in English.'

'A ghost. I seen a ghost.'

'Who Ania, who have you seen?'

'Madeline. I just saw Madeline Eve.'

Chapter 23

Kray covered the phone with her hand. 'Madeline Eve has been spotted.' The other two stared at each other in silence. 'Where are you, Ania?'

'I'm at the Trafford Centre. She is here, I can see her.'

'Where at the Trafford Centre, Ania? Where are you?'

'Outside the Apple shop.'

Kray covered the mouthpiece again. 'She's at the Trafford Centre near the Apple shop. Send a photo of Madeline over to the security control room and get them looking for her on CCTV.' Frost and Tavener scurried into the other room dialling numbers frantically as they went.

'Listen to me very carefully,' said Kray. 'Do not—'

'I can see her! Pieprzone piekło.' Her speech was breathless.

'Try to calm yourself, Ania. What is she wearing?'

'Umm, a blue top and jeans I think.'

Kray cupped her hand over the mouthpiece and called to the others. 'She's wearing a blue top and jeans, relay that to the control room.' Tavener and Frost nodded. 'Ania listen to me. Do not approach her, it is not Madeline. Keep her at a distance and stay on the phone. Do you hear me Ania, stay on the line.'

'Yes okay, I hear you.'

'Where is she now?'

'She is walking away.'

'Where Ania? Where?'

I can see you – the words sing in my head.

With your phone clamped to the side of your head, I bet the conversation is running riot. Have you seen any ghosts lately

Polish lady? I grab tantalising glimpses of your distress as I window shop my way down the esplanade of shops. You look terrified.

I love it when people are predictable. The second Sunday in the month you get in your car and take the sixty-minute drive to stock up on the latest fashions. Looking good is so important to you, but I have to say you're not looking so hot at the moment.

I've been hovering around in the background for the past forty-five minutes waiting for you to notice me. You are not very observant. You glide around the shops in a vacant trance, your eyes fixed on the glittery tops and stylish jackets rather than the faces of those around you. But you got there eventually and the horror on your face was well worth the wait.

'She is walking towards John Lewis,' Ania replied.

'John Lewis, John Lewis … where the fuck?' Kray racked her brains trying to visualise the layout of the mall with its two hundred shops. She burst into the other room and motioned for the other two to listen. 'Madeline is on the first floor heading to John Lewis.'

Tavener conveyed the latest information to the man on the phone, who would be sitting in front of the collage of screens in the security control centre.

'We are getting a photograph over to you as soon as we can,' he said for the tenth time.

Kray returned to the bedroom. 'Can you still see her?' she asked. There was no response. 'Ania, can you still see her?' No response. 'Ania are you there?'

'She's gone,' Ania blurted out.

'Shit,' Kray hissed, holding the phone away from her mouth. 'Where are you now, Ania?'

'I am outside Burton. She was here, I could see her. Then she disappeared.'

'Stay where you are Ania, she's probably gone into a shop. Stay put and wait until she comes out. Try not to let her see you.'

Kray dashed back into the lounge. 'Have the CCTV guys got her yet?'

'No, boss, the station is having difficulties emailing Madeline's picture. It keeps bouncing back.'

'Keep trying.'

There's nothing like creating a drama out of a crisis and in this case all it took was to wait until she wasn't looking. Then I sat down on one of the benches. The middle-aged man next to me, his feet buried deep in a mountain of bags, looks as though he's had enough for the day. I smile, he smiles back.

I can see the Polish girl through the throngs of passing shoppers as she spins on the spot trying to locate me. Her mouth is animated as she barks words into her phone. This is a great sport.

I wonder if they have picked me up yet on the CCTV. With two hundred and eighty-five cameras in the place, I have to appear on one of them. They must be going berserk.

I'll give it a couple more minutes, make that bitch sweat for it.

'They got the photograph, Roz.' Tavener stuck his head around the door. Kray nodded.

'Ania, can you—'

'There she is, I can see her.'

'Okay Ania that's really good. Well done. Where is she now?'

'She is outside Boots and is walking away from me.'

'Stay well back, Ania, don't get too close. We will pick her up on the CCTV any second now.' Kray stepped into the lounge again with the phone clasped between her hands. 'Where the fuck is that CCTV?'

'Coming, Roz, they're scanning the last known position.'

'Is she—'

'Gówno!'

'Ania what is it?'

'She is coming right at me.'

'Ania keep calm and move away. Head to the nearest shop and let her pass. Don't look at her. Do it Ania, do it now.'

I reckon she must be shitting herself.

The look of panic on her face is making me want to laugh my bollocks off. A simple change of direction and the drama needle goes off the scale. I watch her scuttle away and pretend to gaze into a shop window. Her head is flicking nervously around as I close the gap between us. We are level now and I'm fighting every urge in my body to turn and flash her a smile.

'They got her, Roz.' Lucy came into the room. 'The CCTV controller has her on the screen, she's walking back the other way.'

'I know. Tell them to mobilise their security and pick her up. Make it look like they suspect her of shoplifting. Hold her until we can get there.'

Kray returned to her phone. 'Ania, we have her on CCTV now. Can you see her?'

'Yes she is walking into Selfridges.'

'Okay.' Kray waved her hand to Frost. 'She's going into Selfridges, tell the CCTV controller to track her there.'

'He's got her on the screen but they don't have cameras inside the shops.'

'Fuck!' Kray balled her fists. 'Ania listen to me, I want you to follow her but stay well back. We cannot see her inside the store, do you understand?'

'She is inside now. I can see her, she's picking up clothes.'

'That's good Ania, keep talking to me.' Kray cupped her handset once more. 'Where are the security?'

'On their way, Roz, and they have pictures of Madeline.'

Come on my lovely Polish woman follow me like a good girl. I chose this shop for two reasons. The first is that it is not simply a Selfridges store, it's also a Primark store. Which means the calm and orderly shopping experience will dissolve into mad chaos as soon as you cross the threshold. The entire teenage population of Manchester is in here, it's shopping anarchy with a generous side order of raging hormones. The staff are entirely focussed on getting through the day rather than noting who is in their store.

The second reason for choosing this particular shop should be becoming apparent around about now ...

'Hello, Ania? What's happening?'

'She ... I ... clothes, I can't ...'

Kray caught only snippets of her voice as the signal broke down.

'Ania? Are you there?'

The voice on the other end crackled and gurgled before it went dead. Kray looked at the 'Call Failed' message on the screen of her phone.

'Fuck! I've lost her,' she announced. 'Her last known location was Selfridges.'

'That has two exits boss, one on the first floor where she went in and the other is on the ground floor.'

'Get security to cover both.'

I love it. It's utter pandemonium in the changing rooms, there must be twenty garments on the floor of my cubicle. I place the four tops, still on the hangers, on top of the pile and unpack the contents of my rucksack. The mirror attached to the wall is useful as I undress and in less than ten minutes, I'm done.

I slide the latch across on the door and sidle out into the narrow corridor. I pass the shop assistant trying to maintain order amongst the hordes of young shoppers, handing her the garments as she stares at me open-mouthed.

'They weren't right,' I say shaking my head. She struggles to say anything in response.

As I shoulder my way into the main area of the store and notice the Polish woman hovering around, her head twisting one way then the other, like a wind-up toy. She is punching buttons on her phone but that won't do her any good. I ease my way through the knots of teenage girls ransacking the shelves and make my way out into the relative calm of the concourse. A man and a woman dressed in ill-fitting uniforms are standing either side of the door, each one holding a piece of paper.

I pull the peak of my baseball cap down over my eyes and walk past them into the glare of the CCTV cameras. The flood of shoppers carries me along to the escalators and down to the ground floor exit.

After a short wait, I board the bus to take me to the off-site park and ride. The number plate recognition system installed at the Trafford Centre car parks makes driving to the place too much of a risk. Though it is annoying that with spaces for twelve and a half thousand cars I have to catch a fucking bus to reach my car. As we trundle to the roundabout, I see two police cars come screeching to a halt. I settle back and hug my rucksack. The bus is a pain in the arse, but it is better to be safe than sorry.

Chapter 24

When Kray arrived at the Trafford Centre the police had the store sealed off or, more accurately, they had done a good job of ensuring that the occupants were sealed in. The duty manager was kicking up a fuss about loss of trade and goodwill, and a small contingent of irate parents were not buying the line of 'it's just routine'. But on the whole, Greater Manchester Police had the situation under control.

The hundred and fifty kids inside were having a ball with the whole experience. The most popular rumours that were circulating around were mumbles that they had been unlawfully detained, for which they would all receive a sizeable compensation settlement, and the other was that someone had been murdered in the changing rooms.

A crew of officers and PCSOs had swept through the ground and first floors, using pictures of Madeline Eve to screen people out. Also, they turned over every inch of the store to check if anyone was hiding. On both counts they had drawn blanks.

'Nothing, ma'am,' said a sergeant in uniform. 'We've gone through everyone in the store and this person,' he held up the photo, 'is not on the premises. We can't hold them for much longer.'

'Okay sergeant, can you organise for everyone to leave via the first-floor exit and we will conduct one final check.'

'Yes, ma'am.'

Ania Sobotta was still in shock. She was sat on a bench, flanked by a PC, sipping a coffee and staring into the middle distance.

'I need you to help, Ania.' Kray spoke softly.

'It was her. I saw her.'

'No, Ania, what you saw was someone pretending to be Madeline.'

'But it was her …' She grappled with her bag and pulled out a tissue, dabbing her eyes.

'No, Ania, it wasn't.'

'Bóg mnie uratuje, widziałem ducha.'

'Ania, we are going to clear the people out of the shop using this exit and I want you to stand with me and look at everyone who files past. If you see anything familiar, anything at all, I want you to tell me.'

'Okay.' Ania got to her feet and positioned herself next to Kray as the officers funnelled the excited youngsters out into the main thoroughfare. Twenty minutes later the shop reopened, and a fresh band of excited young shoppers spilled through the doors, eager to find out what the commotion had been about. 'There's been a murder.' One of them said in an exaggerated Scottish accent.

Lucy Frost was making friends with the small team in the security command centre. She had located the exact moment when Madeline Eve had entered Selfridges at 11.42am and was combing through the footage of six cameras, each one with a different view of the exits. They scrolled through the images looking for Madeline leaving the store, the clock on the top of the screen said 11.56am.

Kray was losing patience. She was fast reaching the conclusion that picking up clothes off the floor and putting them back onto hangers for a living must make you oblivious to everything else around you. Not a single member of staff had seen Madeline while she was in the shop.

Kray systematically took members of staff off the floor and interviewed them in a side office. She was on her sixth person and was losing the will to live.

'This woman entered the shop at around 11.40am,' Kray said pointing to the head-and-shoulders shot of Madeline Eve laying on the desk. 'Did you see her?'

'No,' replied the assistant.

'Take a good look. Did you see this woman in the store?'

'No. Did someone really get murdered in the changing rooms?'

Kray decided this was not a job for her and called Tavener.

'You take over before I burst a ventricle.'

Kray turned her attention to Ania who was still sitting outside with a PC.

'Tell me again, Ania, what happened in the store?'

'She walked around checking out the clothes. I was trying to reach you but my phone signal had died. I lost her, there was so many people.' She reached for her sodden tissue again.

Kray put her hand on Ania's shoulder. 'It's okay, you did a fantastic job.'

'But why would—' Ania didn't get the chance to finish her sentence as Kray's phone rang.

'Yes.'

'Roz I think we got something.' It was Tavener.

'Good has someone seen Madeline?'

'Not exactly.'

Fifteen minutes later Kray and Tavener pushed open the door to the control centre where Lucy Frost was fast getting square eyes from staring at the bank of screens covering the wall. The clock at the top said 12.14pm.

'Hey,' Frost said, leaning back in her chair and stretching her hands up to the ceiling. 'We have her going into the store.' She pointed to a freeze frame on the bottom right of the screen. 'But so far we've not got her coming out and we are now thirty-two minutes past the time when she was seen entering the shop.'

A petite young woman with purple hair appeared from behind the large frame of Tavener.

'Wow,' she said in a voice that made her sound like she'd been inhaling helium.

'This is Hayley. She works in Primark,' said Kray.

'This is incredible,' Hayley said wide-eyed as she looked around.

'Tell the people what you told my officer.' Kray beckoned her further inside the office.

'Well, you showed me a picture of a girl and asked if I'd seen her in the shop. And I hadn't.'

'Go on,' Kray said.

'Then you left and the man here,' she pointed to Tavener, 'asked if I had seen anything unusual during my shift, you know, anything out of the ordinary.'

'And …'

'We rotate around the store and it was my turn to look after the changing rooms. It's a job that everyone hates because people leave the place in such a mess and people kick off when they have to wait for a cubicle.'

'Tell them what you told my officer.'

'When I was on the changing rooms I had a guy come out of a cubicle and hand me four items of clothing, tops I think they were.'

'A guy?' asked Frost. 'Why is that unusual?'

'He came out of one of the women's changing rooms and I'm sure I didn't see him go in. We are strict about that kind of thing, you know when boyfriends want to go in with their girlfriends – it's a big no-no.'

Kray let the full impact of what Hayley was telling them sink in.

'So Hayley, what I want you to do is sit with Lucy and see if you can identify the man you saw coming out of the changing room. Is that okay?'

'Err yeah, I suppose so. I only saw him briefly.'

'What was he wearing?' asked Frost.

'I don't know, it all happened so fast. I was a bit shocked.'

'Can you remember anything at all about him,' Frost prompted. 'Was he white, was he tall, dark hair, anything you can recall?'

'He was a white guy, about my height, slim build and he was wearing a baseball cap. You know one of those with the stupid wide peaks. He had one of those.'

Kray pulled a chair up for Hayley to sit down.

'Okay Lucy, start again, but this time we're looking for a hat.'

Chapter 25

I edge the car into a side street and kill the engine, still trying to come down from the thrill of the morning. What a rush.

I dig my thumbnail under the rim, lever the lid free from the tobacco tin and remove the white plastic key nestling snuggly in the padded foam. I hold it up against the sunshine flooding through my windscreen, a ball of nervous tension filling my chest.

I wonder ...

My watch says it's a quarter after one, I've got at least a couple of hours. The plods are going to be battling their way through the incoherent statements of a hundred pissed-off teenagers and ploughing through a mountain of CCTV footage.

All the while asking the same question: 'Have you seen this woman?' All the while looking for Madeline Eve. I also suspect that somewhere under the vaulted glass roof of the Trafford Centre a PC will be feeding cups of coffee to a traumatised Polish woman.

I pop open the boot, step out of the car and retrieve a wad of takeaway menus from a bag. After slamming the lid shut, I walk down Dunbar Street and turn right. I step from the pavement onto the brick pathway that cuts through the overgrown foliage in the front garden. I peel a menu away from the bundle and hold it in front of me as I approach the front door. Delivering takeaway menus is a great cover. The key slips into the Yale lock, I push it all the way until the plastic shoulder hits the brass face. I can feel the jagged contours engaging with the tumblers as the springs in the barrel compress. I turn the key – it won't budge.

I jiggle the plastic back and forth maintaining a slight turning pressure. This is tricky. I don't want to damage the delicate plastic edges. Then, with a soft click, the tumbler finally turns and the mechanism disengages. I hold my breath as I edge the door open, listening for the beep of a house alarm. The hallway is silent.

A furtive glance over my shoulder and I'm in, closing the door behind me. I replace the key into its foam cocoon and stand breathlessly still, tuning into my surroundings. Satisfied the house is empty, I make my way down the hall.

The place looks like a show home, with not a thing out of place. It's immaculately clean. The long lounge has an array of scatter cushions arranged across a huge leather sofa and an eclectic mix of ornaments line the mantelpiece. The décor is modern with clean lines and neutral colours. At one time this room was probably intended to be a lounge diner, only now the requirement to dine has long since gone. The kitchen is the same with every surface wiped clean and uncluttered. I press the toe of my shoe on the peddle of the flip-top bin to reveal two bottles that used to contain white wine.

Tut, tut.

I make my way upstairs, nudging the first door I come to with my shoulder. It's the bathroom, filled with soft towels and bath products. The next door along is a spare bedroom and the one opposite is an office containing a shabby desk and a chair, but little else. The door to the right opens up onto the main bedroom, a large space with an en suite off to the left. It is decorated in the same modern style with two double-fitted wardrobes and a matching dressing table in the bay window. A king-sized bed hogs the room with enough pillows stacked against the headboard to furnish a small guesthouse. In keeping with the rest of the house, everything is in pristine condition with not a make-up pad out of place.

Then I see it. My heart leaps in my chest.

Taking pride of place on the bedside table behind the digital clock is a framed photograph. It depicts a couple on a night out, leaning into each other at a dinner table, his arm around her shoulders pulling her close. Their faces beam out of the picture, but it is the happiness in their eyes which makes me blush and turn away – it's like I am intruding on a private moment.

Perfect.

I open the wardrobe and fan my hands through the clothes lined up in regimented order. Dresses, tops and trousers all ready to be picked out. The second wardrobe contains very little, just a gentleman's shirt and a dark blue suit. I go back to the first wardrobe and ease apart each of the garments.

Then I see it. A black plastic suit cover hanging from the rail at one end. I unhook it and run the zip down and the shimmer of emerald green jumps out at me.

I lay it on the bed and remove the dress from the protective cover. It is beautiful, with its fitted bodice and pencil skirt. I hold it against my body and give a little twirl on the spot. No wonder the man in the photograph looked so happy. Any man would feel on top of the world with his arm around a woman who was wearing this dress.

I snap out of my daydream and replace the garment into its cover, hanging it back on the rail. It's time to leave. But before I go, maybe a little mischief ...

Chapter 26

Kray stood in her kitchen, every muscle in her body confirming she'd had a long and tiresome day.

The time she'd spent at the Trafford Centre had been a frantic whirlwind of activity and stress. With Hayley's help, Lucy Frost had found the CCTV clip showing the man with the baseball cap leaving the store. She copied the file and had it sent to the station to run through image enhancement. The high camera angle ensured they had a great shot of the top of his head, but nothing of his face. Still, it was worth further analysis to see if any distinguishing marks became visible.

They had also sat Hayley with a photo-fit guy but she came up with nothing. All she could recall was the damned hat. She could, however, tell them that he was about the same height as she was, slightly built with good teeth.

'I got a thing about people's teeth,' she admitted.

Pity you didn't have the same fixation about the rest of their face.

Ania had continued to struggle coming to terms with what had happened. She seemed unable to process what she had witnessed and eventually Kray sent her home. But to be on the safe side, she'd despatched the PC to drive Ania's car as she was in no fit state to do much, let alone get herself home in one piece.

Kray pulled open the fridge door to retrieve a half-bottle of Sav Blanc. She lifted a glass from the cupboard and headed upstairs to the bathroom. Soon the scent of spun sugar candyfloss and juniper filled the top floor of the house, and steam fogged up the mirrors. Bridging across the rim of the bathtub was a slab of sanded wood with a carved indent to hold a glass and a raised section to hold a book. It had been a Christmas present from Joe. He had wrapped it in sparkling wrapping paper and left it under the tree along with ten best seller books. It was one of his many failed attempts to persuade his wife to take it easy. It had never worked. Nowadays it served the purpose of keeping her wine glass and bottle within easy reach of her mouth while the books gathered dust under the bed in the spare room.

Kray sank beneath the bubbles and let the hot water soothe her aching limbs. Her fingers traced the outline of the scar carved across her body, feeling every lump and bump of the puckered skin. She didn't mind touching her scars, she just didn't want to look at them. In fact, there was something morbidly therapeutic about running her fingers along their length to find out how the sensation of touch was gradually returning to the damaged nerve endings. Submerged below the steaming white carpet of foam, she tried to allow her mind to drift, but despite the soothing effects of the bath, Kray felt uneasy.

She had felt a nagging sense of apprehension as soon as she arrived home. In the car driving back she was tired and pissed off with the day, but she hadn't felt apprehensive. However, she did now and it bothered her. The cold wine tasted good against the back of her throat as she tried to switch off, but there was something gnawing away. She gulped more wine trying to ignore it.

'Fuck, that was close today,' she muttered under her breath. 'Why would he do that? Why would he take the risk?'

The steam was clearing from the bathroom as the extractor fan sucked it away into the night air. The bubbles were up to her chin and the stem of the glass dipped into the water as she brought it to her lips.

Why would you do that? Why would you put yourself in harm's way like that?

Then it struck her like a Blackpool tram.

'Bumping into Ania was no coincidence, it was carefully engineered. You wanted to be seen,' she said to herself.

As the hot water crinkled the skin on her hands, she felt a chill run through her body. She heaved herself from the tub, spilling waves of water onto the floor, and wound a towel around her body. She padded across the landing and down the stairs, her wet footprints flattening the pile of the carpet.

She entered the lounge and her eyes fixed on the cause of her anxiety. It had been there all along. After pulling her laptop from her work bag, she flicked open the screen and hit return. It came to life and she tapped in her password.

Kray looked at the screen and then to the mantelpiece and back again.

The gold carriage clock that had been a wedding present from Joe's parents had its hands pointing to half past eight. The digital clock on the screen was flicking over to 9.31pm.

Kray woke to the sound of her radio alarm going off upstairs. She was still wrapped in the bath towel and was lying across the sofa with her head buried in a mound of cushions. The pips announced that the six o'clock news was about to start. She looked at the carriage clock, with its hands pointing to twelve and five.

She had stayed awake for most of the night tracking the time. Keeping one eye on the minute hand as it swept around the ornate dial and the other on the digital clock on her laptop. For hour after hour the minutes ticked by in perfect sync. Eventually, at some point, sleep overcame her. The same questions rattled around in her head as the newsreader started talking.

Why the hell had the clock lost an hour over the course of the day? And why the hell had it not lost a single minute more during the night?

The clock was exactly an hour out and that bothered her.

Kray jumped from the sofa and snatched the clock off the shelf, flipping off the back cover. The thumb wheel spun the hands forward. She snapped the cover back in place and returned it onto the shelf. This was going to bug her all fucking day.

Chapter 27

Kray drove to work with her mind fixed on one thing. *That fucking clock.* Her intuition was running wild. Why had a clock that had never lost a single minute in two years, a clock that had a new battery installed only three weeks earlier, a clock which waved goodbye to her in the morning and welcomed her home at night, be precisely one hour slow?

The possibilities crashed around in her head as she came to an abrupt stop in the station car park. There was one explanation which kept shoving the others to one side. It was an explanation that elbowed its way to the front of the queue every time. An explanation she didn't want to think about, but it was all she *could* think about.

Kray forced it from her mind and bound up the stairs to CID. Tavener was already at his desk, on the phone. Frost's jacket was slung over the back of her chair but she was nowhere to be seen.

Kray waved 'good morning' to Tavener who, in turn, waved back. He cupped his hand over the phone and mouthed, 'Lucy's in the imaging suite.' Kray nodded and headed off in search of coffee. Her mobile went off in her pocket. It was her mum. Kray ignored the call, she was not in the best place right now to accommodate her mother's daily routine of worries. She had enough worries of her own to contend with.

After a few minutes Kray returned with a brew and perched herself on the edge of the desk.

'Morning,' she said, sipping warily at her coffee and regretting not getting a takeout on her way to work.

'Morning, Roz,' Tavener said, finishing off his scribbled notes, his muscular frame bulging through a shirt which had obviously shrunk in the wash. 'The forensics came back on Wilson's clothes, looks like you were bang on.'

'With what?'

He opened a file and read from the report. 'Short red fibres were found on his shirt, consistent with material used in dress manufacturing.'

'That's a good start to the day.'

Frost breezed in.

'Morning. I've done what I can with the screen dumps from the Trafford Centre.' She had a clutch of grainy black and white images in her hand. 'Not sure they tell us a hell of a lot though.'

'Okay, let's talk things through and see what we've got,' said Kray, marshalling her crèche around her. 'We have a white male aged anything between eighteen to thirty—'

'Great name for a holiday company that, Roz,' Tavener interrupted. The scowl shut him up, it was way too early for that kind of bollocks.

Kray continued, 'that is according to Hayley. He is around five feet seven tall with a slim build. What do the pictures tell us?'

Frost fanned the screen shots across the table. 'From what I can make out he has no tattoos on his hands and doesn't wear rings. He was wearing a wrist watch and carrying a black rucksack. From the outline of the bag I'd say it was stuffed full. Probably his female gear. Other than that, *his* clothes are bog standard, they could be bought in a whole host of shops. There is, however, one detail which is a little out of the ordinary, there is a motif on the back of the baseball cap. I've enhanced it as much as I can but it's still unclear.' She lifted out one of the photographs and laid it on top of the others. 'This is the best I could do. It's a round circle with what looks like a bird's head in it. No idea what that means, but it is something worth following up to see if we get a match.'

'That's good work.' Kray stared at the blurry image. 'The other thing we have to unravel is our suspect being a bit of a shape shifter, able to pass himself off convincingly as a woman. So, we have to presume he has feminine features and is a dab hand with the No.7 and a make-up brush.'

'Bit more than a dab hand Roz, this guy fooled a bloke into thinking he was pulling an attractive woman. Christ, I struggle to achieve that on a night out,' said Frost, immediately regretting giving away way too much information.

'Okay, let me put it another way. Our suspect is an expert when it comes to transforming himself into the opposite sex.'

'He could be a professional make-up artist. Maybe someone who works in a theatre group, or he could work at one of the drag clubs here in town,' said Tavener.

'That's a good point. Let's check them out. He is able to fool people up close, so he must be good.'

'And on that point …' Frost had been busy. 'I went back over the CCTV images from the bar when he was with Joshua Wilson. There is one area where a guy is going to struggle to pass himself off as a woman: his Adam's apple, it's a dead giveaway.' She rifled through the paper on the desk and pulled an image from the pack. 'This is the best angle I could get, it's not great because of the camera elevation but if you look carefully you can see a black line around his neck.'

'He was wearing a choker,' Tavener said.

'Exactly,' said Frost.

'Do you think he could be gay or bisexual? I mean the chances are he snogged Joshua Wilson at some point during the night,' mentioned Tavener.

'Not sure. It doesn't necessarily follow. To him it could be a case of the end justifies the means. Keeping Joshua interested had to be his number one priority otherwise all his efforts would come to nothing. He must have planted the lump hammer in the alleyway, then lured Joshua there. That takes planning. And the whole scenario around the death of Madeline Eve demonstrated meticulous attention to detail, so our guy is an organised killer. He could be married or in a steady relationship, holding down a respectable job and a home owner. This is basic profiling by the way – we need to draft in a specialist to help us,' Kray said.

'He also has a working knowledge of the effects of snake venom,' said Tavener. 'That could mean he owns a snake or he might import the venom?'

'Get that one on the list. In order to own a venomous snake legally you have to comply with the Dangerous Wild Animals Act 1976. To do that you have to register with the local authority. It's a big deal where the fire brigade, veterinary surgeons and the authority have to conduct a suitability assessment before they can grant the license. Not to mention it costs over three hundred pounds.'

'How do you know all that, Roz?'

'We had a case once where a man was refused a license to own a crocodile that he planned to keep in a kiddies' swimming pool.'

'Ha, what a knob, no wonder he was turned down. But why were you involved?' Tavener laughed.

'He punched the inspector in the face when it became clear it was going to be a no.'

The room fell silent, to be broken by Frost trying to stifle a giggle.

'Anyway, enough of that. Let's make enquires with the licensing people and see what we have on our patch. In the meantime, we need to understand what it takes to keep a snake like that.'

'I will check out the exotic pet shops in the area, see if they know of anyone who owns one of these Russell's Vipers?'

'Also have a word with the Zoo, they might have links with any venomous snake societies. The killer is also able to get his hands on Suprane. I'll make inquiries at the hospital, find out what that involves. You all know what to do?' Kray waited for them to nod. 'Good, let's go do it.'

But Kray was not going to the hospital to talk about supplies of Suprane. She was going to see Jackson to make an unusual request.

Chapter 28

I think I must have been about thirteen when Sampson arrived. I can remember my father and a mate bringing the huge glass tank into the house and the banging and clanging coming from the basement as they assembled it.

My father knew nothing about snakes but thought it would be cool to own one. Actually, he thought it would be doubly cool to own one illegally. So, with a couple of hours training in snake husbandry, my father was the proud owner of one of the deadliest snakes on the planet.

I never saw Sampson arrive. All I knew was I got up one Sunday morning and there he was, coiled under the heat lamp in the tank. Looking after the snake was the only thing me and my father did together. He was an abusive fucker for ninety percent of the time but when it was just me, him and Sampson down in the basement, he behaved like a proper dad.

I feel the cool air pinching at my skin as I make my way naked down into the cellar, my left hand skimming against the plaster wall. I can hear the freezers hum, and the green glow of the LEDs illuminates the bottom of the stairs. Sampson tastes me in the air. I can see his tongue flicking against the scent. He is grumpy, he knows what's coming.

The glow from the heat lamp is all the light I need. I glance up and can see the shadow board now complete with the lump hammer back in its rightful place. Good, it's nearly time.

I pull the table out from the wall, position it in front of the tank and slide the top back to hear Sampson hissing his displeasure. On the table is everything I need. I arrange them in order as I've done a thousand times before. I have a three-foot-long aluminium rod with a hook on one end and a similar instrument which has a hand-operated grip. I place the glass jar down onto the table top and stretch a latex membrane across the mouth of the container. A thick elastic band holds it in place.

Sampson doesn't like being handled. He darts his head forward as I ease the hook between his coils and lift him clear of the tank. With my other hand, I gently grab him behind his head with the calliper and lay him down on the bench.

I can feel his muscular body flex as he tries to escape my grasp. I run my fingers along his body. My thumb and forefingers clasp him just behind the head. I release the metal grip and lift him into the air. He is beautiful, with his flattened triangular head and blunt snout glowing yellow, orange and black.

I turn him to face me and I swear he always has the same look in his eyes. It's a look that says *one day you will slip and I will have you*. But I never slip, my father trained me well.

I pick up the jar and hold it in front of Sampson's face. I move his head to and fro, bringing the glass just in range only to move it away at the last second. I can feel a surge of power as he fights against my grasp. The glass comes close and he jerks his head, but I take it away. His body tenses and strains. Then I bring the rim of the jar up to his mouth and he strikes. His long white fangs unfold from the roof of his mouth and the pale membrane pulls back to reveal his instruments of death. They plunge through the latex and a flood of yellow liquid coats the inside of the glass. I feel my own rush of blood and my cock stiffens. I pull Sampson back and he goes again. Slamming his fangs through the plastic, pumping venom into the jar. I massage the venom glands located just behind his eyes. Droplets of the golden nectar fall into the container. He is done.

A single milking delivers enough venom to kill five men. Just the right amount for what I have in mind. I lower Sampson into the tank and point his head away from me, releasing my grip. As the top slides back into position he slithers around protesting the inconvenience of this ritual until he is coiled back up in his favourite corner glowering at me through the glass.

One day you will slip and I will have you. It's written all over his face.

I shove the bench back into place against the wall and take the container upstairs. My heart is pounding as I put it on the shelf in the fridge. That will keep it cool and fresh. Not long to go now. Almost time to play.

'Carl Rampton!' Jackson spat coffee onto his desk.

'Yes, that's right,' Kray replied, trying not to look at the morass of pens lying in front of her.

Jackson pulled a ball of tissues from his pocket and mopped up the spillage.

'Why the hell do you want to visit Carl Rampton?'

'If you wanted to get high around here he was the man to go to. He could lay his hands on anything. Suprane can be used as a recreational drug in the same way people do Nitrous Oxide. If anyone knows how to lay their hands on Suprane, it's Carl Rampton.'

'Okay I get that, but why you? Can't you send one of the others?'

'No, it has to be me.'

'I don't know Roz, you've barely got your feet back under the table and now you want to sit opposite Carl fucking Rampton. I say this is a bad idea.'

'I know him.'

'He might refuse, he might not want to talk to you. Have you thought of that?'

'He can't refuse to meet with me because this is police business,' she lied. 'He'll talk to me, I know he will.'

'Where is he?'

'Garth prison.'

'Okay if you're sure. But you have to be very careful with this bastard, you have a prison officer in with you at all times. Do you hear me?'

'Yes. So, can you make the request?'

'Yes, I'll email the GM and make a formal request. I know the prison governor, see if she can speed things up. I'll keep you in the loop.'

'Thank you.'

Kray left Jacko's office with her mind not on the job. It was on that fucking clock.

Chapter 29

HMP Garth is a category B prison for adult males near Leyland. It houses around eight hundred inmates in six wings and holds the accolade for once putting out a contract on a police dog because of its success rate in finding drugs. Kray didn't give a shit about any of that, all she knew was it housed Carl Rampton.

She weaved her way through the flood of pedestrians migrating across the car park on their weekly pilgrimage and parked up at the far end. She joined the mass of people and entered the front of the building under a huge sign that read 'reception'.

There was something about jails that gave her the creeps. She could never put her finger on why. Maybe it was the high walls or the cells with barely enough room for one person, let alone two. Or maybe it was the air of desperation and fear that permeated the very fabric of the place. The waiting area was rammed full of women and kids, the noise made Kray wince as she pushed open the door. The smell of cheap perfume and stale crisps hung in the air.

She threaded her way to the desk and handed over a letter. Her hand was visibly shaking. The clock on the wall read 1.45pm. Visiting time commenced at 2pm.

The man gave the letter to a second guard. 'Okay, ma'am if you would like to follow me, I'll show you where you need to be.' Fifty pairs of eyes followed her out, each one thinking the same thing - *who the fuck is she?*

The officer walked Kray through a set of double doors into a corridor with white washed walls and a grey floor. The soles of his boots squeaked against the polish as he walked. The walkway opened up into another waiting area with an airport style metal detector and a series of tables. A small group of prison guards were milling around awaiting the onslaught of visiting time. She placed her bag onto a tray along with her phone and removed her jacket. An officer waved her on and she stepped through the arch, collecting her things at the other side.

'This way,' the man said.

Her anxiety rocketed with every step. They made their way down a rabbit warren, through another two sets of doors that miraculously unlocked just as they approached and finally arrived at a small room. Inside was a table and two chairs. Kray took the one facing the door and unpacked her bag, removing a pen and notebook.

She sat with her hands in her lap spinning the gold band on her finger round and round. She felt sick. After several minutes she could hear the familiar squeak of rubber soles on shiny floor and her heart rate spiked.

'In here,' said the guard.

The gangly figure of Carl Rampton came around the corner.

'You were the last person I was expecting to hear from, Detective Inspector.' Rampton folded his lanky frame into the chair opposite and slouched back in his seat, his arms dangling down. He looked like an adult sitting in a playschool chair.

Kray tasted bile at the back of her throat. She forced it back and fixed him with a stare. He had lost weight since she had last seen him, with his hair sleeked back and a stubbled chin, he looked a lot healthier. But then, even with the proliferation of drugs in prison, he was probably shooting up only a fraction of what he did while he was on the outside.

'I couldn't say no, could I? Not with you having written such a nice letter to the Governor and everything.' He held his long, tattooed arms out in a welcoming gesture.

Kray looked at the attending officer. 'You can leave if you like.'

'Of course you can my man, me and the Detective Inspector here are old friends. Looks like she just wants a friendly chat,' said Rampton. He was still a cocky shit.

'Can't do that, protocol says this has to be a supervised interview.' The officer was having none of it and stood in the corner.

'So come on Roz, you gotta be pleased to see me. How long has it been now? Oh wait a minute I know the answer to that, it's been nineteen weeks and three days exactly. Nineteen weeks and three days since I last saw you in court when the judge sent down.'

'Yes that's right.'

'He sent me here for five and a half years, I'll be out in under three if I keep my nose clean. Just think of that, Roz.'

Kray wanted to plunge the pen into his throat and rip the arteries from his neck.

'I want to ask you some questions that relate to a current case.'

'Why? So you can stitch me up with that one as well.' His left eye twitched.

'No, it relates to a new drug which we believe is being used in the Blackpool area.'

'Oh, what is it?'

'It's called Suprane, have you heard of it?'

Rampton shook his head 'Suprane? Never heard of it. Why are you looking for it?'

'Can't tell you that. It's an anaesthetic, are you sure you don't know it?'

'Yeah. I can tell you about Special K or Hippy Crack, I can tell you about a load of shit, but I've never heard of this Suprane stuff. Why do you want to know?'

'Because we do.'

'You gotta give me more than that for me to cooperate.'

'That's it. Have you heard of it?'

'No, I've not fucking heard of it.'

Kray fell silent.

'I've never heard of Suprane.' Rampton leaned forward. 'But you know that already. You've worked the streets long enough to know what's on the market and what's not.'

Kray held his gaze, her ring spinning furiously on her finger.

'What the fuck is this about? Cos it sure as hell is not about some fucking new kind of high.' His left eye spasmed and he dabbed it with his hand to keep it still.

Kray took a rasping intake of breath, sat back in her seat and started to cough. She hit her chest with her right hand and stood up. The guard moved forward as she coughed and barked, her shoulders rocking back and forth.

'I'm okay,' she croaked in between wheezing. 'I'm okay.'

'Would you like some water, ma'am?'

Kray nodded, bringing the coughing bout under control. The officer left the room. Kray sat back down, put her elbows on the table and stared into Rampton's face.

'Are you planning on finishing the job?' Kray asked. The cough completely gone.

'What?'

'Are you planning on finishing what you started?'

'What the fuck are you talking about?'

'Because I'm telling you now, if that's your game then you won't be walking out of here in two years, three years, maybe not even five years' time. Do you get my drift?'

'No, I don't get your drift. What are you on about?'

'Oh I think you do. If you come anywhere near me or my house again I will have you back in court faster than you can say 'parole denied'. Do you hear me?'

'How the hell can I get close to you? It might have escaped your notice but I'm locked up in fucking prison.' His eye spasmed again.

'You got one of your boys to pay my house a visit.'

'What?'

'Trying to put the frighteners on me? Well I'm telling you now it won't fucking work.'

'This is stupid.'

'Is it your intention to finish the job, Rampton?' Kray pulled her shirt to one side to reveal the dark red scar slashed across her shoulder. 'You going to get someone to do a proper job this time?'

Rampton jumped from his seat.

'And why the fuck would I want to do that? You stitched me up you bitch. I spent six months inside because of you. You had it coming.'

Kray followed suit. The two of them facing off against each other like a pre-fight press conference.

'That's bollocks! How the fuck did I stitch you up? I wasn't even working your case. You were arrested as part of a major drugs bust called operation Clean Sweep. It was Brownlow who sent you down for possession with intent, not me. You were peddling this bullshit during your trial. It makes no sense.'

'You turned me over, I know it. You planted those drugs to get me taken off the streets and that's why you had to be dealt with. And now you think I'm coming after you to finish the job? Why the hell would I want to do that? I've had my revenge – you and me are square.' Kray could feel droplets of spit land on her face. She clutched the pen tight in her hand, clicking the nib in and out. 'You had me put away and for that I cut you up, I just happened to corpse your husband for good measure. It was an accident like, but I've had my revenge, why the fuck would I want more?'

'Because it was me you were after not my husband.'

'Yes it was, but I reckon it's a fair swap. You're barking up the wrong tree lady, the slate is clean between us, if someone has been in your house it wasn't cos of me. It must have been some other poor fuck you've stitched up.'

'Why do you insist on saying I planted evidence on you? I didn't.'

'Yes you did and I'm not the only one you've fucked over.'

'What are you talking about?'

'Look all I'm saying is I know that you've planted evidence on other cases. People talk and for that you had it coming.'

'But I didn't, I swear to you.'

'People talk, enough said.'

'But I didn't …' She could fight back the tears no longer.

'Oh, poor little copper going to cry now? You fucked me over the same way you fucked others and you had to be stopped. You had to pay. I'm not interested in you any more, you're old news. I've moved on. You should do the same.'

'I swear I didn't ...'

The guard entered the room carrying a plastic cup of water. His eyes popped out of his head seeing the two of them standing toe to toe.

'Wow, you both need to sit down.' He slopped water onto the floor in his haste to step between them.

'I've had enough of this shit, take me back.' Rampton flung his hands in the air and made for the door. 'Oh yes I forgot.' He turned tapping the side of his head with his index finger. 'You can't move on can you? Because you and me will always be connected – I'm the one who put your husband in the ground. Why don't you suck on that thought while you're screwing over some other poor shit?'

The officer took Rampton by the arm and led him through the door. Kray stood in the centre of the room still clutching the pen as tears stained her face.

Chapter 30

I have the day off today, you know how it is, things to do, people to kill.

My car trundles along the country lane flanked with hedges and trees. The road is listed as a B road, but it is only a single lane track for much of its journey through the countryside. I have no idea where it eventually ends up. It probably just comes to a dead stop in a field somewhere.

Dappled sunshine bursts through the trees, forcing me to shield my eyes. It's a beautiful day to meet up with friends. After about a mile and a half there's a hard-left turn. It is not signposted, it simply appears as a gap in the hedge. My front suspension complains as it hits the broken tarmac and I slow my speed to a walking pace as I bounce and bang my way along. There are portions of the road up ahead where the tarmac surface has completely lifted off. My car thinks this track is trying to kill it. The road is straight but my view is obstructed by overgrown vegetation, as vines and shrubs scratch at the wings of my vehicle. This used to be a service road that cut a path across the landscape leading to a housing project - forty affordable homes to be built in the middle of nowhere. No wonder it never got off the ground. I continue my journey until the hedgerows run out and the road disappears to be replaced by an expanse of derelict ground. While the developer never got round to building any houses, he did however build twenty-one garages. Three rows of seven. The ravages of nature, and people with a homebuilding project to complete but no materials to build with, are sorely evident. Most of the garages have no roofs, no doors and large swathes of brickwork is missing. At least that description fits twenty of them. Mine is fine.

I roll the car slowly over the rubble to the first line of garages and reverse into position. I climb out of the car, retrieve my kit from the boot and walk over to the door. The small key turns half a step clockwise and when I twist the handle the mechanism springs open. I put the paper mask around my nose and mouth and loop the elastic over my ears. It is more of a ritual than anything else, it certainly doesn't help.

The other garages occasionally suffer from renewed bouts of theft and damage caused by kids, but mine remains unscathed. That's because mine reeks of death.

The fetid stench of rotting flesh smacks you full in the throat, it passes straight through the dust mask, that's for sure. Still, the stomach churning stink is a great security measure keeping unwanted visitors away.

The door swings up to reveal a brick interior and a concrete floor. I've been coming here for years to tend to my flock. Truth be told, they look after themselves, I'm more of an interested bystander.

Against each of the walls stands three large glass tanks. Lying at the bottom of each are slabs of pork and chicken. Not just any old meat, this meat is infested with maggots and pupae, gradually dissolving the carcasses into a putrid liquid. The most beautiful sound washes over you, invading your very being. It's the sound of hundreds upon hundreds of wings beating in unison. Hordes of flies.

I yank down the door, pull a couple of camping lamps from my bag and suspend them from hooks in the ceiling. Their incandescent glow gives the pace a welcoming feel, that is if you ignore the stink of the dead.

The tank to my left is ready for harvesting. I unscrew the top from the large plastic cookie jar and place a metal cup inside. I pour from the thermos flask, filling the cup a third full with boiling water, then leave it to stand. I open the cool box and take out a bag of dry ice nuggets. Using a set of tongs, I drop cubes into the hot water and replace the lid. The dry ice begins to boil, filling the cookie jar with vapour. I then switch on the flat circular fan fitted into the back of the cookie jar. The rubber tube leading from the side of the jar immediately spews cold white vapour onto the ground. I attached it to an inlet pipe at the base of the tank. I sit back and watch the show.

The dry ice blows like a billowing white carpet across the floor of the tank and gradually fills the volume. The flies try to escape the creeping fog but they are inevitably swamped by the chilled mist. The sound of buzzing gradually diminishes until there is silence.

I turn everything off, release the catches at the base of the tank and pull the false floor towards me. The cloud of dry ice vapour falls to the floor, nipping at my legs and feet. At this stage in the process the stink from the rotting meat has been known to make me gag. I lay the tray on the garage floor and wait for the fog to clear.

There at the bottom of the tray lie hundreds and hundreds of flies who have been forced into a state of hibernation by the cold. They are unharmed, it's a natural process that occurs every winter.

I grab my soft brush and gently sweep them into a pan, then deposit them into another container. The flies are perfectly fine. When they warm up they simply wake to find their living quarters are far more cramped than before.

It's a nice little trick I taught myself after watching a YouTube video showing how street magicians bring back to life flies that appear to be dead. I simply industrialised the process.

When I'm done harvesting, I slide the bottom back into the tank and leave the lid off. Within a week I will return to a new community of flies each one intent on rearing their young in the rarefied environment of ready food and safety. All I do then is replace the top on the tank and I have a new set of pets.

I place the container with the sleeping flies into the cool box, open up the garage and reload the car. My clothes now stink of rotten meat. Soon my car will stink of rotten meat, but that's okay … it's almost time.

Chapter 31

'What the hell were you playing at?' Jackson was stomping around his office. His voice boomed down the corridor as Kray came into view. She marvelled at how fast bad news travelled when you didn't want it to.

Kray had spent the afternoon touring around, catching up with the crèche, after her disastrous meeting at the prison. She couldn't face going back to the office. She had met Tavener, who was hunting around sports shops looking for a baseball cap that matched their description, and later she tracked down Frost who was having her eyes opened by chatting to the people at the Bosom Buddies Cabaret Bar, where Craig, a six-foot-one-inch former brick layer, was a fountain of knowledge when it came to speaking on his favourite topic – men dressing up as women.

Kray let out a huge sigh and veered off to the left towards the sound of Jackson's voice.

'It got out of hand,' she replied stepping into his office.

'Out of hand? What was the very thing I told you to do?'

'I know, I know.'

'Have an officer in attendance at all times. That's what I said.'

'He went to get me some water, I was choking to death.'

'And he came back just in time by the sound of it, before you and Rampton choked each other to death. What were you thinking?'

'I let him get to me.'

'That's for sure. And now the governor has been on my back, tearing strips off me because she'd done me a favour and now she had an incident report on her desk to say thank you.'

'That lanky shit Rampton must have shot his mouth off.'

'It wasn't Rampton, it was the prison officer. He said he could hear you two going at it from way down the corridor. Something about you stitching him up with fabricated evidence and how everything was square. What the fuck happened?'

'I went there to ask him about Suprane and it all went tits up.'

'I should never have let you go.' Jackson was rattled by the complaint. 'If this gets on the Chief's desk I won't be covering for you.'

That's it Jacko, think about your own reputation. Kray knew she had no choice but to stand there and take it.

Jackson slumped back into his chair.

'I could do without this,' he said to no one.

'The important thing is Rampton had never heard of Suprane so the chances are it is not a drug you can pick up off the street. Our killer must be getting it from another source.'

'You mean Gorgon.' Jacko was determined to make his new name stick.

'Yes, I mean Gorgon.'

'Did you know that already before you went to see him?'

'No, I didn't,' Kray lied.

'Because it sounds like you went to see him to talk about other things. Did you?'

'No, I went to ask him if he knew about Suprane and it went pear-shaped after that. I'm sorry. I shouldn't have remained in the room after the guard left. That was my mistake.' Kray needed to shut down the discussion, Jacko tended to stop once people had rolled over and surrendered.

'Yes it was a mistake. Mis-use of a police interview request with a prison inmate is serious shit. I just hope to God the Chief is busy right now and this fuck-up passes him by.'

'I got the confirmation we needed, it was a legitimate line of inquiry.' Kray could feel a swell of anger rise in her chest. She drove it back down, this was not the time nor the place.

'Got anything else?' Jacko asked.

'Still working on the most recent leads, it's early days.'

'Okay, keep me posted. Oh, and BT have been onto us asking if they can have their phone box back?'

'Yes we got what we could from that. They can have it now.'

Kray went to the office to stare at the evidence board and to sift through the influx of paperwork. The niggle wouldn't leave her mind. *If it wasn't Rampton then what the fuck happened to that clock?*

Her mouth smears a half kiss of cherry red across the rim of the mug, her long fingers dancing on the surface of the china to avoid the heat.

She pulls her phone from her bag and flips open the case. Her gel nails peck at the screen, switching images in a blur of captured moments past.

She parades a picture in front of her friends. They peal with laughter. Her head is thrown back and I can see the regular pattern of her glistening teeth. Teeth that have not suffered the close attention of the dentist's drill. Bright white against the blush of her skin. Her features are perfect. The narrow nose, defined cheek bones and elegant jawline makes her perfect. But her eyes are the clincher - big and bright, set slightly wide apart.

She tugs at the hem of her skirt, struggling to make it decent. It barely makes it to midway up her toned and slender thigh. A consequence of it having spent too much time in the tumble dryer. They shriek like tortured cats as she waves the phone in front of their dumb faces. From my booth in the corner I can see her lips moving. But the clatter of the kitchen behind me ensures I cannot hear her words - I'm sure she is mouthing 'you need to take me.' Over and over. I'm sure of it.

She turns her head and stares right at me, placing her fingers in her mouth and sucking hard. Her tongue laps across the tips of her fingers. 'Not long to wait now,' she mouths. I'm sure that's what she does. I'm sure that's what she says.

Reaching into her bag again, she draws out a set of keys. I imagine the sound as she drops them onto the table, striking the

Formica. A Vauxhall Micra car fob, a Sea World charm, a photo-booth picture of her sister and a silver Yale key. The same shaped key I have tucked away in my pocket.

Her flat is a fifteen-minute drive from here. On average it takes her eight minutes to say goodbye to her friends. That gives me at least seven minutes of bliss as I wait in the darkness. Dressed in her clothes. I've chosen carefully.

It could have been the silk top from her aborted date with the guy from HR, or the skirt she wore at the birthday bash when she fell off her high heels in the street, or the underwear from her hectic date with Mr Right. But in the end, there was only one choice. I have to go now.

I slide a five-pound note onto the table, gather my coat in my arms and head for the door. As I pass, I glance her way and the whole world goes into slow motion. She tosses her head to one side, her tongue wetting her lips, she looks right through me.

I'm the invisible person, with the invisible life and invisible needs. You would never think tonight has been almost a year in the planning and she's stared right through me more times than I've cut myself.

All that is about to change. She will stare at me tonight, as I cut her.

Chapter 32

I scrub the tyres tight against the kerb, the road is narrow and I don't want an accidental bump to draw attention to my presence. The car door swings open and I step out into the cool evening air. The indicator lights flash orange as the door locks and I walk down the uneven pavement towards Rothschild Avenue. A grand name for a place that is such a shithole. It suits her. She fits in perfectly with her cut-price dresses, tatty shoes and supermarket make-up. I suppose people gravitate to their own level.

I slide the plastic key into the lock and with a soft click the door opens to welcome me in like an old friend. My senses are coated with the familiar scent of Yankee candles and hairspray. The hall is dark but there is no need to fumble for a light, I know where I'm going.

In the semi-darkness, I see the collage of pictures strewn across the lounge wall to my right. Even if I close my eyes I can see them. I see them in all in their pathetic glory. The drunken university photos crammed with too many faces and the cringing snaps from the year abroad. At Niagara Falls she is surrounded by like-minded fuckwits. And then there is the scrum of pictures taken in a pretend jungle. South America is so overrated. What a waste.

I skirt around the sofa, to the bedroom. The smell of White Linen gives way to the gagging reek of perfume. A double bed, wardrobe and dressing table are crow-barred into the poky space. The carpet is threadbare from a hundred casual occupants. Some of them bringing protection, most of them making use of the condom slush-pile lying in the bedside table.

I close my eyes and see her lying on the duvet, the guy from HR pawing at her naked body. She's not enjoying it - I can tell.

Then his phone bursts into life and it's all over as fast as you can say 'Shit that's my girlfriend'. Clothes are hastily pulled over sweating bodies as the headlights of her car swing into view and she arrives early to pick him up. She should learn to pull her curtains shut tight. Too late now.

I open the wardrobe and lift the hanger from the rail. The dresser drawer holds a multitude of soft delights. I strip naked and choose carefully.

The silk feels cool against my skin and the shoes pinch a little. I'm laying out the toys for tonight as I hear the key in the front door. She's made good time.

The clip-clop of heels on laminate flooring echo down the hallway, then the bouncing clatter as they are discarded in the corner with the others. A moment of silence is broken by the first strains of Adele booming out from the living room. Her shrill voice screeches to the music as she demonstrates that even after five months, she still can't get the words right.

I wait in the dark. Tucked between the wardrobe and the wall. My breath is shallow. It needs to be. Listening.

I hear the padding of poorly manicured feet approaching and the slam of the bathroom door. It's time for her to discard the clothes of the day into the pale-yellow basket at the side of the sink. The wailing continues.

The sound of water cascading into the sink fills my head louder than the rush of blood thumping in my temples. All of my senses heighten to bursting point.

She squeezes toothpaste onto a frayed toothbrush she should have changed months ago, her nightly routine playing out for the last time. I hear the bathroom door open and the sound of disappearing footsteps. The music stops.

Any moment now.

My head spins as the lack of oxygen fogs my brain. Water droplets blur my vision. The plastic bag doing its job. I tighten the cord around my neck. The door swings open and she is in the room. She sits at the dressing table and layers night cream onto her face. A futile routine designed to make her more beautiful for tomorrow. I feel the cold liquid soak through the cloth in my hand. She's running a brush through her hair, the colour of burnished bronze, and wiping dark make-up from her eyes. She's naked in front of the mirror. The curves of her waist and breasts are plain for everyone to see. Slut. She draws the soft pad across her face and sees my reflection in the mirror. She screams and half turns.

My right arm wraps around her throat while my left arm locks it in place. My left hand pushes hard against the back of her head and I squeeze. She seizes my upper arms with her clawing fingers and I drag her from the stool onto the floor. She kicks out, toppling it over. I lay back, wrap my legs tight around her waist and wait. She bucks and twists like a rodeo bull. I lock in tight and enjoy the ride. She's strong and she's a fighter. Any second now. Two, three, four – and she's out.

I relax my grip, forcing the sodden cloth over her nose and mouth. Her chest heaves as she draws the vapour deep into her lungs and into her bloodstream. I feel her body melt into mine. My head is buzzing on a cocktail of adrenaline and endorphins.

After a while her hands start to twitch as she comes back to the surface. I remove the cloth and lock my arms around her neck again. Two, three, four – and she's out. The cloth is back in place. The cold liquid doing its job. Her soft body is limp.

By now I am tripping out as the excess nitrogen and carbon dioxide surges through my body. The thick plastic clinging to the contours of my features. With my spare hand, I tear at the plastic bag and heave air into my burning lungs. She is lying on her back on top of me, both of us staring at the ceiling. My breathing is short and erratic. My face damp from the condensation. The familiar feel of a sticky mess in my pants.

I lie there in the afterglow, the bag discarded on the floor. Her body twitches again. My arms lock in place. Two, three, four – and she's out.

It's playtime.

Chapter 33

Kray found herself stuck at the hospital reception desk talking to what looked like a fourteen-year-old boy in a suit.

'I'm sorry but Dr Aldridge is unavailable,' he said replacing the receiver.

'But I called yesterday, spoke to someone and booked an appointment with him first thing this morning.' It was bang on 8am.

'We are trying to locate him. If you would take a seat.'

'This is a police matter.' She flashed her warrant card in frustration, the lad looked unimpressed.

Kray did not want to take a seat, she wanted to talk to Aldridge about Suprane. She sloped off and sat on a plastic chair against the far wall.

By the time she had got home the previous night, the events of the day had all but wiped her out. She was emotionally drained. She had held it together until she opened her front door. Then she had collapsed onto her knees in the hallway and burst into tears. She couldn't contain the outpouring of emotion and time after time she leaned forward, slapping her hands against the wooden floor. This wasn't crying, this was wailing.

She remained that way until exhaustion overcame her and she could wail no longer. The palms of her hands were red, and rivulets of tears streaked the floor. She had curled up into a ball in her hallway and prayed for numbness to set in.

After ten minutes she pulled herself together and went to find the one thing guaranteed to bring on the numbness. With a bottle of Pino in one hand and a glass in the other, she headed for the bathtub.

An hour and a half and three refills of hot water later, the wine had gone and she was feeling much better. She had forced the meeting with Rampton to the back of her mind and had given herself a stiff talking to. The clock was one hour slow because … it just was. Don't know why, don't know how … it just was. And the conspiracy theories about someone breaking into her home and altering it were the product of her galloping paranoia. She had also realised that in her eagerness to concoct elaborate theories around why the damned thing was slow, she had conveniently ignored the fact that there had been no evidence of a break in. She had berated herself with every swear word she knew. She had to get a grip, she had a case to solve.

She squirmed around on the hospital chair clutching her takeout coffee that had cost her nearly four pounds and was feeling rejuvenated. Today was going to be a good day, or at least it was until Aldridge started playing silly buggers.

The receptionist beckoned her over.

'He sends his apologies and said he would give you a call.'

'But I phoned ahead and spoke to one of the lab techs, he told me he was free this morning. He told me to come over.'

'I'm sorry you've had a wasted journey. Dr Aldridge is a very busy man.'

'Yes I'm sure he is, but I was told he wasn't busy this morning and that's why I'm here.'

'I appreciate that, but things must have changed. Maybe you can reschedule when he calls.'

Kray was not happy at being given the brush off. She left the waiting area without thanking the poor boy. She rounded a corner heading for her car and caught sight of a familiar looking bald head dashing across the car park.

'Dr Aldridge!' she called after him. 'Harry wait, I need to talk to you.'

He looked back and cursed under his breath.

'Oh, DI Kray. Sorry I have an urgent meeting.'

'I spoke to your lab technician and he told me you were free this morning. Did he mention that?'

'Err yeah, he did. But I got a call and have to shoot off I'm afraid. Can we do this at another time?'

'I guess we have to if you're not going to be here. I need to talk with you about Suprane.'

'What of it?'

'Who supplies it? How do you lay your hands on it? Things like that.'

'Yes that would be fine. Now if you'll excuse me I do have to rush.'

'Could a member of the public buy it?'

'No you would have to be a licensed practitioner. Look I'm terribly late, can we do this another time?'

'Do you stock Suprane at the hospital?'

'Yes we do, under a strict stock control regime. Now if you don't mind, I really do have to dash.' And with that he hurried to his two-seater sports car, revved the engine, and was gone.

Kray was back at the station sifting through the license information, supplied by the council, identifying the people who kept dangerous animals. The same thought barged into her head every time she read the scanned documents. *Why the fuck would you want one of those?*

The clock in the office ticked over to midday and in walked Tavener wearing another one of the shirts he'd shrunk in the wash.

'Hi, Roz.'

'Hey, Duncan, how are you doing?'

'Pretty good, better than Lucy it would appear.'

'Why?'

'She called in sick this morning, didn't sound at all well, apparently.'

'Oh, I'll give her—'

'It looks like Gorgon likes baseball,' Tavener interrupted.

It took Kray a while to cotton on to the change of topic. 'Well, he wears a baseball cap but that doesn't necessarily mean—'

'The Blue Jays,' he interrupted her again.

'What is?'

'The emblem on the back of his cap, do you remember the circle with a bird's head in it? It's the symbol for the Toronto Blue Jays.'

'How did you find that out?'

'I drew a complete blank with the sports shops around here so went online and chatted to a bloke in London. He knew straight away when I described it to him. What about you?'

'I had a meeting with Dr Aldridge at the hospital first thing this morning to discuss Suprane and he ran away from me. And this lot …' She pointed to the documents on the screen of her laptop. 'Do you know that within a thirty-mile radius of where we are right now, there is one King Cobra, two Capuchin monkeys, six wild boar and an ostrich.'

'An ostrich?'

'Yup.'

'Why the fuck would you want one of those?'

'Exactly.'

'So we pay the King Cobra guy a visit?'

'We can but it's the wrong snake. The cobra produces a neurotoxic venom which attacks the nervous system. What we are looking for is hemotoxic which attacks the blood.'

'Ah, not that simple then, eh?'

'Nothing ever is.'

Tavener laughed, slung his jacket over his arm and walked towards the door.

'How do you mean 'it would appear'?' said Kray.

'What?'

'You said you were better than Lucy 'it would appear'.'

'Yes that's right, she called in sick.'

'What's wrong with her, did she say?'

'I didn't talk to her. The desk sergeant downstairs handed me a note when I arrived this morning. She must have rung the station.'

'Why would she do that? Why didn't she call one of us?'

Tavener shrugged his shoulders.

'Don't know Roz, I was going to give her a bell later.'

Kray dialled her mobile. 'Her phone goes through to voicemail.'

'I'll catch up with her this afternoon. Right now, I've got an appointment with a drag artist who wants to educate me in the finer arts of theatrical make-up.'

Tavener turned to leave and almost crashed into a man coming the other way.

'Hey Roz I got a present for you from BT.' It was Alex Devereux, a new addition to CID. He was waving a small clear plastic bag.

'What is it?'

'A bloke from BT was in reception asking for you. He was about to leave this behind the desk marked for your attention.' He handed her the bag.

Kray held it up to the light, inside was a pound coin.

'He said it's the money from the phone box.'

'What phone box?'

'He said something about recommissioning a public pay phone and finding this in the cash drawer, so he thought he'd better hand it in. He said he picked it up using gloves and put it straight in the bag. A BT engineer with CSI skills, whatever next.'

'But we already have the pound coin from that call box. It's been through the forensics lab,' said Kray.

'Presumably this is a new one,' said Devereux.

'Are you sure? Did he specifically mention Albany Road?'

'That's the one, found it this morning.'

'But that phone has been cordoned off with police tape for days.'

Devereux shrugged his shoulders and raised his hand in a gesture of goodbye. Kray reached for her mobile and pressed redial, toying with the coin on the desk. The phone clicked through to voicemail. Kray's head spun and her whole world went into free fall.

Chapter 34

'Are you sure about this?' Tavener said, hanging onto the dashboard with one hand and the seat with the other.

'No, that's why it's just me and you,' answered Kray, her eyes fixed on the road.

'Shouldn't we call it in?'

'Wacko Jacko already thinks I've lost the fucking plot. This isn't going to help.'

Kray jumped her second red light of the trip and hurtled around the corner, the tyres screeching on the tarmac as she juddered to a stop. Kray and Tavener spilled out and scanned up and down the street.

'Which one?' Kray asked.

'This one.' Tavener pointed to a new build conversion about thirty yards away.

They burst in to find flat five. It was on the ground floor at the north corner of the building. Tavener got there first and banged on the door. There was no answer. He banged again. Nothing. Kray held her hand up for him to be quiet and dialled her phone. She put her ear to the door.

'I can hear it ringing.'

She stepped back and nodded to Tavener.

'Are you sure?'

'I'll pay for the damage myself.'

Tavener's size eleven boot crunched against the front door. It shuddered on its hinges but stayed in place. He took a step back and thudded another boot against the wood. The door bounced back. The third stomp shattered the lock from the frame. A neighbour opened her door to see what all the commotion was about. Tavener went to reassure her. Kray was first into the flat.

The door opened up onto a short corridor with an archway leading into the lounge. It was the middle of the day but the flat was in darkness. Kray hit the light switch on the wall – nothing. Her stomach turned over. She made her way through to the living room, a small space comfortably furnished with a couple of two-seater sofas, a TV and a sideboard. The mobile lay on the coffee table. The kitchen was off to the left. Kray stepped around the table and flicked on the torch on her phone; the bright cone of light cut through the gloom illuminating a wide hallway with three doors leading off. There was a bathroom situated to the right. Kray pushed open the door, it was empty. She stopped in her tracks. She could hear a buzzing sound coming from the room opposite. Kray eased down the handle and as the door cracked open, the sound grew louder. The bottom of the door skimmed across the carpet as she opened it up. The curtains were shut and the room was bathed in a purple glow as sunlight fought its way through the drapes. Flies were everywhere. Clouds of them billowing in the air. They landed on her face, neck and hands as she tried to swat them away. A double bed with a white duvet commanded the centre of the room. The shaft of light from her phone landed on a stool lying on its side next to the dressing table. Flies pitched into her hair, fighting to free themselves.

As she skirted around the bed, Kray saw a pair of feet. Then the shins, then the thighs. Laying on the floor was the body of a naked woman. Flies danced off her skin, swirling in the bright light. Kray clasped her hand to her mouth. There were no marks on her body, no signs of a struggle. She was stretched out with her arms by her sides. Kray could hear the sound of Tavener entering the room behind her. Kray dabbed away the tears clouding her vision with the back of her hand.

'Get SOCO and Jackson here asap and lock down the area,' she said.

The sound of buzzing raged inside her head. Her skin crawled with the touch of marauding insects. The woman lying at her feet had no face. On the bedside table was a family picture taken in a Christmas setting. Nestled among the smiling faces was Lucy Frost.

Chapter 35

The office was filled with a crushing silence. Tissues were being plucked from a box sitting in the middle of the table by male and female officers alike. Kray stood out front with her hands locked together behind her back. The fingers of her right hand spun the ring round and round. She gazed into the faces of ten members of the Lancashire constabulary, each one of them in a state of shock.

Twenty-four hours had passed since the discovery of Lucy Frost's faceless body. The forensics had yielded a set of results that were a carbon copy of the killing of Madeline Eve. The cause of death was massive organ failure brought on by her blood coagulating to the consistency of raspberry jelly. The post-mortem had revealed a single needle mark piercing her jugular vein and slight bruising around her neck. Her finger nails were scraped clean and Suprane was found in her lungs. Her face had been removed with a series of clean incisions made by a sharp scalpel-like blade. The flies had not yet had time to putrefy her body.

All eyes were on Kray as she stood in front of the evidence board which was now adorned with photographs depicting the horrific murder of one of their own. Jackson was absent. He was with the Chief, meeting the parents.

'Do I need to run through the details of Lucy's death? I think you are all well briefed but I want to be sure.' Kray looked around the room at ten shaking heads. 'Okay I know this is difficult but we have to stay focussed. If anyone feels the situation is too much, you can talk to me or we have a liaison officer you can speak to. Is that clear?' The heads nodded. 'Right, the clock is ticking. Following the death of Madeline Eve, the killer impersonated her and picked up a man named Joshua Wilson in the Purple Parrot. He then proceeded to drug the victim with Rohypnol and bludgeoned him to death with a lump hammer in an alleyway.

'Our working assumption is that he will follow the same pattern. Joshua Wilson was killed one week after the death of Madeline. The time lapse might be significant but we cannot rule out that he might kill sooner. The killer used the call box on Albany Road to phone the station in the same way he called Madeline's place of work. So, what we can assume is that he's working through a predetermined game plan. We have a lot of ground to cover if we are going to stop that happening.'

A young man at the back of the group raised his hand.

'Yes,' said Kray.

'I read in the briefing notes that Gorgon used articles of Madeline Eve's clothing to impersonate her. Are we expecting the same thing again?'

'That's a good point, which leads me on to the tasking for today. I want three teams – the first will make an inventory of Lucy's clothing. I want it cross-referenced with her friends and social media photographs. If he's going to follow the same MO, we will find items missing. The second team, I want you to focus on finding a connection between the two women. The killer does not choose his victims by accident, it will be against a specific set of criteria; find out what that is. I want the third group to bang on the doors of all the clubs and bars in the area and circulate Lucy's picture. Set up a hotline for them to report anything suspicious. Stress to these guys if they see anything out of the ordinary, no matter how small, they must call in. Is that clear?'

'Yes, ma'am,' was the unified response, apart from Tavener who called her Roz.

'You have each been allocated to a team and Duncan Tavener has the tasking list.' Everyone got up and converged on Tavener. 'And I will be talking to the hospital about how the killer might lay his hands on Suprane.' Her words were lost in the hubbub of anxious chatter. *More specifically I'll be pinning a bald doctor to a wall.*

Kray entered the reception hall at the city hospital and strode right past the fourteen-year-old behind the desk. He looked up without a flicker of recognition.

She reached the bank of lifts, pressed the second-floor button and exited into a mass of people staring at a board listing the whereabouts of the various departments. They parted enough for her to squeeze through and she headed down a walkway signposted 'Mortuary, Bereavement Office and Pathology'.

After several more doors she entered a corridor with the faint-but-familiar smell of rotten chicken and disinfectant. Kray was just about to shoulder open another door when she glanced through a glass panel and saw who she was looking for – Dr Harry Aldridge.

He was sat with his spectacled face glued to a VDU screen, his fingers tapping away at the keyboard. She barged in without knocking. Aldridge nearly fell off his chair.

'Oh, err, DI Kray, I mean Roz. How are you?'

'You said you would give me a call when you were free?'

'Err yeah, I've been busy.'

'Are you too busy now?'

'Umm yes, I have to go to a meeting. So, if you don't mind …'
He rose from his chair stuffing papers into his bag while fiddling with the mouse to save his work.

Kray reached into her inside pocket and brought out her mobile. She hit some buttons, pressed speaker phone and placed it on the desk. The sound of the ring tone filled the small office.

'Yes, Roz?' It was Tavener.

'Can you send a squad car to the front of reception at the hospital.'

'Sure, right away.'

Aldridge stopped and stared at Kray with his mouth gaping open.

'I need to bring Aldridge in for questioning in relation to the Madeline Eve and Lucy Frost murders.'

'This is outrageous!' Aldridge exploded.

Kray reached forward and pressed the mute button. 'Do you mind keeping it down, can't you see I'm on the phone?' She re-pressed the button. 'Quick as you can.'

'Okay, okay,' said Aldridge holding up both hands in a sign of surrender.

'Tavener? Cancel that.'

'Will do, Roz.'

She clicked the off button.

'So now do I have your attention?'

'I will be making a formal complaint to your superior.' Aldridge was brimming with indignation.

'Well, the way this week is panning out, you'll have to get in the queue.'

'You are over-stepping the mark, Detective. I will have you know—'

'It's Detective Inspector, now sit down and talk to me about Suprane.'

Aldridge was weighing up his options; should he continue with 'what he would have her know' or do as he was told. He sat back in his seat and did as he was told.

'We have no use for Suprane down here for obvious reasons, but they do in the operating theatres. It comes in via a number of different suppliers, is held in a central store and allocated depending on demand.'

'How is the stock controlled?'

'The same as any other drug held at the hospital.'

'Show me.'

Aldridge went to protest and Kray held up her mobile.

'Follow me.' He scuffed his chair along the floor as he shoved it backwards, stomping out of the office. Kray hurried along close behind, his long legs causing her some difficulties in keeping up.

'This is stupid,' he said over his shoulder.

'As far as we can determine Suprane is not finding its way onto the streets. This hospital is the only source in the immediate area.'

'Bloody ridiculous,' was all Aldridge had to say on the matter.

Soon they arrived at what looked like a giant pharmacy. The main thing that distinguished it from anything on the high street was the counter to ceiling Perspex glass and steel meshing.

A woman in her mid-forties with bright eyes and long hair pulled into a ponytail sat behind a gap in the security screen. Her name badge read 'Mandy Hawthorn'. Aldridge pointed at her and huffed his displeasure.

'Ask away.'

Kray flashed her warrant card. 'Could you help by answering a couple of questions relating to the way you control the stock of Suprane?'

'Of course.' She hit a button and the door in the corner buzzed open. Kray nodded for Aldridge to go first.

'It's pretty standard stuff,' Mandy said. 'We get deliveries from suppliers which we draw upon depending on usage. When the stock reduces to a certain level, the system automatically triggers another order. BanKan or something it's called, we went on a course about it.'

'How do you reconcile the stock?'

'We kind of do a mass balance. We know how much comes in over the month from the delivery dockets and we know our opening level of stock. The demand is deducted and on a monthly basis we do a physical stock check. It's always right, everything balances. Take a look …'

Mandy opened up another window on her screen.

'The dockets are scanned into the system - here is one. This is the stock record showing the daily usage and at month end we check everything. I hate doing the monthly stock take, it's a pain in the—'

'Can you go back?' Kray interrupted, spinning the gold band round and round on her finger.

'To where?'

'The docket, can you pull up the docket again?'

The delivery note flashed onto the screen.

'What is this?' Kray pointed to a row of figures where the number had been crossed out and a handwritten figure scribbled in its place.

'Oh, that's a manual adjustment.'

'How does that work?'

'Occasionally we order a certain quantity and the supplier confirms the order. But come the day of delivery the company does not have sufficient product to fulfil the order. But the paperwork has already been produced. So, they change it, and we work off the amended figure. It all adds up at the end of the month.'

'Thank you for taking me through that, I appreciate your time,' Kray said. 'One last question: have you ever had a stock discrepancy with Suprane?'

The woman shook her head. 'No never, and I've been working in here for three years.'

'Seen enough? Because I've got work to do,' Aldridge barked at Kray, marching out of the door.

She let him go and stared at the docket on the screen.

The gold band went round and round.

Chapter 36

'It's black.' Tavener entered the incident room.

'What is?' Kray said while doodling on a scrap of paper. The office was deserted.

He slapped a photocopy down on the table in front of her. 'The dress that's missing, it's black.'

Kray looked at a medley of three pictures, each one showing Lucy Frost with a gaggle of friends. One was in a bar, another in a club and the other around the table in a restaurant. In each case she was wearing a black dress with three quarter length sleeves and a scooped neckline.

'Are you sure?'

'Yes, these pictures are from her Facebook page all taken within the last four months. This dress is not in the clothing inventory.'

Kray held the sheet of paper in her hand, staring at the happy face of Lucy Frost.

'It's not your fault,' said Tavener pulling up the chair next to her. Kray looked away. 'I know what you're thinking and it's not your fault.'

'Then why does it feel like it is?'

'Because you care, Roz, everyone cares.'

'But not everyone had the responsibility to keep Lucy safe.'

'And you did, while she was at work. You cannot hold yourself responsible for what happened.'

'Hey it's me that should be doing the counselling, not the other way around.'

'When Wacko gave this case to Brownlow the whole station thought he needed his fucking bumps feeling.'

'Hey, that's DCI Jackson to you.'

144

'Okay, everyone thought *DCI Jackson* needed his fucking bumps feeling.'

Kray stifled a laugh.

'You are the best DI in the place. It's a privilege to work with you, Lucy thought it was a privilege. You will catch this fucker.'

'Yes Duncan, we will.'

Their tender moment was interrupted by a horde of noisy coppers entering the room. Kray looked at her watch, it said 4.45pm. Wash-up time.

People took their seats, unpacking bags and pulling out notebooks. Kray made her way to the front.

'Thank you for being prompt. I want to touch base on how your inquiries have gone and set the stall out for the remainder of today and tomorrow. Let's start with—'

She got no further. Everyone in the room rose to their feet as Jackson walked in, followed by the Chief.

I'm on parade.

I am tripping out on endorphins and dopamine. Those people who shoot chemicals into their veins or powder up their nose should try this, at least once.

Lucy Frost was a perfect choice, made even more so when I discovered she was a copper. I can only imagine the mayhem taking place right now in the police station and it's about to get worse. Much worse.

My high heels click on the concrete as I walk along the Promenade. The sea breeze feels surprisingly warm as it hugs around me, pressing my newly acquired little black number into every contour of my body. It's a gorgeous dress, fits me perfectly.

It's early. When I parked up the clock on the dashboard read 4.50pm. No taxi for me today, I might need to make a sharp exit. Consequently, there are no groups of men to ogle me as I make my way along the Prom, no turning heads as I sway my hips, no cat calls to raise my pulse. But that doesn't matter. This is a high octane walk if ever there was one.

The police must be out looking for me. They must have joined the dots up by now. My assumption is they will be looking for somebody who looks like Lucy, wearing her stolen dress and posing for the CCTV cameras. I am assuming they will have circulated photographs of her to the bars and clubs. At least I hope they have, or all this will be for nothing. It's time to shock.

My favourite bar comes into view as I round the corner. The door staff don't come on duty until six so I will have to open the door for myself. There will be no beefy doormen in tight T-shirts to rub themselves against me as I squeeze past. Oh well, a girl can't have everything.

The traffic along the seafront is heavy. I smile as male drivers crane their necks to get a better look. The ones travelling on their own are blatant, twisting their heads around for a good eyeful. Those driving with the wife and kids in the car give a short sharp glance, as if checking for traffic, but I know they are checking me out.

I push against the glass door to the Purple Parrot and step inside. Bouncers are trained to notice things that might cause a danger to patrons and letting a killer into the premises would definitely fall into that category. Bar staff on the other hand want to serve drinks and get through their shift without being yelled at or covered in beer. They are less likely to hit the alarm bell.

The bar is half full. The clientele is mostly families resting their aching feet and refuelling with wine, beer and soft drinks. The music is more subtle than in the evenings, when you cannot hear the person right next to you. That will all change later.

I settle myself at the bar and order a large wine. The young woman hardly notices me as I hand over the cash. The table I want is unoccupied and I make my move. The last time I was here I had that beautiful looking man pushing his hard body into mine as we squashed ourselves together. He was lovely. I so enjoyed caving his head in.

I place my bag on the table and slide onto the high stool. My heart is bursting through my chest and I can feel the blood pulsing in my temples. Three minutes. I've given myself three minutes.

My eyes are everywhere. Checking out the faces of the bar staff for the faintest hint of recognition. Somewhere in this building is a photograph of my face with the strict instructions not to approach me.

I pick up the glass and hold it in mid-air as if I'm about to take a sip. But I lift my face and look directly down the lens of the CCTV camera perched high in the corner and tip the glass in a silent toast.

The seconds are ticking away. A minute and a half to go.

I scan the faces of the bar staff once more – nothing. No one is taking the slightest interest in me. A gang of lads barge in, much the worse for an afternoon on the beer. The noise levels rise as they fight their way to the bar. I can see fathers telling their kids to drink up, looks like family time is over. One of the group looks over to me.

'You alright, darling?' he shouts and sways against his mates. 'Where's your boyfriend?'

I'm thrilled with the attention. It's about time.

'Fancy another drink?' his friend calls out as he props himself against the others.

I shake my head and smile. My heart is racing. If the bar staff hadn't noticed me before, they have now.

The minute hand on my watch says there's fifteen seconds to go. Maybe it's because of the renewed attention but a couple of the bar staff are looking over at me. Or are they? My senses are running riot. One young woman is definitely stealing furtive glances in my direction as she puts pint glasses onto a shelf.

Five seconds to go.

The guys are eyeing me up: a pretty, lone female drinking in a pub on her own has got to be worth a crack. Three, two, one – I ease myself off the stool, take my bag in one hand and the wine in the other and head off to the toilets.

Through the door and down a set of stairs. I toss a coin in my head and choose the gents. I push open the door, the room is empty. I hurry into one of the cubicles and lock it behind me.

My hands are shaking. I can't control the adrenaline surging through my body.

I fumble with the bag.

The zip won't open.

Why won't the fucking zip open?

Chapter 37

'Please sit,' the Chief said striding to the front. 'Afternoon Roz, good afternoon, everyone.'

'Afternoon, sir,' the group replied in unison.

'Sorry to disturb your briefing Roz, would it be okay for me to say a few words?'

Kray liked the Chief. He was in his late forties with silver hair and the demeanour of an overseas diplomat rather than a copper. During her rehabilitation he had been a constant support, often dropping in on her to see how she was progressing. Kray liked the Chief a lot. The room fell silent.

'This is a particularly difficult and challenging time for us all. We deal with callous and cruel acts every day we come to work, but when those acts are targeted towards one of our own, it is hard to endure. But as much as we feel that pain it is nothing compared to the agony of Mr and Mrs Frost, Lucy's parents, and her brother James. We have just returned from meeting with the family and they are devastated.'

The Chief gave a speech that touched each and every one of the team. No one was left in any doubt about how proud the family were of Lucy Frost and how it was everyone's duty to keep focussed and bring this evil bastard to justice. The Chief then handed over to DCI Jackson.

Jacko did not possess the same magical eloquence as the Chief. *What the fuck is he going on about?*

Kray watched the clock on the wall tick its way past 5.15pm. Jacko was delivering something that was less like a pep talk and more like a pulpit sermon. There was an ominous shuffling of paper and checking of mobiles under desks.

'Quality policing is about quality people,' he droned on. 'This investigation team will win in the end because, to quote Aristotle, the whole is greater than the sum of its parts.'

He's fucking lost me now. Kray wanted the fire alarm to go off to bring this torture to an end. Instead, the phone rang. No one moved. Tavener held up his hand. 'Sorry I have to get that.'

Jackson looked put out at being interrupted mid flow. He stopped his inane wittering and waited, tapping his foot.

'Hello Detective Tavener, how can I help you?' The voice on the other end sounded slow and deliberate. 'Okay, and when was this?' He reached for a pen and paper. 'Do you have security on the door?' There was a pause. 'We'll be there right away.'

Tavener put down the phone and Jackson saw that as his cue to begin talking again.

'So to quote Aristotle—'

'Sorry, sir,' he interrupted, 'we've got a sighting of Lucy Frost.'

Why won't this fucking zip open?

My fingers grapple with the tag but it won't budge. Boiling panic consumes me. I hear the outside door bang against the wall and rowdy conversation echoes off the walls.

'That's the trouble when you break the seal, I'm going to piss like a race horse every twenty minutes now.'

'Did you clock the totty sitting at that table? Man that was nice. Did you see where she went?'

'You got no chance my son. Not with the size of that thing anyway.' The place erupted into gales of laughter.

'I'm cold, okay?'

'You must be fucking Baltic mate with a stub end like that.' More raucous laughter filled the air.

I am sitting on the toilet with the bag clamped tight between my knees. I yank with all my might at the zip and the tag breaks off.

Fuck, fuck, fuck.

The commotion on the other side of the door continues, but I'm not listening. I force my finger into the gap between the zipper and the material and pull. The plastic teeth shred themselves apart and the bag opens up. I am freaking out – the clock is ticking.

I unpack the bag, laying items onto the seat and hanging clothes on the back of the door. I feel sick. My hands won't do what my head is telling them to do. I hear the door bang against the wall and the sound of disappearing voices as the men troop back to the bar. I'm alone once more.

I tear at the clips anchoring the wig in place and fumble my way out of the dress. My shoes are kicked to one side and I squeeze make-up remover onto a pad. I scrub my face, looking into a small compact mirror. I'm drowning in my own panic. My breathing is short and sharp. I feel light-headed.

I stuff the dress, wig and shoes into the bag and try to steady myself. I fiddle with the bra clasp and it springs free.

'I have time,' I whisper to myself over and over, 'I have time'. My lungs are burning.

I step into the jeans and force my feet into trainers. The T-shirt slips over my head. I am nearly there …

There was a moment of hesitation, then the whole station burst into action. Coppers raced down the stairs to get into patrol cars, not waiting for the lift. The building evacuated faster than the end of shift on Christmas Eve. Kray flew into the driver's seat and was already pulling away when Tavener hurled himself in beside her.

'Purple Parrot, go down Gladstone Street to avoid the congestion on the Prom,' he ordered, but Kray wasn't listening. She already had her preferred route and it was a shit load faster than Gladstone Street.

The blue lights in her grill flashed and the siren blasted out as they hurtled across a junction causing other motorists to slam on their brakes. Tavener hung on for dear life. Cars slammed into the kerb to get out of the way as Kray powered her way through gaps in the traffic. Tavener stared at his boss. *Fucking maniac.*

Through another red light, the road finally opened up. The speedometer was touching seventy as the blur of houses and driveways flew past the window. Then Kray stood on the brakes and slewed the back end of the car around a bend and skidded to a halt.

They both leapt out.

'You take the back, I'll take the front,' Kray said pointing to the pub.

Here they come. Like flies around shit.

I can see her running to the door. There is a man outside holding a sheet of paper, he stops her and they have a conversation. That must be a picture of me, or to be more precise, the person I was nine minutes ago.

The ice cream tastes good. A ninety-nine with all the sprinkles and toffee sauce has always been my favourite. I lick around the edges, savouring its sugary delights. My heart is still beating hard as I sit on the bench looking out to sea. Well, half turned looking out to sea, so I can also watch the show unfold.

A second car screeches to a halt about fifty yards from where I'm sitting. Three people pile out into the bar. I would love to be a fly on the wall right now. Kray would be talking to the barmaid who recognised me from the mug shot. The other plods would be searching the place high and low looking for the woman in the picture, while others attempt to take statements from drunken bystanders.

I crunch through the biscuit cone and get a bad case of head freeze. The sugar is helping me to come down from my exertions. Another car arrives and more coppers jump out, scampering inside.

I munch the last piece of cone from my hand and check my bag. The torn zip gapes open, displaying the dress, wig, shoes, tits, underwear, mirror, cream …

Then at the bottom of the bag I see it. My heart stops.

A two-inch square of plastic with a perforated top containing a surgical wipe.

Fuck, fuck, fuck.

Chapter 38

Question: How do you get twelve police officers to cram themselves into a small imaging suite? Answer: Tell them they're going to see CCTV footage of a dead colleague, who is seemingly alive.

'Shit there she is, there's Lucy,' one man said putting his hand to his mouth.

'It's not Lucy, it's the sick bastard who killed her. Note what he's wearing,' said Kray.

'The dress from the photographs,' Tavener added.

'Jesus that's exactly like her,' said another, still trying to fathom that it wasn't Lucy they were looking at.

'That's why I wanted you all to see what we are up against. The man is a pro, not some happy amateur with a liking for women's clothing.'

They were glued to the black and white images on the screen.

'Stop. Rewind a few seconds,' said Kray.

The guy operating the equipment did as he was told.

'Now I want all of you to watch this very carefully. Press play.' The killer picked the glass from the table and raised it, staring straight into the lens.

'Pause. I want you all to take a good look, remember this is not Lucy Frost. This cheeky bastard is raising his glass to us. He did it last time, sat at the very same table in the very same bar. He raised his glass and said cheers. Now watch as the suspect leaves the table and heads off towards the toilets. Fast forward ...' The operator rotated the thumb wheel and the figures in the bar rushed about.

A group of guys who were congregated at the bar beetled off in the direction of the toilet, then came back again to resume their onslaught on the bar staff.

'Watch,' ordered Kray. 'Now freeze.' The image on the VDU was of a slightly built man carrying a rucksack slung over one shoulder. He was wearing a white T-shirt and jeans. You couldn't see his face because it was hidden below the wide peak of a baseball cap. The figure eased his way through the jostling crowd and disappeared out of camera shot.

'That's our man,' Kray said. 'That's the bastard that killed Lucy. We will be circulating screen grabs from the footage.'

'Boss can you rewind to when Lucy, err, I mean the suspect, gets off the bar stool?' Kray spun around to see who was speaking. A thirty-something-year-old man with floppy hair and greying side burns pushed his way to the front. 'I'm Craig ma'am, Craig Forrest.'

Kray motioned to the man with his hands on the buttons and the film went into reverse.

'There,' Craig said.

'There what?' replied Kray.

'The suspect leaves the table carrying a wine glass. It's in the hand farthest away from the camera but I'm sure he does.' The tape spun backwards and forwards. 'Look, the glass is there in this frame and then it's not.'

'Nice spot Craig, he took it with him.'

'Boss, I found a glass of wine in the gents' toilet. It was on the floor in one of the cubicles.' Craig was on a roll.

'Where is it now?'

'I bagged it. I thought it was odd having a wine glass in the gents, beer glasses I could understand but—'

'Is it in the evidence room?' Kray cut him off.

'I guess so.'

'Get it down to the lab and get it dusted right away. And check the rim for DNA,' Kray said. 'I think our boy might have made his first mistake.'

Fuck, fuck, fuck. It's all I can say to myself as I drive home.

I can't believe I messed up. I had the disinfectant wipe with me, and in all the commotion with my bag, I forgot to use it. I have to assume they have the glass of wine and when they realise what they've got, they will have my finger prints within hours. It seemed like a good idea at the time, to use the glass to wind up the coppers, but that only works if I clean the bloody thing first!

What a dickhead thing to do.

My mind is running amok. *Did I drink from the glass?* I don't think so, I wasn't meant to, but in the heat of the moment I can't really remember. *Get a grip and calm down.* I have to keep my mind focussed on the prize, remind myself why this is important.

I bring the car to a stop and get out. Slinging the bag over my shoulder, I slide the key in the lock and reach the sanctuary of my home. I'm still rattled by my stupidity, but there is nothing I can do about it now. I put the bag in the hallway, strip off my clothes and open the door to the cloakroom under the stairs. The skirting board lifts away to reveal the key and I'm standing on the top step gazing down into the darkness. My cock begins to stiffen in anticipation of what's to come.

The wooden steps are cold on the soles of my feet and the back of my hand keeps in contact with the wall as I descend into the cellar. I am welcomed at the bottom by the green glow of the freezer lights and the soft orange warmth of Sampson's tank. He eyes me from his coiled position in the corner and tastes the air. He is sleepy and not interested in trying to kill me today.

I shuffle along to the upright freezer and pull on the handle. The suction gives way with a whoosh and the door swings open. The cold air hits my skin but does nothing to diminish my erection. I curl my fingers around the shaft and rub back and forth in time with the rhythm as I chant the lines.

'To chill her blood, how so divine,
Walk in her shoes, her face is mine,
With evil dripping from your pores,
The next face I need to take

… is yours.'

On the top shelf is a frosted back mannequin's head covered with the white puckered skin of Madeline Eve. I chant the words over and over as I rub my cock.

'To chill her blood, how so divine,

Walk in her shoes, her face is mine …'

On the middle shelf is another head, lightly dusted with ice crystals, and framed with the freshly sculptured face of Lucy Frost.

'With evil dripping from your pores,

The next face I need to take …'

On the bottom shelf is a naked mannequin's head – ready and waiting.

'… is yours.'

Chapter 39

For the second time in a week, blades of grass clung to Kray's shoes as she crested the brow of the hill to gaze down at the riot of colour. The early morning dew dampened the bottom of her trousers. In her hand was a brown paper bag, the Costa brand emblazoned on the side. She made her way along the rows of headstones and turned right, walking along to the fourth one from the end. She stopped midway and took out a coffee and a bran muffin.

'Hey,' she said into the wind as it tugged at her coat. 'I'm having a shit week so I thought I'd meet you for breakfast. The weather woman said it's going to be sunny today, she even used the word 'hot'. Which means it will probably reach a sweltering fifteen degrees for us.' She took a tentative nibble at the muffin and gulped some coffee.

'The bastard killed one of my team, you know the one I told you about, the pretty girl, the runner. He fucking sliced her up like he did with Madeline. The whole station is devastated. Then the cheeky twat goes walkabout in her clothes in the centre of town, posing for the CCTV cameras. Made us all look like wankers.' Kray took another bite. 'We scrambled everyone we could, but he slipped away.

'And don't get annoyed but I went to see Rampton. I didn't tell you because you would have told me not to. I had to look him in the eye when I asked him the question. That didn't end well either, turns out it was nothing to do with him. Fucking stupid clock. It was the ravings of a mad woman, and before you say anything, I know you're not surprised. I got into hot water with Wacko-Jacko though, he was fizzing mad.'

She laughed to herself and slurped at the hot drink.

'Funny thing happened at the briefing. The Chief wanted to say a few words to the troops and did a great job. Then Wacko decides to do the same – what a bloody car crash. No one knew what he was on about, it was hilarious. That is, if anything at all this week could be described as hilarious. Anyway, I thought I'd come and share my shit week with you. How have you been?'

Kray paused, every time she asked that question she expected her husband to respond. She stared out to sea at the array of windmills in the distance. They looked like a child had planted them there and forgotten to come back. Jackson's words barged their way into her consciousness and a phosphor bomb of realisation went off in her head.

Kray marched past the hospital reception boy who was playing Candy Crush on his phone. She emerged from the lift on the fourth floor and looked for the signs that read 'Pharmacy'. She retraced her steps from the other day when she had been trailing along behind a tall, pissed-off pathologist. The place was a whitewashed maze of corridors and hallways and she asked for directions twice.

She arrived at her destination and pushed open the door. At her post behind the counter was Mandy Hawthorne.

'Hi Mandy, I'm DI Roz Kray, we met the other day.'

'Oh yes, I remember. You were interested in Suprane.'

'That's right, would it be okay if I asked you a few more questions?'

'Well I'm due to go on my break shortly, but I'm fine for a few minutes.'

Mandy pressed the button and the door to the side clicked open. Kray wandered in.

'Can you bring up the delivery note we looked at last time? The one with the manual adjustment.'

'Umm, I'll try to find it. It was pure chance that one came up.'

The VDU in front of her came to life with a series of windows showing scanned documents. After a while Mandy sat back. 'You mean this one?'

Kray looked at the document. 'Yes that's the one. Now can you bring up the associated documents that correspond to that delivery.'

'How do you mean?'

'You know, the purchase order, the invoice, things like that.'

Mandy's hand sped around the mouse mat clicking hot buttons on the screen. 'So, what we have here is the PO stating the amount of material requested, the cost and the delivery date. And this is the matching invoice.'

'May I?' Kray moved her hand towards the mouse. She clicked between the documents tallying up the figures.

'Is that it?' Mandy said, looking at her watch.

'Can I see another please?'

'Okay let's see if I can find one.' The screen dissolved into a blur of electronic paperwork. After a couple of minutes Mandy sat back again. 'Here's one.'

Kray looked at the delivery note with the quantity crossed out and replaced with a handwritten number.

'Can you find the corresponding paperwork to go with that? Like you did before.'

Mandy made a point of looking at her watch again. 'It's my break time now and the Pharmacy has strict opening hours. If I miss it, I don't get to take it later.'

'Please, it's important.'

The mouse moved even faster than before. The documents came alive on the screen. Kray scrutinised the figures – they checked out.

'And one more, the last one I promise.'

'I really do have to go or I'll miss my break.'

'Please Mandy, this is the last one. You've been so helpful.'

Mandy interrogated the records further and brought one up. The delivery quantity had been amended and a new figure was scrawled in its place.

'Now can I see—'

'I know, I know,' Mandy interrupted.

Kray scanned between the documents.

'Can you print these off for me?'

'I suppose so.' Mandy was now giving it the grumpy schoolgirl routine. 'Why do you want them?'

Behind a filing cabinet a printer spooled out the sheets of paper. Kray picked them up and spread them across the desk in front of Mandy.

'Here is the purchase order for fifty-two boxes of Suprane, placed on the third of February. This is the delivery note for that order number showing an amended quantity of fifty-one boxes, received on the eighth February.'

'Yes so?'

'This is the final invoice showing ...' Kray didn't bother completing her sentence.

'Fifty-two boxes,' Mandy said in hushed tones.

Kray folded the sheets of paper together and left Mandy staring at the screen with her mouth open. It looked like she wasn't going to have her break after all.

Chapter 40

The poky room resonated with the sound of buzzing which seemed to go on for an eternity – then it suddenly stopped.

'For the purposes of the tape, present in the room are DI Kray and Detective Tavener with Kevin Chamberlain and his solicitor Cheryl Paignton. Mr Chamberlain has been previously read his rights and is still under caution. Do you understand, Kevin?' Kray asked.

A short stocky young man with angular features sat opposite her dressed in a sweat shirt and ripped jeans. He shuffled around in his seat and said nothing.

'For the purposes of the tape Mr Chamberlain has nodded his head,' Kray continued. 'Can you tell us what you do for a living, Kevin?'

Kevin looked sideways at his brief who nodded her head.

'I work at the hospital.'

'What specifically do you do at the hospital?'

'I work in the stores.'

'What do you do in the stores?'

'I do lots of things but mostly I look after the deliveries and make sure the stock is in order.'

Kray looked at Tavener who produced a plastic folder with a sealed red top. Inside was a document. 'This is a docket dated the eighth February for a delivery of Suprane. It shows a quantity of fifty-two boxes, but this has been crossed out and overwritten with a new quantity of fifty-one boxes.' Tavener slid the evidence in front of Chamberlain. 'Is that your writing Kevin?'

Chamberlain shrugged his shoulders and said nothing.

'It is customary,' Tavener continued, 'for documentation to be altered to correspond to the actual delivery quantities received. That's correct, isn't it?'

Chamberlain said nothing.

Tavener pulled two new pieces of documented evidence from a folder. 'These are also delivery notes, each one has the quantities manually crossed out and a new figure written in its place. Is this your hand writing Kevin?'

Kevin looked at his brief, then at the papers spread out on the desk, then back at his brief.

'Yes, I suppose it is,' he replied.

'I am now showing Mr Chamberlain the corresponding invoices for each of the deliveries.' Tavener produced more documentation and arranged them on the table so the order numbers matched up. 'You can see in these two instances the invoice amount matches the altered delivery quantity, however, in this case the delivery quantity was amended to read fifty-one boxes but the invoice amount is still made out for fifty-two boxes. How do you account for that, Kevin?' asked Tavener.

'I don't know.' Chamberlain screwed his face up.

'We checked with the supplier and their paperwork confirms that fifty-two boxes were despatched from their warehouse.' Tavener pulled another piece of paper from a file and laid it on the desk. 'They are certain that quantity of Suprane left their warehouse but when you took delivery of that order into the hospital, you changed it to read fifty-one. The company sent an invoice for fifty-two boxes because that's what they believe was delivered. Why did you alter the quantity, Kevin?'

'Because that's how much there was.' He held out his hands, palms facing up, in non-verbal sign of honesty.

'Did you alter the delivery quantity with the intention of stealing the Suprane?'

'No, I never did that.'

'This is your writing isn't it, Kevin? It matches the other manual adjustments.'

'Yes it's my writing but I didn't steal any Suprane. And anyway, if I did it would show up at the month-end stock check. And they are all fine.' He sat back in his chair folding his arms across his chest as though that was the end of the matter.

'We will come on to the stocktake in a minute, Kevin. Let's stick with the dockets for a moment.'

'But the results of the stocktake are critical here Detective,' Cheryl Paignton intervened. 'My client has explained to me how the process works and it would seem that any discrepancy would have been detected, and from the hospital records, all stock is accounted for. If he had stolen Suprane it would have shown up. My client has denied the accusation that he stole from the hospital and the stock control system verifies that to be true. It would appear that the most likely explanation is an administrative error on the part of the supplier. I do not see why this is being handled in such a heavy-handed manner. This is obviously an internal matter for the hospital to resolve with the supplier.'

'Thank you but I would rather hear from Kevin,' said Kray stepping into the discussion.

'I am merely representing my client. He is finding this extremely stressful and has difficulties clearly articulating his thoughts.'

Kray glared at her and leaned forward placing her elbows on the table. 'Do I have to remind you, Ms Paignton, that this is a triple homicide investigation and your client may be heavily implicated? That is why it is absolutely *not* an internal matter for the hospital to resolve. Your client does understand that, doesn't he?'

'My client is cooperating with your inquiries, Inspector and I fail to see how you can seriously accuse my client of stealing Suprane when the checks and balances which monitor and control stock levels are clearly all in order.'

'Firstly, it's *Detective* Inspector, and secondly, I agree with you the stock checks are in balance. But they only take into account the quantity of stock that has been physically checked into the store. Kevin knows that. He amended the paperwork to read fifty-one boxes when in actual fact fifty-two were delivered. He stole one box of Suprane and covered his tracks. Now the documentation shows that fifty-one boxes were delivered to the hospital and the same number were checked into store. When it comes to the end of month stock take, they are only looking for fifty-one boxes. The checks and balances do not include tying the delivery paperwork back to the original purchase order which does not match to the invoice. They simply take fifty-one boxes into stock and that's all they check against.'

'Are you suggesting the stock control system in the hospital is flawed, Detective Inspector?'

'No, I'm not suggesting it, I'm telling you it is.'

'But that is preposterous!' Cheryl Paignton was either hell-bent on defending her client come what may or hadn't grasped what she had just been told.

'No, no, no,' Chamberlain butted in. 'The stock take is fine. I can't have taken it or it would show up at the end of the month.'

'The stock control procedures do not look at the full picture and you know that, Kevin,' said Kray.

'Know what? What do I know?' Chamberlain was struggling to make sense of things. 'The physical stock check balances, so I can't have taken it.'

'Kevin the way in which the stock take is carried out is incomplete and you know that. You know that if you take Suprane from the order and amend the paperwork then the stock will still balance at the end of the month.'

'But the stocktake says everything is okay, so I can't have stolen it.'

'What did you do with the Suprane, Kevin?' asked Kray.

'The stocktake is fine. I didn't take it.'

'Can we take a break?' Cheryl Paignton butted in. The penny had finally dropped.

Tavener declared the interview adjourned, gathered up the paperwork that was strewn over the desk and switched off the tape. Kray got up from the table and stomped out, followed by Tavener. They huddled together a little way down the corridor.

'He took the Suprane, I'm convinced of it,' Kray said.

'I was watching him when you were describing the holes in the stocktake regime and he didn't understand.'

'I know and that's where he got careless.'

'I'm not sure Roz, he doesn't strike me as someone smart enough to work a way around the system.'

'How do you mean?'

'I'm not saying Chamberlain is stupid but he's not exactly a candidate for Mastermind. Can you honestly see him figuring this out for himself? I reckon he's stealing to order. Someone else is pulling the strings.'

'You think there is a second person involved? Someone who saw the holes in the system and is telling him what to take?'

'It's possible. Chamberlain is obviously not the man who killed Madeline or Lucy but I'm sure the Suprane he took got into the hands of the killer.'

The door to the interview room opened and Cheryl Paignton stuck her head out.

'We are ready when you are?'

Kray smiled and held up her hand. 'She's getting right on my tits,' she said through gritted teeth.

'Before we go back in, how did you know the stock control process was wrong?' Tavener asked.

'It's tenuous. It only makes sense to me,' Kray continued walking.

'No Roz, I want to know. How did you work it out?'

'It was something Jackson said when he was talking bollocks about Aristotle.'

Tavener shook his head. 'What?'

'He said the whole is greater than the sum of the parts.'

'I still don't get it.'

'Okay, in our case the whole should be greater than the sum of the parts, in other words, greater than the sum of the deliveries.

Because Chamberlain is skimming product off the top before it makes its way into the stock control system. In other words, the whole of the stock should be greater than the sum of the amended deliveries.' Kray looked at the blank expressions on Tavener's face as her words came tumbling out. 'See, I told you it would only make sense to me.'

'Not sure it makes sense at all. And you say Jackson was talking …'

Kray shot him one of her death stares.

They trooped back in and took their seats. Tavener hit the button and the sound of the machine buzzing filled the room again. He went through the introductory routine once more.

'What did you do with the Suprane, Kevin?' Kray began from where she had left off.

'My client now understands how the stocktake can be in balance when items could have been removed at the time of the delivery.' Cheryl Paignton ignored the question. 'He also understands the gravity of the situation—'

'That's great, now what did you do with the Suprane, Kevin?' Kray interrupted.

'If you would allow me to finish, Detective Inspector.'

'Who did you give it to, Kevin?'

'Detective Inspector!' Cheryl Paignton was losing her rag. 'My client now has a far better understanding of the situation he finds himself in—'

'Who, Kevin, who did you pass the Suprane on to?'

'This is intolerable—'

'Who, Kevin, who did you give it to?'

'I am terminating this—'

'Harry Aldridge. I gave the stuff to Harry Aldridge.'

Chapter 41

Kray was itching to leave. When she should be out chasing bad guys, she was cooped up in an expensive office chatting to a shrink. Jackson had made seeing a shrink a condition of her return to work. Forty-five minutes, once a week, each session scheduled into her diary for the next three months – it was like sticking hot needles in her eyeballs.

The room was comfortable and dimly lit. Dr Gilbert sat in a winged arm chair while Roz slouched on the couch. This was her fifth session.

'I saw him,' said Roz.

'When was this?' asked Gilbert.

'The other night. I woke at around 3am to drink some water and when I dropped back off to sleep he was there.'

'Was it good?'

'Yes, it was good.'

'What was he doing?'

'He was in our kitchen, dressed in his favourite apron preparing dinner.'

'Was he happy?'

'Yeah we were both happy. I was smiling, he was smiling. He was scoring the fat of a duck breast and drinking beer.'

'Did he like to drink beer?'

'Always. If he was cooking at home he always had a knife in one hand and a beer in the other. I was drinking beer too.'

'Did you speak?'

'Not much, I just watched as he prepared food. He was talking, I could see his lips moving but I couldn't make out what he was saying.'

'How did it feel?'

'It felt like summer. We were warm and the sun spilled through the window splashing sunlight across the worktops. The BBQ was on and he was putting the finishing touches to a salad or something. He had that rolling chopping action going on, the one that shreds the vegetables really thin.'

'That sounds good, but how did you feel?'

'I felt hungry. Like I hadn't eaten for a week. I was starving.'

'Did you eat, Roz?'

'No I never did. He kept chopping and washing food the whole time, cutting vegetables and marinating meat. He was chatting and I was listening, but I couldn't hear what he was saying. We just smiled at each other and drank beer.'

'How did he look?'

'He was tanned and relaxed, like this was all he had to do - cut vegetables and prepare meat.'

'You said you didn't talk much, can you recall anything you said?

'Yeah there was something.'

'What did he say, Roz?'

'Every now and again he would look at me and say, 'We can have dinner whenever you're ready, Roz. I have all the time in the world to cook dinner. When you're ready, Roz, when you're ready.'

'And what do you think he meant by that?'

'I'm not sure. I think he meant when I was ready we could have dinner together.'

'And how do you think that would happen, Roz?'

'We would have dinner together when I die.'

'Long term goals are important, Roz but it would be more productive if you focussed on something more positive.'

'Maybe not, there are times when I think having dinner with him soon would be good.'

I killed my mother when I was fourteen years of age. I didn't mean to kill her, it just happened that way. However, I did watch her die while sitting on the top step of the cellar. Her body lay in a crumpled heap on the concrete floor below. Her head crooked over to the side at a weird angle.

It was during one of her fits of rage when she stripped me naked and ordered me into the cellar. But on this occasion she was in such a frenzy she forgot to lock the door. I can recall waiting for the sound of the bolt to be drawn across. I held my breath while I waited, but it never came.

I could hear her screaming upstairs and smashing crockery. Then it subsided and all was quiet. I sneaked up the stairs and nudged open the door. It creaked in protest like it was signalling my escape. I stood in the cloakroom listening to the noises outside – all was quiet. I cracked open the second door leading to the hallway and the light burned the backs of my eyes. I slid my slender frame through the gap and closed it behind me, she was nowhere to be seen. I could hear her moving around upstairs and the toilet flushing. This had never happened before; my heart was racing with anticipation and excitement. If she caught me I would be in deep trouble. The metallic sound of the pinking shears opening and closing grated in my head. I was frozen to the spot.

What was I going to do next? I had unexpectedly gained my freedom but had no idea what to do with it. Suddenly I heard her thumping around on the landing and the bedroom door clicking shut. She was on her way down. I panicked. My first reaction was to hurry back to the security of the cellar, but that damned door would give me away with its creaking hinges.

Fuck, fuck, fuck. She's coming. What the hell am I going to do?

I fled into the kitchen and hunkered down behind a cupboard next to the bin. The wood and wallpaper felt cold against my exposed skin as I pressed myself tight into the corner. I heard her slippered feet on the hard wood floor in the hallway. She shuffled into the lounge and switched on the TV.

Shit, what am I doing?

I needed to get back to the cellar but my route took me past the living room door. What if she saw me? What if she met me in all my nakedness on my way under the stairs? And then there was that fucking door with its squealing hinges waiting to give me away...

I heard the lounge door swish across the carpet and her footsteps on the wood, they were getting further away. She must be going back upstairs. This was my chance. I sneaked a glance around the unit to see her walking away from me towards the front door. Maybe she was going out? No, not in her slippers, she would never leave the house in her slippers. Then she turned and I ducked away. I heard her open the door to the cloakroom under the stairs and then the house was filled with the most terrifying scream. It curdled my blood and numbed my senses.

'What the *fuck* are you doing?' my mother shrieked. The door to the cellar was ajar. I could feel the warm trickle of urine against my leg as fear consumed me.

'Where are you, boy?' she yelled yanking the door open and staring down into the blackness. 'Answer me you little shit. Answer me!' I could hear her banging around in the cloakroom and then the kitchen door burst open against its hinges.

Fuck!

'You little shit!' she yelled. Drawers were being yanked open and banged shut along with the sound of cutlery clanking together. Then the noise that I dreaded most – metal shearing against metal. She had found the pinking shears.

'Where are you, boy?' she cried as she snapped the blades together. I felt more piss drip onto my feet as I crouched behind the unit, shaking. 'I have something for you.'

She left the kitchen and went back to the cloakroom. I could hear the echoed tones of her voice as she yelled down the stairs into the darkness.

'Get ready boy, cos I'm gonna fucking cut it off this time. I'll make you a proper girl yet.'

I broke cover and ran through the kitchen to the hallway. I could see my mother stood in the doorway staring down into the cellar with the shears in her hand. In that split second I thought about running out into the street, showing the world what an evil bitch my mother really was, showing the whole world what they steadfastly chose to ignore.

The thought only remained in my head for an instant before another thought took hold. A much better option.

I veered to the right into the cloakroom and shoved her in the back. I think she must have heard me coming because her head turned to the side, but it was too late.

My mother tumbled through the doorway. Her right hand grasped at thin air, reaching for the handrail to arrest her fall. But there was no handrail. She toppled sideways from the top step and landed with a bone crunching splat on the floor below. I stared into the vacant space which, milliseconds before, had contained my mother, but was now nothing more than a gaping black hole.

I sat on the top step staring down to the floor below and listened. Nothing. The grey outline of her body stood out against the dark concrete.

I sat like that for two hours watching her die. Occasionally she regained consciousness enough to croak and moan but she soon slipped back under and the peaceful silence wrapped around me once more. At one point I thought I saw her looking up at me, mouthing something I couldn't hear.

The back of my hand grazed along the plaster, keeping tight to the wall, as I descended into the darkness. I flicked on the light and found the pinking shears that had been tossed against the back wall. I knelt beside her. She was all twisted and limp, her eyes were open. I put my ear to her chest – everything was still. There was a smear of matted blood on the side of her head. She looked happy.

I made my way back upstairs, replaced the shears in the drawer and retreated into the living room to watch TV while eating breakfast cereal from the box. The phone lay beside me. After several episodes of my favourite TV show, I pulled on some clothes and dialled 999. The paramedics arrived quickly. Then the police turned up and the questions started.

The coroner reached a verdict of accidental death and I gave a stunning performance as the grieving son. The court put me into foster care until a suitable guardian could be found, which was a joke. Whoever fucking decided my uncle Greg was suitable for anything wants shooting. For the next four years I fended largely for myself at the family home while he pissed the allowance money up against the wall.

I never did get around to fitting that handrail to the stairs leading down to the cellar. Even now, when my left hand touches the cool plaster as I descend into the darkness, it is a glorious reminder of my freedom. And when the house is deathly quiet I can still hear her moaning in the cellar. It makes me smile.

Chapter 42

Kray marched into the interview room, which seemed even smaller with the lanky frames of Tavener and Aldridge shoe-horned in behind the desk. She was late, courtesy of the shrink.

'Am I being arrested?' Aldridge asked.

'No, we have a couple of questions we want to ask you in relation to the theft of Suprane from the hospital,' Kray replied taking a seat opposite him.

'Not that again, don't you people have better things to do?'

'As it stands at the moment, Harry, this is precisely what we need to do. You can have a solicitor present if you wish but you are not under caution.'

'Get on with it.'

'Firstly, when we arrived at your home we found you packing a bag into your car. It looked like you were about to take a little trip, Harry. Where were you going?'

'What does that have to do with anything?'

'I checked with the hospital and you have not booked leave for today but you appeared to be going away somewhere in a hurry.'

'I'm employed by the Home Office not the hospital. I have a stressful job and occasionally I like to take off to the countryside and leave it all behind me.'

'Without letting your employer know you're going? They must be very accommodating.'

'We have cover arrangements in place; it's not a problem.'

'So, you weren't intent on doing a disappearing act?'

'No.' Aldridge furrowed his brow and shook his head.

Kray eyed him and spun the ring on her finger. She opened a folder and pulled out a series of documents lying them on the table in front of him.

'These are the delivery documents for three shipments of Suprane made to the hospital in January, February and March of this year. You will note that in each case the delivery notes have been overwritten with a lesser quantity. These are the corresponding pieces of documentation from the supplier along with the matched invoice for each order. All the paperwork refers to the full amount of product apart from the delivery dockets which are amended. This paper trail, along with the physical stocktake, tells us that on the three months in question, Suprane was stolen from the stores.'

'As I have already told you, Detective Inspector, I have nothing to do with the stores or with the administering of Suprane. This is ridiculous!' Beads of sweat were visible on his balding head. 'This is the second time—'

'Yes, it is, Harry,' Kray interrupted. 'But this is the first time we have hard evidence that Suprane was stolen from the hospital and, as you are well aware, that drug played a major role in the murder of two women.'

'So, you've uncovered the supply? That's commendable but I have to stress it has nothing to do with me.'

'On the face of it, that's correct. You do not administer the drug and neither are you responsible for the store where it is kept.'

'Then I'm pleased that's cleared up.' Aldridge got to his feet. 'Now if you don't mind I have better things to do.'

'You are, however, responsible for making three payments to Kevin Chamberlain totalling six hundred pounds, which you paid him to steal the drug for you.'

Aldridge stopped in his tracks. Half-moons of sweat stained the underarms of his shirt.

'So you see, Harry, it very much does concern you and we would like to know more.'

Aldridge sat back down and put his head in his hands.

'Harry? Do you have anything to say?'

Aldridge raked his fingers back and forth across his scalp.

'That is an outrageous claim!' He looked like he was about to burst a blood vessel. 'I have nothing to do with bloody Suprane and I don't even know a man called Chamberlain.'

'Well he knows you and he's given us a statement that he has been stealing the drugs for you in return for three cash payments of two hundred pounds each.'

'He's lying.'

'Why would he do that?'

'To divert the blame. You probably told him that the Suprane had been used in two murder cases and he panicked. He must have seen me around the hospital and blurted out my name. You should be talking to Chamberlain, not me.'

'Oh, we will be talking more with Kevin but for now we needed to put the accusation to you. And you're telling me that Kevin Chamberlain made up the entire story. He fabricated the whole scenario about you approaching him and offering money, how he upped the price because he could see you were desperate and he thought he could screw you for more cash. I mean come on Harry, your initial offer of fifty pounds a pop is hardly worth doing now is it? So, Kevin Chamberlain saw his opportunity and upped the ante to two hundred. He threatened to expose you if you didn't stump up the money. A regular little organised crime boss is our Mr Chamberlain. He took you for a ride, am I right?'

'This is complete nonsense!'

'Chamberlain was very convincing in his statement. He even fessed up to what he spent the cash on. A set of tuned exhausts for his car – whatever they are. Now you had better start to talk to me or I am going to think the worse.'

'He's lying, can't you see that? He's shifting the blame.'

'Yes, he's doing that all right, but what I want to know is what did you do with the Suprane?'

'I didn't do it I tell you, I didn't.'

'What did you do with it? Did you sell it on? Was it stolen to order? Where is the drug now?'

'This is fucking stupid. Can't you see he's lying? Can't you see he's setting me up?'

'I'm going to ask you one more time. What did you do with the Suprane?'

'Fucking hell, why don't you listen.'

'Harry Aldridge I am arresting you on the suspicion of—'

'I'm being blackmailed, okay? I'm being fucking blackmailed.'

Chapter 43

'Talk to me, Harry,' demanded Kray.

'It happened about six months ago. I started receiving threats in the post.'

'Threats about what?'

Aldridge stared into the distance, watching helplessly as his career was about to plummet off the end of a cliff. Tears welled in his eyes. 'I'm a heroin addict.'

'What? You don't look like an addict.'

'That counts for nothing.'

'Who is blackmailing you?'

'I don't know.'

'Come on, Harry, are you seriously expecting me to believe that you are a junkie and some unknown person is putting the screws on you?'

Aldridge stood up taking his jacket off the back of the chair. 'Let's go.'

'Go where?'

'I'll show you.'

Twenty minutes later Aldridge was opening the door to his stylish flat in Stanley Park. He was followed inside by Kray and Tavener.

'Let me get it, I won't be a minute.'

Kray put her hand on his arm. 'You are implicated in a triple homicide you're not going anywhere unaccompanied.' She nodded to Tavener who followed him down the hallway to the bedroom at the end. He reached up and pulled a suitcase down form the top of the wardrobe and laid it on the bed. He unzipped the top and flipped it open, then ran his fingers around the bottom of the case and lifted out the lining to reveal a stack of papers. Aldridge picked them up and walked back into the lounge.

'I received this in the mail in December last year.' He handed Kray an envelope. She tipped out the contents into her hand. It contained a photograph showing Harry Aldridge and another man: Harry had a packet in one hand and money in the other.

'Is this your dealer?'

'Yes it's one of them. A week later I received this.' Aldridge handed Kray a second envelope which also contained another picture.

'Same dealer?' Kray asked.

'Yes, same one.'

'Then I got this.' It was an envelope and a note. The envelope was addressed to the CEO of the hospital trust. The note read:

> *I have an envelope just like this one. Find a way to obtain Suprane from the hospital stores or I will fill my envelope with photographs and mail it off. You have one week to comply. Put a vase of fresh flowers in your bedroom window when you have figured it out.*

'What happened next?'

'I approached Chamberlain, he is well known around the hospital as a bit of a wide boy and is always short of cash. He showed me how the stock control system worked and it was a simple matter of skimming product off the deliveries and amending the paperwork.'

'And then?'

'I put flowers in my bedroom window. I was fucking terrified, whoever did this was watching my place.'

'And then?'

'I received instructions telling me the quantity to steal and a series of P.O. boxes to mail the drugs to. I paid Chamberlain the money, he lifted the Suprane and I posted it. That was it.'

'Was there any more interaction between you and whoever this person is?'

'No, none, apart from me having to put flowers in the window every time I posted off a consignment of drugs. I was so scared.'

'Two more questions from me. Who would want to blackmail you?' said Kray.

'I don't know.' He shook his head.

'Who knew you were an addict?'

'I don't know.'

'Arrest him.' Kray shot Tavener a glance and walked out.

Chapter 44

Kray sat alone in the incident room. It was way past the end of her shift and the sun was dipping ever closer to the Irish Sea. On the wall were three boards, each one containing a starburst of interconnecting images. At the centres of the sprawling mass of information hung the mug shots of Madeline Eve, Lucy Frost and Joshua Wilson.

Kray fiddled with her pen and spun the ring around on her finger. She was so engrossed she failed to notice Jackson until he was standing next to her.

'What do you see?' he asked.

'Jack shit. We've only found one thing that connects the two women and absolutely nothing linking them to Wilson. We've trawled their Facebook, Twitter and Instagram accounts, phone records… and have amassed all this detail.' She waved her hand at the boards. 'And the only thing that connects the two women is they belong to the same Facebook group. That's it, nothing else.'

'What is it?'

'What's what?'

'The Facebook group?'

'Something to do with magic, nothing that rang alarm bells, the guys will look into it in the morning. They've been at it for days now and that is the only common thread.'

'I hear Aldridge coughed.'

'Yes, we have the blackmail paperwork with forensics but I'm not sure they will find anything. Gorgon is too clever for that.'

'Hey, you said Gorgon without being prompted.' Jackson felt vindicated at last.

'Yeah maybe its growing on me.' *And maybe it's fucking not.*

'I can't get over Aldridge being a high-functioning drug addict, who'd have thought it.'

'Takes all sorts I guess.'

'Gorgon must have been watching him for a long time.'

'Single bloke living on his own with money to burn, he's got to have a few vices he'd rather keep under wraps. We need to question him more thoroughly.'

Jackson scanned the boards and clicked his tongue against the roof of his mouth. 'There must be something. He selects them for a reason.'

'I know, that's the frustrating part.'

Jackson paused. 'You okay?'

'No not really.'

'You'll get a breakthrough, but it will take time.'

'No, it's not that.'

'What is it?'

'I have a terrible feeling that he's not going to wait.'

'How do you mean?'

'He killed Josh Wilson seven days after he killed Madeline Eve. My gut feel is telling me he won't wait that long. We've got extra patrols out on the streets and Lucy's photograph is in circulation but …'

'But what?'

'He's going to kill again, boss, and soon. I know it, and we're not doing enough to stop him.'

I'm on parade.

I hand five pounds to the driver and motion for him to keep the change. He watches me slide across the back seat and step out onto Parsons Way. Today is different. Madeline was coy and demure, subtlety was the name of the game. Lucy is a little different. Shy and retiring doesn't get you laid and she had a wild streak a mile wide. Madeline was all 'butter wouldn't melt in her mouth', while Lucy has a mouth that could melt pig iron.

I look amazing, if I do say so myself. There is something about being Lucy that fits me perfectly. The dress caresses my curves as the breeze reminds me that I live on the north-east coast of England. It's chilly but I feel hot, my skin is on fire and my heart is racing. I clip-clop my way down Ferron's Avenue and hang a left into Beresford Road.

They see me coming.

A new girl on the block is never welcome because it brings something new to the party and something new always results in a drop in trade. A fresh piece of eye candy causes alliances to be broken and faked relationships dissolve into mush with the bat of an eyelash. I look stunning in the fitted dress and killer heels, more like Hatton Gardens than Beresford Road. Eight pairs of eyes drill into me as I saunter to take up my spot at the end of the line. I walk in a small circle swaying my hips – their look says it all. I glance up at the other girls all doing the same circular walk. I have zero competition.

A car comes into view and the girls edge to the kerb bending forward at the waist to see who's cruising. A couple of the hookers turn away, it must be someone they know. Someone who they are in no rush to know again.

The driver spots me and speeds up passing the others as they look on. He coasts to a halt with his passenger window wound down.

'Hey, love,' he calls out. 'You open for business?'

I peer into the car. He is a big bloke with a week's stubble colouring his chin. The car is a mess of food wrappers and cans. I shake my head and step away. He curses and speeds up to make another pass at the other girls. He was too big and too confident. I'm looking for someone different. A second vehicle comes into view.

Kray spoke to the small group of officers in clipped, hurried tones.

'This is the person we are looking for.' She handed out photographs of Lucy. 'He's a slippery bastard and very dangerous.

If you get eyes on, do not try to apprehend him on your own, call for backup. We have to make sure he doesn't do another disappearing act on us. His MO is that he picks up a guy in a bar, drugs him and lures him to a secluded place where he bludgeons him to death. Are we clear?'

'Yes, ma'am,' was the collective reply.

'Here is a list of venues we believe he went to last time, he might repeat his route. But I also want as much coverage as possible. I realise that's a tough ask but we need to find this person before he kills again.'

'What about blow job alley, ma'am, where he killed his second victim?'

'I want someone posted there permanently. Got it?'

They all nodded and headed off into the delights of Blackpool by night. Jackson had listened for once.

Twelve minutes later Kray was flashing her warrant card at the bouncers on the door of the Purple Parrot. Memories crammed into her head as she scanned the interior. She forced them from her mind to focus on the people in the bar. None of them were Lucy.

I watch as the latest punter pulls up and chats to one of the girls standing three away from me. They obviously know each other, and I can hear her laughing as she leans into the car. Repeat business is always welcome. She opens the door and slides into the passenger seat. She glares at me as they drive by.

Fifteen minutes later, another car pulls onto the street. He seems tentative as he checks out the hookers. I watch their reaction and come to the conclusion he must be new. He stops and one of the girls thrusts her bursting cleavage at him through the window. They chat for several minutes and he pulls away. Maybe he's not a tit man – this could be promising.

He clocks me and makes a beeline to my spot. I slink to the kerb and wait; he stops next to me with the window down. He leans over, placing his hand onto the passenger seat. 'Erm, how much, love?'

'That depends.' He is early forties and looks like he could do with several square meals inside him. His arms are scrawny and I get the faint whiff of polish as I peer through the window. I can see a wedding ring on the third finger of his left hand.

'How much for oral and straight sex?'

'That depends.' I lean with my elbows against the window ledge to get a better look at him. He looks petrified.

'Depends on what?'

'How long do you usually last?'

I can see the cogs whirring: *do I tell the truth or do I lie?*

'Oh you know, the usual.'

'In my experience, there is no such thing as *usual.*' He's stroking his crotch with his right hand as he stares into my eyes. He's actually doing the maths in his head.

'Thirty minutes, how about half an hour?'

I lick the tip of my finger. 'Not sure.'

'Why?'

'I'm more than you could handle in a hundred years of trying. If you want to satisfy me I suggest you bring a friend. I'm not like the others, you can tell that right?

'You look gorgeous.'

'I do this for the kicks not the cash. I'm not interested in a ten-minute quickie where you make a mess on my dress and I get nothing in return. You up for that?'

I can see his erection straining against his jeans.

'That sounds good,' he croaks.

'I'm not sure about you, I'm here for my regular guys. They're like puppy dogs waiting for treats.'

'Then why did you come over to speak to me?'

'I'm always on the lookout for a new puppy dog.'

Chapter 45

Kray arranged beer mats into a tower, knocked them down only to build them back up again. The clock behind the bar counted down another five minutes, this was killing her.

Where is he?

A man with a rockabilly haircut wearing leathers squeezed in beside her.

'Hello love, not seen you in here before. Not drinking?'

Kray got up from the table, pushed through the crowd and onto the street. The Promenade was filling up with groups of happy, pissed people. She headed back to her car.

I know you're out here somewhere. Where are you?

Sitting in the driver's seat, she reached for the radio.

'This is Kray, has anyone got anything?'

'Nothing.'

'All quiet.'

'Nope.'

The answers came rolling in, every one of them telling the same story.

Kray slapped her hands against the steering wheel. The scar on her cheek tingled.

Where the fuck are you?

'Do you want to be my new puppy dog for thirty quid?'

'Yes.'

'You do understand that I want something out of this as well, don't you?'

'Yes, I understand.'

I pull on the door handle and step into the car.

'Where to?'

'Drive, I'll give you directions.'

He pulls away and we head up the road to the T-junction at the end.

'Make a left, we're heading for the park.'

'Okay.' His eyes are feasting on my legs. The hem of the dress is hitched up providing a glimpse of lace from my stockings.

'Better watch the road or we'll not get there,' I tell him as we speed along.

'You don't do this as a regular thing then?'

'I do it when I feel like doing it. I post cryptic messages on social media and my puppy dogs come running.'

Park View is a sprawling expanse of green with pockets of woodland dotted around, there are visitor attractions and cycle paths. I motion for him to turn left into the car park with a public toilet at the far end.

'Keep going, to the left of the building.' The road runs out to be replaced with a dirt track that sweeps in an arc to the back of the toilet block. 'Keep going straight ahead.'

The track meanders along for a few hundred yards and terminates in a copse of trees. He comes to a stop under the cover of low hanging branches. The sun has dipped below the horizon and the foliage above almost puts us in the dark.

'What is this place?'

'It's where the twitchers come to have fun.'

'Twitchers?'

'Bird watchers, there are hides around here and they come to look at birds.'

'Oh.' He's not looking for birds, his eyes are welded to my legs.

'You ready to play?' I lean over and kiss him deeply, leaving him breathless.

'I'm ready.'

Kray had abandoned her post at the Purple Parrot. She was cruising around in her car causing traffic mayhem.

'I fucking know you're out here,' she said to herself over and over. Up and down the sea front she drove with a queue of frustrated motorists tagging along behind.

'All units, all units. I don't think he's here, I don't think he's in town.' Kray had pulled off the front and was dashing between the side streets.

'Roz this is Jackson, why the change?

'I don't know, this doesn't feel right.'

'Come on Roz, he has a pattern. We can't change course on a whim.'

'He's not here, this doesn't feel right.'

She slapped her hands against the steering wheel once again.

I pull away from him sharply, his hand is on my breast.

'How ... what ...' he stutters.

'Pull the seats forward and get in the back.'

He bolts for the door and is sitting in the back seat by the time I get out of the car. I slide along the seat beside him, he lunges at me.

'Whoa there puppy, haven't you forgotten something?'

He scrunches up his face, then reaches into his back pocket and pulls out the money.

'Put it on the back window ledge.'

He slaps the notes onto the shelf and throws himself at me again. His hands explore my body and his tongue feels hot in my mouth. I reach down to feel his cock bursting through his jeans. I shove him away.

'Steady on there puppy or you're gonna pop your cork too soon.' He's breathing hard, desperate to please. 'You heard what I said, you got some work to do first.'

I ease myself back against the door and open my legs. My hand pushes his head down and he slides from the seat into the foot well. His hands caress my thighs, sliding up my dress to expose my stocking tops.

'You going to please me?' I say seizing two handfuls of hair.

'Yes, yes.' He begins to kiss my inner thighs, panting like a good puppy.

I wrap my legs either side of his head and lock my ankles.

'If you want to please me you're going to have to work for it.'

I squeeze my thighs together. He makes a gurgling sound. He tries to prize them open but he can't. He is so desperate to please.

'Try harder,' I taunt him as he struggles. He shuffles around in the footwell, trying to get better leverage. He likes this game.

I reach for my bag and delve inside. He writhes around between my legs.

I let him get close to his prize only to push him back down and clamp him in place. His face is red with exertion and my stockings are laddered from his grasping hands.

'Work harder puppy, show how much you want to please me.'

My fingers find what I'm looking for. He is too busy trying to reach my crotch to notice. His eyes are closed. I can see his tongue darting out of his mouth. The cold point of the screwdriver touches his temple and he stops.

His eyes flick open to portray a mixture of confusion and pleasure.

I drive the screwdriver into the side of his head. His eyes burst from their sockets and his jaw drops open. His arms spasm against the seats.

I watch the life drain from the face between my legs. He emits a gargled retching sound and tremors run through his body. I slam the heel of my hand into the handle and ram the driver all the way in. The shaking stops. His lifeless eyes stare at me. His mouth gaping open. He tried so hard to please.

Chapter 46

Kray was drained. She hadn't slept a wink. Instead she had spent the night staring into the darkness of her bedroom, picturing where the killer could have been. She was angry that an evening spent racing around the streets had yielded nothing. She had despatched the team of officers to every nook and cranny but they had come up blank. She felt like shit and what she didn't need was to be sat in Jackson's office to receive a 9am lecture. But she was getting one anyway.

'I was prepared to cut you some slack, Roz. We deployed more officers because you had a hunch that he was going to kill. But then you turn it on its head mid-operation for no apparent reason, give me a break!'

'He was out there I know it.'

'How Roz? How do you know it?'

Kray shook her head, spinning the ring on her finger, feeling as though the word 'idiot' was etched on her forehead.

Jackson continued. 'We pulled officers from other assignments to stake out the previous locations where Gorgon had been sighted, I get that. But then we abandon the plan in favour of scattering them around town with zero co-ordination and fuck all rationale? That, I don't get. What happens when we need to call for reinforcements again?'

'I'm sorry. I just had a feeling he had changed his pattern. I know he was out there somewhere, we just weren't in the right place.'

'Yes well I've got a feeling that we made ourselves look like dicks. This is bound to move up the chain and it's me who will have to deal with the shit when it starts raining down.'

Yeah that's it. Never mind about the fact that we were trying to prevent a fourth murder, you think of yourself. Kray kept her mouth shut.

'The ACC wants a briefing at ten o'clock and I'm struggling to know what to tell her. She's getting impatient for results and the Chief wants to put out a statement. My problem is I've got jack shit other than we had officers chasing around town on a wild goose chase.'

'I'll tell her if you would prefer?' Kray offered knowing what the answer would be.

'No, it's my job to keep them updated. I just wish I had something positive to say.'

There was a sharp rap at the door. It was one of the new members of Kray's team, Jackie Marsden.

'Excuse me, sir.' She stood in the doorway. 'Ma'am you need to come and see this. I might have something.' Kray didn't need a second invitation and followed her down the corridor to the incident room, not waiting to be dismissed.

'What is it?' Kray asked as Marsden returned to her seat behind her laptop.

'Do you remember I said yesterday that the only thing we could find connecting the female victims was a Facebook group?'

'Yes, and please call me Roz.'

'The group is linked to a website called Boston Magic. It turns out Lucy and Madeline were members and accessed it often, sometimes two or three times a week.'

'What's it about?'

'Well, it has nothing to do with conjuring tricks,' said Marsden. 'Take a look.'

She spun the laptop around to face Kray.

'What the hell is this?'

'Boston Magic is a make-up tutorial site specialising in highlighting, contouring and sculpting.'

Kray looked at Marsden blankly. 'You realise I don't understand what you just said, right?'

'It's a method of applying make-up that alters your face. The results are startling - it can accentuate your cheekbones, make your face appear narrower, change the shape of your nose, alter your jawline. The techniques can completely change the way a person looks. It also sells products sourced from America at exorbitant prices. I think that's where they make their money.'

'One hundred and twenty dollars for a tube of foundation? You're not kidding. You said they were members?'

'Yes, fortunately Lucy kept a record of her passwords in a coded form on her phone. I worked through them and managed to hack in. That gave me access to the members only pages and that's where it gets interesting; I found this tab called *he2she*.'

'What to what?'

'To promote how good their products are, they use guys as models.'

'Okay but blokes wear make-up these days, that's not unusual.'

'This is different. They transform these men into women.' Jackie brought up a gallery of 'before and after' faces.

'Are you sure? They can't be the same people.'

'They are.' Marsden clicked on one of the thumbnails to bring up a sequence of photographs. 'This is the man before and this is him made up as a woman.' The images showed a man in his late twenties with a stubbled chin, bright eyes and a cheeky smile posing for the camera. The second set of pictures were of a stunningly beautiful woman.

'Bloody hell, I don't look half as good as that when I go out,' Kray said running the mouse over the frames. She clicked on one. It took her to a video showing the process the man had gone through to achieve the transition. 'That is incredible.'

'The company's claim is, if we can make a guy look this beautiful think how good it's going to work on you. But that's not all ...' Marsden clicked on another tab and scrolled down. 'It encourages people who subscribe to the site to post pictures of themselves in return for free advice on how best to apply their make-up and which products will suit them the most.'

An array of photographs filled the screen, and Kray ran her eyes down the images.

'Fucking hell.' Kray traced her finger along the rows of passport-like faces. Staring out at her, three rows apart, were Madeline Eve and Lucy Frost.

'Get this up on the TV. I want everyone to see.' Marsden did as she was told and inserted the HDMI cable into the port. The large flat television on the wall came alive. 'Listen up everyone, we've got a breakthrough,' Kray announced. 'Go through that again.' She gestured to Marsden. The team dropped what they were doing as she reiterated the latest discovery.

Kray stared at the images. The bright smiling faces of two attractive young women beamed at her from across the room. She looked at the mug shots on the wall of Lucy and Madeline, then back to the screen.

'So that's the connection,' Kray muttered. All heads turned her way despite Marsden being in mid flow. 'We've been looking for a link between the two women when it's been staring us in the face all along. They both have the same facial features. Disregard the hair style, ignore the make-up, forget about the colour of their eyes - they have the same narrow face with high cheekbones. They both have large eyes, set slightly wide apart, a slim nose and thin lips. While they don't look like identical twins they have the same basic facial features.'

Tavener had been watching his boss and was doing the same, glancing back and forth at the pictures. 'You're right Roz, that's uncanny.'

'This website links the two women but the main thread linking the female victims is they have the same facial characteristics as the killer. He selects women who look like him.'

'But that doesn't account for why he would crack open Wilson's skull with a lump hammer?'

'It doesn't, but let's take one step at a time. I reckon he finds his female victims by surfing the pictures on this site.'

'It's a bit of a coincidence that he selects two women who both live in the same area,' said Tavener.

Marsden enlarged the images on the TV. 'Not much of a coincidence at all.' The picture was grainy due to the poor resolution but beneath each photograph was written – 'Blackpool, England'.

'Shit,' uttered Tavener.

Kray got to her feet and stood next to the television. 'I want every one of these followed up. Concentrate on women living within a fifty-mile radius—'

The phone rang. Tavener answered it.

'Roz, sorry to interrupt,' he said. 'They have found a body in Park View. Forensics are at the scene, it could be our man again.'

'Park View? Where is that?' asked Marsden.

Kray put her hand up to her mouth. 'It's in Lytham St Annes, about a mile and a half from my house.'

Chapter 47

Kray came to a halt twenty yards short of the hive of activity taking place in front of her. She got out of the car and the mid-morning sun pierced her eyes. She fished out her sunglasses. It was a beautiful morning to wish to God you were wrong.

She tugged on a pair of overshoes, a white paper boiler suit and bobbed beneath the yellow tape cordoning off the area. A cluster of people in similar dress busied themselves with cameras and evidence bags. Ahead of her she could see a blue Ford Fiesta parked under overhanging branches. She recognised the balding head of Mitch peering over the roof of the car with two guys working beside him to erect a tall white screen.

Kray waved and walked over.

'Roz,' said Mitch in his customary abrupt manner.

'Mitch, what do we have?'

'Brian Dukes, forty-one years of age from Blackpool. A bunch of kids found him this morning while riding their bikes.' He jerked his head in the direction of a PC standing twenty yards away chatting to four lads, their bikes discarded on the floor. 'They approached the car and saw this.' Mitch pointed to three ten-pound notes lying on the back window ledge. 'They thought the car had been abandoned, opened the door to take the cash and found him dead.'

Roz looked inside the vehicle at the contorted figure crumpled into the footwell behind the driver's seat.

'Time of death?'

'Between nine o'clock last night and midnight is my best estimate.'

'Cause of death?'

'At first I thought he'd been shot. He has a round hole in his left temple, but I doubt it was made by a bullet, it's too small. There is no exit wound and no blood spatter on the interior. My guess is it's a puncture wound and my other guess is, when we conduct the post-mortem, we're gonna find it goes deep into his brain.'

'Have you finished?' said Kray, pulling on a pair of blue latex gloves.

'Yep we're just about to move the body.'

'Give me a minute.' Kray moved to the front of the car and put her left hand under the passenger seat. Then she leaned between the gap in the seats and examined Dukes' left hand; his right was tucked beneath him. His eyes stared at her from between the seats and his tongue protruded from his mouth.

'The blood stains are only as high as the back seat.'

'I know, looks like he died in the footwell.'

What the fuck were you doing down there? Kray held his dead gaze.

'Mitch! Do you have a torch?' she called out. He handed her one, she flicked on the beam and shone it on his face. 'Did you notice the discolouration on his cheek? It looks red.'

Mitch popped his head into the car. 'No I didn't see that.' He beckoned to the two men in white boiler suits. 'Let's get him out.'

'Ma'am, are we okay to move the body?' asked the crime scene supervisor.

'Wait.' Kray spotted something reflecting in the torchlight. She leaned over the body, slid her finders down the back of the seat and levered out a mobile phone. She swivelled it in her hand and touched the screen - fifteen missed calls. She motioned to Mitch who held open an evidence bag for her to drop it into.

'That's Dukes' phone.' She nodded to the men crouched at the back door. 'You can move him now.'

They expertly manoeuvred the dead man out of the passenger door on the driver's side and laid him on a plastic sheet. Mitch knelt down beside him to examine the wound on the side of his head.

'Yes it's definitely a puncture wound, we're not looking for a gun.'

'Let me see.' Kray tilted his face away from her to examine the entry wound. 'What do you make of this?'

Kray pointed to the side of his face. Mitch moved the victim's head from side to side.

'Don't know, but there is a slight abrasion on each cheek. What do you think, Roz?'

'Not sure about the discolouration but there's one thing I am sure about—'

Tavener appeared from around the screen. 'Roz, Dukes' wife reported him missing last night when he failed to return home from work. He was supposed to be back by ten thirty and when he didn't show she rang 999 and reported him missing around midnight.'

'Where was he supposed to be?'

'She said he was on a late shift.'

Kray spun her wedding ring round and round as she stared at the lifeless body on the ground. The scars running across her back began to burn.

'What do you think?' asked Mitch.

'I think Dukes told his wife he was working late and took the opportunity to have casual sex with a stranger instead. Both front seats are pulled forward which would suggest there was going to be some action in the back. The vehicle is parked undercover and there's thirty quid on the back window. Doesn't take a rocket scientist to work out what happened.'

'Do you think this is …' Tavener left his sentence hanging.

'I don't *think*, I know. Dukes' finger nails are scrubbed clean and that hole in the side of his head is going to be caused by a tool of some kind. Maybe a screwdriver or a drill bit. The thirty pounds has been left behind because this was not about money.'

'You think he used a tool like he did with the lump hammer?'

'Exactly. And when forensics get hold of this car I bet you the last bottle of wine I have in my fridge the back seat is covered with short black fibres.'

'How do you know that?' asked Mitch.

'Because that was the colour of the dress the killer took from Lucy Frost's apartment.'

Kray stripped off her gear and stuffed it into a bag, then strode back to her car barking out orders, with Tavener in hot pursuit. 'Check out the CCTV in the area. Find out where the victim worked and run an ANPR on all routes linking it to here. I found his mobile which should tell us the route he took. Also get a photo of Lucy in front of the local hookers to see if anyone noticed a new girl, and if they did, who picked her up.'

There was the screech of tyres on tarmac. They both looked up to see two people get out of a car and run towards them. One was carrying a camera and the other a microphone attached to a rucksack by a cable. A second vehicle came to a stop, carrying the same cargo.

'Oh, and keep the press away.'

'On it, Roz.' Tavener peeled off to confront the story seekers.

Kray's self-control lasted long enough for her to reach her car. She flung herself into the driver's seat, slammed the door shut and grasped the steering with both hands, almost tearing it from its mountings.

'Fuck!' she yelled at the top of her voice as she wrenched at the wheel. Then Kray collapsed forward with her head resting on her knuckles. Tears of anguish ran down her face.

'I fucking knew it! I fucking knew it!' She was yelling at no one. 'We were looking in the wrong places!' Saliva droplets speckled the dashboard as her shoulders slumped. 'I could have ...' Her voice tailed off to nothing.

Images crammed their way into Kray's mind, her thoughts tumbling together. She could see the phone box outside her house and pictured the killer feeding a pound coin into the slot. She could see her favourite table at the Purple Parrot where she and

Joe went every Friday night to kick-start their weekend with a few beers. She pictured the two of them walking hand in hand around Park View in the sunshine after their Sunday lunch.

The colour drained from her face and bile filled the back of her throat. The whole world swam by on a swirling torrent of memories. Kray opened the car door and vomited on the grass. As she gasped for breath and stared down at the putrid mess splashed on the ground, the cold and terrifying realisation welled up inside her.

The killer knows me.

Chapter 48

Kray was back at her desk ploughing through the deluge of paperwork, forcing the latest demons to the back of her mind. She had work to do and that sort of craziness wasn't helping.

The policing gods were not on her side. The forensics report on the glass found in the toilets of the Purple Parrot had come up with nothing. Smudged prints and not a trace of DNA. The Royal Mail had confirmed three deliveries to the P.O. boxes used by Harry Aldridge, which was good, but all three locations did not have CCTV installed and the paperwork had yielded nothing – which was bad. In addition, the forensic analysis of the documentation used to blackmail him was also clean. The only thing they could confirm was that Aldridge had handled them.

Not only were the policing gods not on her side, to Kray it felt like they were laughing their bollocks off at her expense. She straightened the pens on her desk so they lay parallel to her laptop. *It's difficult to imagine how this could get any fucking worse.*

Her newsfeed came up in the right-hand corner of the screen. It showed a very harassed DCI Jackson on the steps outside the station, pinned down by a forest of microphones being shoved in his face. Scrolling at the bottom of the picture were the words: *'Breaking News – Body found in Park View, Police say the killing is linked to previous murders.'*

Kray stared boggle-eyed at her screen trying to take in what was in front of her. She hit the sound button.

'We can confirm that a body was found in Park View earlier this morning. The family have been informed and at this time we are not giving out further details as the investigation is ongoing,' Jackson announced to the nation.

'Is it true there have been three other murders?' said a reporter.

'Is this killing linked to the others?' piped up another.

'I am not prepared to give further information as—'

'Why is the general public being kept in the dark about these murders? Don't you think they have the right to know?'

'As I said, this is an ongoing investigation—' Jacko was drowning in the full glare of the media.

'So all four murders are linked. Are you looking for a serial killer?'

'That is not what I'm saying.'

Kray stared through the screen. *Get out of there. Get the hell out of there.*

Her phone vibrated on the desk. It was Tavener.

'Roz have you seen—'

'I'm looking at it now.'

'How the hell did they get hold of this?' he asked.

'Let me call you back.'

Jackson was still under fire. 'How many other murders has this serial killer committed?'

'We are following up several lines of inquiry. As I said the family has been informed and we would ask the public to be vigilant ...'

Kray closed her eyes and wished she was somewhere else.

For fuck's sake stop talking.

'How can you expect the public to be vigilant about something they know nothing about?'

'Do you have a description of the killer if you're asking for the public's help?' The questions came thick and fast.

'No, what I'm saying is that we confirm that a body was found in Park View earlier this morning. The family have been informed and at this time we are not giving further details as the investigation is ongoing.'

'So, what about the other murders? And do you want the public to be on the lookout for the killer?'

'That's all for now.'

Jackson held up both his hands, turned and forced his way back into the station. Kray had her head in both hands staring down at the desk.

What a car crash.

She could hear the sound of heavy footsteps in the corridor and a door slamming shut. Kray looked at the time stamp on the video, it had happened forty minutes ago. Rage boiled inside her.

What the hell is going on?

She leapt from her desk, bolted for the door and met Jackson coming the other way.

'With all due respect William, what the fuck was that all about and why was I not consulted as the senior officer in charge?'

'Come with me.' He turned and walked back to his office.

'William, I insist that you discuss this matter with me.' Kray followed him into his office to find ACC Mary Quade sitting at the oval table in the corner.

'Sorry ma'am, I didn't realise you were here,' Kray apologised.

'Take a seat, both of you,' the ACC said in a flat tone.

Quade was a scary monster with epaulettes. She was new in post and had come from GMP with a fearsome reputation. About the same age and height as Kray, she probably tipped the scales at twice her weight. Her management style could best be described as 'vicious'. Jackson took a seat at the table, he looked like he'd just shit his pants.

'Ma'am I wanted to ask DCI Jackson why I was not informed that a press conference was about to take place. And how did they draw the conclusion that the murders were linked? We have maintained a news blackout on this for the specific reason—'

Quade raised her hand in a signal for Kray to stop talking.

'They were chancing their arm. The press have been making their frustrations known about the blackout but we have refused to budge. When this latest murder was discovered they jumped straight in and didn't wait to be told not to report it. They knew if they played up the link to the murders, we would be forced to respond.'

'But why was I not informed, ma'am? I am the SIO and I could have helped provide a more cohesive view.' She glowered at Jackson who looked away. 'Instead we now have a situation that we cannot contain. We cannot be led around by the press. We have to get out in front of this story and manage it.'

'Yes we do, we also have to manage the investigation.'

Kray furrowed her brow. 'I don't understand, ma'am.'

'Give me an update on progress,' Quade asked, fixing Kray with piggy eyes.

Kray was taken aback by the question. 'Err, well, we are following several lines of inquiry. There is a definite link between the two women. We know the killer assumes the identity of the women to murder the men. I believe this latest victim was murdered with a tool of some kind in the same way as Josh Wilson. We have clear forensic evidence of fibres from the dress of Madeline Eve on Wilson. I believe we will find the same evidence of dress fibres in the back of the car of the latest victim. We have confirmation from the Royal Mail that—'

Quade held up her hand again. Kray stopped mid-sentence.

'All of this I know. What I don't know is, are we any closer to catching the bastard who is doing this?'

'Ma'am we are exploring every avenue.'

'The force is pushing manpower at this at an alarming rate and what I am not hearing is anything that gives me confidence that we are using them in the right way.'

'I disagree.'

'We have a ton of forensics and hypotheses but that hardly constitutes as progress. When am I going to be able to give the Chief a date?'

'A date, ma'am, I don't get it?'

'Or a timetable?'

'Ma'am you've lost me.'

'I need to be able to tell the Chief that we have a cohesive plan. I need to be able to say we have these many officers working these many hours on these lines of inquiry and we expect to have the suspect in custody by this date.'

'But ma'am, it doesn't work like that.'

'Yes it does Roz and that's my problem with this whole investigation.'

'I must protest in the strongest possible terms and you need to back me up here, William.' Jackson stared down at the table top, fiddling with the cuff buttons on his shirt. 'We need the additional manpower because this is a complex case.'

'Yes I agree, but my concern is the way that manpower is being deployed.'

'They are all tasked in support of our lines of investigation, ma'am. I cannot see how—'

'What about the other night? You had a crew of officers staking out the known haunts of the suspect in line with the pattern of the previous murder. Then on a whim you abandon that strategy and scattered them all over the place.'

'I knew the suspect was out there, ma'am, and I realised he was about to break with his previous pattern.'

'You realised? How precisely did you decide to rip up a perfectly sound surveillance operation in favour of a hit and hope approach of deploying officers all over the place?'

'I knew something was wrong, ma'am and I was proved right. The killer did strike again and I was also right about it being in a different location to last time.'

'Yes, Roz you were right. But we cannot run a multiple homicide case on gut feel and intuition. We don't all possess your crystal ball. We have to demonstrate due diligence and proper policing methods, and this case has none of those qualities.'

'William, you need to say something. Tell the ACC how I have conducted the investigation, tell her that it is based upon solid policing. Tell her William ...'

Jackson said nothing.

'I need to be able to tell the Chief we are making progress. We need to be able to hold a press conference and tell the public we are making progress and I'm afraid with you in charge Roz that is not going to happen.'

Kray looked at Quade trying desperately to hold back the tears and stop herself from punching her in the throat.

Quade continued to twist the knife. 'I am not denying you delivered some useful insights in the beginning, Roz. The snake venom, the way in which Suprane was being stolen from the hospital and the way the flies were screwing the timeline. But that's it and I'm afraid that is not a substitute for old-fashioned, knocking-on-doors-style policing. You came back to work too early Roz and this case is too big for you.'

'No, ma'am that's not true. I am ready for this, we are making progress.'

'I've seen the latest report from Dr Gilbert. He was so alarmed he took the unusual step of reporting it up the line because he deemed you a suicide risk.'

It took Kray several seconds for the words to sink in.

'No, no, ma'am, I was messing with him. The counselling is a waste of fucking time, I was spinning him a line.'

'I understand the severity of what you went through, Roz, I really do. But this cannot be allowed to go on. Your judgement is flawed and it is damaging this investigation.'

'No, ma'am, my judgement is sound. Say something, William, back me up here!'

The buttons on his cuffs were subjected to even more fiddling.

Quade went in for the kill. 'Then how do you explain upsetting the apple cart by going to see Carl Rampton in prison. Talk me through that one. You see him on the pretext of pursuing a line of inquiry, end up discussing something completely different, and we all have egg on our faces. This can't go on, Roz.'

'But ... but, the whole Rampton thing was a misunderstanding. He thought I was—'

'I've heard enough, Roz. As of immediate effect I will be overseeing the day to day tasking of this case with DCI Jackson as the SIO. You have two choices – you can either sign yourself back on the sick or we will re-assign you to another role pending a further doctor's report. For the record, the Chief shares some of the responsibility for bringing you back too early, Roz and he wants to do the right thing. I want you to do the right thing.'

Jackson looked petrified at the prospect of being accountable. Quade looked delighted she had savaged a member of staff and Kray wanted to curl up in a corner and die.

Chapter 49

Kray cleared her belongings from the incident room, avoiding eye contact with those who were there, and relocated to an office across the hallway. She offloaded her laptop and reams of paper onto the desk and closed the door. She stood in the centre of the room shaking.

What the fuck just happened? That fucking Wacko set me up for a fall. He threw me under the bus to save his own skin.

Outside, she heard Jackson barking orders in his best Metropolitan voice. 'Right I want a briefing in ten minutes, bring with you everything you have, be prepared for a drains-up review.' She heard the sound of feet scurrying about.

She shuffled behind her desk and sat with her head in her hands considering her options. The prospect of being sidelined was a difficult pill to swallow, she could get her head around that, but signing back on the sick would be like giving up. The voice of doubt chirped away on her shoulder. *Maybe the ACC is right, I have come back to work too soon.*

She could handle the loss of face in stepping down, her battle was with herself. Had she got it so wrong? She was just starting to get into the head of the killer, beginning to think like him, anticipating his moves. Or was she deluding herself and all her gut feel and intuition were actually the product of a crazy woman?

There was a sharp knock on the door and Brownlow's face appeared. 'Morning, Roz,' he said with a smile so wide it nearly cut his head in two. He disappeared, leaving the door ajar not waiting for a reply. She heard him enter the incident room. 'Sorry I'm late, boss, what have I missed?'

'Fucking typical!' Kray said under her breath. 'That's just like Wacko to bring in a wing man so he can divert the blame if things go wrong.'

I've had e-fucking-nuff of this.

Kray stormed from her office and out of the station to the coffee shop down the street. She needed to put distance between her and those wankers, and she needed strong coffee.

She sat at the back of the shop as far away from everyone else as she could get. Two mugs stood empty in their oversized saucers on the table. She gazed into the distance, spinning the wedding ring on her finger.

Her mobile buzzed in her pocket. It was a text.

Do you want another?

She looked around to see Tavener standing in the queue. She texted back.   Cappuccino.

After a while he heaved his large frame into the seat next to her and removed the drinks from the tray.

'I got you a large,' he said as Kray's eyes widened at the sight of the swimming pool of coffee in front of her.

'You did that alright,' she replied, noting the double handles required to pick the mug up. She lifted it with both hands, it weighed a ton.

'How did you find me?'

'You drink coffee when you're under stress or need to think, and from what I've just been told you must be doing a shit load of both. I'm sorry, Roz.'

'Yeah well, sometimes shitty things happen.'

'So now we have the dynamic duo of Wacko and Brownbag running the show. We all need to wear our underpants on the outside of our trousers to compensate for that pair.'

'Maybe a fresh set of eyes will make all the difference.'

'Yeah, and maybe it won't. Who amongst them has that copper's instinct? The insight you brought to the investigation was genius, Roz.'

'Not sure the ACC sees it that way. My instinct has well and truly bitten me on the arse this time.'

'Brownbag is getting us to—'

'Whoa there, Tonto.' She held up both her hands. 'I don't want to know. That investigation is nothing to do with me now and that's the way it has to stay.'

They both took a sip.

'Is it okay to take this personally?' Tavener asked. 'Because I want to catch that fucker so much I can taste it for what he did to Lucy.'

'No it's not okay but despite what a large portion of the general public might think, we are human.'

'The problem is I'm not sure we will catch the bastard now.'

'You will.' Kray took another slurp of coffee. She could feel the excess caffeine kicking in.

'What are you going to do?'

'Not made my mind up yet.'

'Don't throw in the towel.'

'Maybe it's for the best.'

Tavener shook his head. 'Excuse my language ma'am, but that's bullshit.' His phone rang; he answered it. 'Yeah, okay I'll be there in ten.' He looked across at Roz. 'Sorry I have to go, the ACC wants to give us a pep talk.' He screwed his face up.

'Then you need to go.'

Tavener eased himself out of the booth with his coffee in hand and asked the man behind the counter for a takeout cup before heading back to the station. Roz went back to staring into the middle distance. After a while she pushed the bucket of coffee away from her, collected her things and left.

She had things to do.

Back at her office Kray closed the door and flipped open her laptop. Her fingers tapped away at the keyboard and a series of mug shots scrolled across the screen. Aggravated burglary, assault with intent to wound, domestic violence – the cases flashed before her.

She remembered 2014 was a hectic year but 2015 was even busier. Face after face came into view at the click of her mouse. Some were angry, some were blank and others defiant. But they all had one thing in common: they had all helped Kray to rack up an impressive arrest rate, propelling her to the rank of Detective Inspector. She buried herself in the past, each time skirting over the details of the case focussing instead on the individuals involved.

Tavener might be a promising detective but he was crap at reading people. Kray wasn't in the café pondering on her professional future. She was there with one thought, and one thought only.

She was so engrossed that she failed to notice Jackson stood in the doorway. 'Looks like you've made your decision.' Kray rubbed her eyes and glimpsed at her watch. She'd been at it for over two hours. She closed her laptop.

'Yes I have. I can't go back on the sick Jacko, because I'm not sick.' She immediately regretted using the name he liked to be called the most. He would see it a sign of friendship and reconciliation. 'It's best if I stay in work.'

'Hey, I know that, Roz. You're a real asset to the force.' He leaned against the doorframe, positively simpering.

Shame you didn't fucking say that in front of the ACC.

'If it's still okay with you I want to be reassigned,' she said balling her fists under the desk.

'That is the sensible option, Roz. I'm glad we could reach a satisfactory conclusion.'

I swear if he calls me Roz in that tone of voice one more time I'll ...

'I have a shed load of paperwork to complete so I thought I'd get that out of the way first. If that's okay?' she said.

'Yes of course take your time, we have everything covered.' He bounced himself off the woodwork and swaggered away.

Patronising twat.

She opened her laptop to resume her search. A single thought crashing around in her head. *The killer knows me.*

Chapter 50

It was late and Kray was regretting that her diet today had consisted solely of a shit load of coffee and three biscuits. She had a banging headache and her stomach would not stop growling in protest. She rubbed the sting from her eyes and closed her laptop. She had turned up a big, fat nothing.

She had examined every case going back three years but no one fitted the description; narrow face, high cheekbones, large eyes set slightly wide apart. In fact, no one came close, not even the women. Her trawl back through the years had yielded nothing. She was tired and needed to acquaint herself with a hot bath and a bottle of wine.

'Roz have you got a minute?' bellowed Jackson down the corridor.

How the fuck does he know I'm still here?

She tore herself away from her thoughts and trudged to his office. He looked frayed around the edges.

'Uniform have called in a sudden death. It looks like a drugs overdose and they want us to give it a once over.' He handed Kray a slip of paper. 'Here are the details, it looks straight forward.'

Kray took the note. 'Are you sure? I thought you wanted me to—'

'Don't make a drama out of this, Roz. We are really up against it. Every man and his dog is working on the Gorgon investigation and I need you to deal with this, okay?'

'Sure, I just thought—'

'Well don't.'

'I'll take care of it.' Kray turned and walked back to her new office, leaving Jackson shoulders-deep in paperwork. She left the station pausing only to buy a packet of crisps from the vending machine and chomped on them as she cruised towards the less salubrious side of town. The flat in question was buried in a high-rise block on the Crown Estate. Not a place where people went to live by choice.

She got out of the car and brushed the crumbs from her suit. The estate should have been levelled twenty years ago, but the council decided against that when they realised they would have nowhere to house the dregs of society. It stood as a constant reminder that when it came to providing safe and secure social housing, the local authorities didn't give a toss.

She found the tower block and walked straight past the lift, choosing instead to walk to the third floor to avoid her clothes stinking of piss. A gang of kids were hanging out on one of the landings and took off when they saw her coming. Isn't it strange how, for some children, 'how to spot a copper from thirty yards' is an essential part of their upbringing.

Kray flashed her warrant card at the uniformed officer standing sentry at the door and walked in.

'SOCO are on their way, ma'am,' the officer said. Kray nodded her response.

The living room looked like a pound of C4 had gone off and no one had bothered to clean up afterwards. The carpet was ripped in places exposing bare floorboards and half a sofa sat against the far wall. The walls had the blackened appearance of having once been in a fire and there was a broken TV stand in the corner, minus the TV. The flat stank of dirty clothes and fag smoke.

The body of a man was slouched in an armchair with his head tilted forward. In front of him was a coffee table with all the paraphernalia you would expect to see in a drug den. Balls of tinfoil, a mirror, a handful of credit cards, cotton wool balls, a set of scales and a bottle of talc all lay strewn across the top.

The dead man was dressed in a T-shirt and jeans with nothing on his feet. His hair had fallen forward covering his face and a trail of vomit ran down his front and onto his legs. A used syringe and rubber tourniquet lay beside him.

Kray looked around the chair, reached down and patted the man's pockets with her gloved hand. She looked up into his face, he looked familiar. *Where the hell have I seen you before?*

Her thoughts were interrupted.

'His name is Richard Moore, Richie to his friends,' said the uniformed PC emerging from the kitchen on the left. 'He is well known to us for all sorts, petty theft, D and D, that kind of thing. Looks like old Richie here had made a step up to dealing. We pulled him a couple of times for possession but couldn't make it stick.'

'I'm DI Roz Kray.'

'Graham Chapel, ma'am.'

'What are the circumstances?'

'We got a 999 call from a male saying they had discovered a man in the flat. The caller refused to give their name and hung up. When we got here the door was open and Richie was dead in the chair.'

Kray crossed the room and examined the door.

'I'm presuming nothing has been touched?'

'As you see it now is exactly how we found it.'

Kray crouched down, took her phone from her pocket and flicked on the torch, shining it under the chair. She moved around each side, repeating the process.

'Looks clear cut to me. Richie decided to give himself a little treat and overdid it. Someone shows up wanting a fix and finds him dead. Calls it in because they are an upright citizen.'

Kray stood up and switched off the piercing beam.

'Is it heroine?' Kray asked pointing to the white powder on the table.

'Not sure until it gets run through the lab, but it looks like it to me.'

The SOCO team arrived outside and started gowning up.

'Self-inflicted. Killed by a taste of his own medicine,' said Chapel with the air of a man who's seen this a thousand times before.

'Not sure about that,' Kray said handing him the torch. 'This is now a crime scene.'

Back at the station Jackson was coming apart at the seams. 'A suspicious death?' He was red in the face and on his feet.

'Yes, sir.' Kray had decided to address her boss formally to avoid calling him Jacko.

'I send you to a bog-standard overdose and you turn it into a suspicious death. For Christ's sake, Roz, I've got enough on my plate.'

'No, sir.'

'No, sir, what?'

'No, sir, I didn't turn it into a suspicious death. The person, or persons, who were present when Richard Moore took a massive overdose turned it into a suspicious death.'

'Don't be fucking clever with me, Kray. I've had it up to here. This is going to take resources we don't have. How the hell are we going to cover this?'

'I'm on the job, I'll handle it.'

'I suppose so. I've had the ACC in here every hour on the hour wanting updates on progress and Brownlow has gone back to square one with reviewing the evidence. It is soaking up every last drop of manpower we have.'

'That must be tough.' Kray was laughing her tits off on the inside.

'And now we have this to contend with. Why the hell do you believe Moore's death was suspicious? He overdosed on his own gear. What's the problem?'

'The initial report confirms he administered a fatal dose of heroine intravenously using a syringe which was found by the side of the chair.' Kray slid a photograph across the desk. 'We both know that's cooked up by holding a flame under a spoon, dissolving the powder in a small amount of water and drawing it up through a cotton wool ball.'

'I do not need a lesson in basic drug taking.'

'I appreciate that, sir. But as these photographs show, there was no lighter. Everything else is accounted for but where is the lighter?'

'Did you check his person? Is it in his pocket?'

'I checked sir, nothing. I looked everywhere in the flat and found nothing that could have been used as a naked flame. He even had an electric cooker. That would suggest to me there was someone with him when he overdosed and they took the lighter when they left the scene.'

'Okay so there was someone with him, that doesn't necessarily make this a suspicious death.'

'And then there is the front door. Whoever called 999 had found the body when they walked into the flat. The door had no signs of a forced entry and had a perfectly functioning lock. Here is a copy of the transcript from the call into the control room, it says, *'The door was open so I went inside and found him dead'.*'

Jackson shook his head. 'So?'

'Who shoots up with the door open? Plus, there is something else you need to know about Richie Moore—'

'I don't fucking believe this!' Jackson interrupted, throwing himself back into his chair with his eyes closed and his hands linked together on top of his head.

'Sir there is something else you need to know—'

'Are you sure about this?'

'We can't ignore the evidence, it warrants a full investigation.'

'What does?' It was ACC Quade filling the doorway.

'Oh nothing ma'am, I'll update you later.' Jackson was now sitting bolt upright.

'Okay, tell me later then. What have we got?'

Kray skirted around the desk. 'We were just finishing up ma'am, I'll leave you to it.' She waited for the substantial bulk of the ACC to move, allowing her a gap big enough for her to get the hell of there.

Jackson looked like someone had let the air out of him. 'Ma'am, it's only been an hour and a half—' His words were cut off mid-sentence by the closing door.

Kray left for home, once again laughing her tits off, on the inside.

Chapter 51

Having drawn a blank with her cold cases, Kray was beginning to doubt her own sanity. She had slept very little - which didn't help matters - and when she did, her dreams were filled with phone boxes, the interior of the Purple Parrot and relaxing walks hand in hand in the park with Joe. While her rampant intuition continued to scream that the killer somehow knew her, the rational side of her brain was telling her she was fucking losing it.

She had enjoyed the intervention by the ACC the previous day. That woman had Jackson by the balls and was making him squirm. Deep amongst the shit and turmoil of yesterday it had provided a glimmer of payback that had made her smile.

Kray pulled into a slot marked 'visitor' and stepped out into the morning sun. It was a cloudless sky but with little warmth in the air. She crossed to the reception and approached the front desk. After a brief exchange she was escorted down a series of hallways, through a metal detector and shown into a poky interview room. There had been no time to go through the niceties of due process, a direct approach mixed with a dose of feminine helplessness had done the trick.

'Thank you,' Kray said, taking a seat facing the door.

A few minutes later she could hear the squeal of rubber soles on polished floor. Two men entered the room: one looked dishevelled in a sweatshirt and jogging bottoms, the other wore dark blue trousers and a light blue short-sleeved shirt. The man in the blue shirt took up his position near the door. The second man folded his lanky frame into the chair opposite and slouched back in his seat, his arms dangling. He looked like an adult sitting in a playschool chair.

I was on the early shift this morning which means I'm back home by 10.30am. I'm on a massive high and can't come down, and I need to have a cool head. The chatter and gossip from the ugly people at the studio was all about the murders in Blackpool. Their theories ran riot. As I brushed and puffed their blemishes away my hands were trembling with excitement. They were too busy to notice I had made mistakes, too busy speculating. That fucking idiot who spoke to the press on the steps of the police station has lit the blue touch paper. I said one day they would be talking about me and today is the day. It's a massive turn on.

Despite the fact that I only got a couple of hours' sleep, I am totally wired. My dreams were a ragged collection of snapshots from my time in the car. The money on the back window ledge, his face red with exertion and his eyes popping from his skull as the last vestiges of life drained away.

The light from the freezer cuts a wedge of white across the basement floor. The cold air tumbles from the cavity to chill my naked legs.

'To chill her blood, how so divine, walk in her shoes, her face is mine,' I chant as the pretty face of Madeline Eve winks at me from her shelf and runs her tongue around her lips.

'With evil dripping from your pores,' Lucy is smiling at me and flashing her come-to-bed eyes. She is such a tease.

'The next face I need to take,' I feel my knees tremble and my short breath condense into clouds.

'… is yours.'

Drops of semen splash onto the concrete floor. It is my third ejaculation since I got back. I need to come down, I need a clear head.

Sampson is watching me, coiled into his favourite corner. His tongue darting out, tasting the air. It's nearly feeding time, but I want to delay it. I don't want his venom wasted on a dead animal. It needs to be a full load. Not long now.

I say goodbye to the girls and close the freezer. Darkness envelopes me as I make my way up the stairs to the cloakroom above. I continue along the hallway and up the stairs to my mother's bedroom. The scent of lavender wafts over me as I slip the cotton dress off the hanger in the wardrobe, and jasmine drawer liners add to the fragrant cocktail as I select underwear from the drawer. I put them on. The clothing feels cool against my chilled skin as the smell of my mother permeates the air.

I sit at the dressing table and apply make-up. My mother's face is looking out at me from a photograph. It's a picture of her and my father taken while they were on holiday in Spain before I was born. They both appear tanned and relaxed, sitting at a bar against the backdrop of Barcelona.

But you can still see it. There is no mistaking that look. It is the face of pure evil. She smiles at me brazen as you like with her high cheek bones, slim nose and thin face. Her large eyes, set slightly wide apart. Why can no one see the filthy, savage bitch for what she is? Why no one else can recognise it is beyond me. Not my father, not my aunty Joan, not our neighbours who came around for coffee and a chat. Not the people who met her in the street – no one. Nobody could see what I could see. The face of pure unadulterated evil. And these women walk amongst us today – bold as brass. These women who are the very image of my mother are going to pubs, holding down responsible jobs, having relationships and no one, not a single person, can see the evil they are capable of. No one that is, except me. It's my job to show the world what they are truly like. Evil sadistic killers.

I fix the wig in place, brush out the fringe and smooth the creases from my dress. My reflection stares back at me. I reckon my mother was twenty-four when she went on holiday to Spain. I look like I'm twenty-four, I look like I'm enjoying my first holiday abroad in sunny Spain. But the sun isn't ready to shine on me yet. My job is not complete - there is one left to go.

I slide my feet into a pair of black court shoes lying at the front door and pull a light top coat around my shoulders. The weather is so unpredictable these days, it would be a shame to get caught in a shower, wearing such a pretty dress.

I leave the house and walk to my car parked a few yards away. The indicator lights flash as I unlock the door. Despite cumming three times, I am still on a high. I picture the hiatus of activity down at the station with coppers running around trying to look competent. That press interview on the steps was a shambles. Still, it made me laugh.

I drive like I'm taking my test – extra careful. I don't want any mishaps while en route.

After twenty minutes, I pull up at the side of the road, get out and retrieve a rucksack from the boot. I check the contents – Chinese, Indian and pizza takeaway menus, all freshly stolen last week. I walk up the street with a clutch of them in my hand. It's time to have some fun.

Chapter 52

'I must say DI Kray, this is twice in a matter of days. People will talk you know?' Rampton sneered at her, showing his discoloured teeth.

Kray's scars burned, she felt like she was on fire. She eyed him, impassively spinning the ring on her finger.

'I wasn't sure you would see me at such short notice.'

'What and deny myself the pleasure of your company, come on Roz what do you take me for? We are almost friends now. How can I be of service?'

Smarmy bastard, if it wasn't for this guard standing behind me I'd ...

'You might be able to help with an ongoing inquiry.'

'Oh come on Roz, not more fucking Suprane, is it?'

'No it's not about Suprane.'

'Do you still think I'm trying to finish the job? That was a weird assumption even for you.'

'No, it's not that.'

'By the way, I hope you got a rap on the knuckles for last time. It was very clumsy.'

She ignored the inferred question. 'I want to talk to you about Richie Moore.'

Rampton's expression changed in an instant. His left eye went into a bout of involuntary twitching.

'What about him?'

'That's the question I wanted to ask you.'

'I don't know anyone by the name of Richie Moore.'

'Come on Carl, you can do better than that.' Kray leaned forward studying his every move. His left eye went into overdrive. 'You and Richie go back a long way.'

'You have me mixed up with someone else.'

'Don't think so, Carl. You and Richie shared a cell for six weeks in 2011 when you were both banged up on drug offences. Then the pair of you shared a bedsit for three months when you were released. Is this ringing any bells?'

Rampton sat with his arms folded across his chest and said nothing. Dabbing his eye with his hand trying to make it behave.

'You and Carl were best buddies. Inseparable, people say. That is until you attacked me, killed my husband and ended up in here, leaving Richie to look after the business while you're away.'

'You're talking shit, Kray. All that bereavement counselling must have gone to your head. You're making stuff up which, let's be fair, is not unusual for you now is it, DI Kray?' His jovial demeanour was cracking wide open. Kray ignored the comment, determined this time not to be drawn into a fight.

'Am I? Am I really? You and Moore were friends and business partners and my sources tell me he's been running the shop while you're indisposed. You had built up a profitable network on the outside, it would be a shame to let all that hard work go to waste. Eventually you'll get out of here and you need to have something to come home to. That's right isn't it, Carl?'

'I'm saying nothing.'

'Come on Carl, I thought we could help each other, I mean one good turn deserves another.'

'What good turn?'

'I thought I could give you some much needed business advice and, in return, you could help me out by answering a few questions about Moore.'

'Why don't you ask him?'

'Yes I agree that would be a better option, but there's a problem.'

'What problem?'

'Now I want you to pay attention, Carl, because this is where I hold up my part of the bargain and give you some sound business advice.'

'I don't need anything from you.'

'You might want to consider getting a new business partner.'

'What the fuck are you on about?'

'Richie is dead.'

'What?'

'He took a massive overdose and died yesterday. So, I thought it was only right that I come and tell you that your empire may be falling apart. With us being nearly friends and all that.'

'Wh-wh ...' Rampton's head was whirring, struggling to work out the ramifications of what he'd just been told. His left hand was permanently stuck to his face, rubbing his eye.

'I can see there is a lot to take in. Maybe I should give you a couple of minutes before asking you about Richie.'

Rampton was red in the face and now holding on to the table with both hands. For Kray, it was a sight to behold.

'I don't believe you, you're lying!' he said.

'Come on Carl, why would I lie about something like that? Now it's only fair that I get to ask you about Richie - did he have any enemies?'

'No, no, no, if he was dead I would have heard about it. You're lying. You're trying to make me say something.'

This was not the line of response Kray was expecting. 'Carl, look at me, Richie *is* dead. He died from an overdose. I want to know if there was anyone who would want to do him harm. Who might that be?'

'Richie would never overdose, he's been shooting up since he was a kid. Amateurs overdose, not Richie.'

'He shot enough shit into his vein to kill two people. What do you know about it, Carl?'

'You're trying to fit me up.'

'What?'

'Richie's dead and you're trying to say I had something to do with it.'

'What?' Kray was having a dreadful feeling of déjà vu. 'No, Carl, I want to know—'

'You're doing it again.'

'Rampton that's nonsense. He OD'd and I want to know who might want to do him harm.'

'That's bullshit, you're trying to pin his death on me.'

'Now who's talking shit?'

'You fucking stitched me up before and now you're doing it again.'

'Not that again, give it a rest. You were arrested and convicted of drug offences as part of a major drugs bust operation. I wasn't even on the team. You know all this.'

'You set me up by planting drugs in my flat and now you are trying to implicate me in Richie's death.'

'No Carl, that's bollocks. I had nothing to do with that operation and I am not trying to implicate you in Richie's death. I simply want to know about Richie.'

'You set me up, you bitch, and now you are trying to do it again.' Rampton was on his feet, the prison officer moved forward, grasping his arm.

'For the fucking last time, I did not set you up then and I'm not trying to set you up now. I want to know about Richie Moore, that's all.'

'You fucking set me up!' Rampton lunged forward and the officer pulled him away.

'That's enough,' the officer said.

'Why the hell would I do that? You had enough gear in your flat when you got busted to get half of Blackpool high.'

'No, no, no, you planted more drugs because you are pure evil.' The guard was wrestling Rampton out of the door. 'He said you were poison and he was right, you fucking evil cock sucking bitch. I had nothing to do with Richie's death. You're setting me up again, just like last time.'

'Who said that, Carl? Who said I was poison?'

Another guard arrived and Rampton was frogmarched out of the door and down the hallway. His voice echoed off the walls as he was led away. Kray sat back down, her hands were shaking. *Shit!* It had all gone tits up again. Yesterday, Jackson didn't want to know about the connection to Rampton, but there was an odds-on chance he would get to know about it today.

Then a bolt of realisation went off in her head. Her stomach turned over and she could taste her breakfast coffee in the back of her throat.

Rampton didn't attack me because I set him up, he attacked me because someone told him I did.

Chapter 53

Kray could not get back to the station fast enough. Her head was a jumble of half facts and conjecture, all served up with a large side order of galloping paranoia. She knew exactly where to start - in the same way Rampton recruited Moore while they were in prison together, someone planted the seed in Rampton's head and turned him against her when he was in jail. This had nothing to do with the recent murders, it had no connection to Moore's death - this was personal.

Kray flipped open her laptop and began her search. She knew where to look but she had no idea what she was searching for; she just hoped she would know it when she saw it. It was needle in a haystack time because Rampton was not exactly a model prisoner. Fights and unruly behaviour ensured he was moved around a lot. Fortunately for Kray he had always been held at the same jail, so she only had to trawl a single data base. But there was a shit load of it to work through.

It was mid-afternoon, and all Kray had to show for her hard work was a headache. There was a rap on her door and a fresh-faced PC with a ginger bob popped her head around the door.

'Excuse me ma'am, sorry to bother you. I need to speak with DCI Jackson or DI Brownlow, it's urgent.'

It took Kray a split second to click her brain into gear. 'You can find them around here somewhere, probably in the incident room.'

'Yes ma'am, I know where they are.'

'Then go speak with them.'

'No ma'am, you see, I've been tasked with—'

'If you know where they are why are you speaking to me? And please call me Roz.'

'Okay err... Roz.' She edged open the door. 'I've been tasked with tracking the movements of Dr Aldridge and I found something odd. I need to run it past either DI Brownlow or DCI Jackson before I proceed.'

'But if you know where they are, ask them.'

'They are in the incident room with the rest of the team. I missed the briefing because I was out when they called the meeting. ACC Quade is also in there.'

'If it's urgent, interrupt.'

'Not sure that would be good, ma'am, I mean Roz. It sounds like world war three has broken out in there.'

'Can't it wait?'

'They've been in there for a while, could you take a look?' The PC was obviously shitting herself at the prospect of entering the lion's den.

Kray couldn't help herself.

'What is it?'

'DI Brownlow has a theory that Aldridge is in contact with the killer. He doesn't buy the story about being blackmailed.' Kray didn't catch herself in time before she raised her eyes to the ceiling and shook her head. A gesture that wasn't wasted on the PC. 'We can't hold him because he is up for receiving stolen goods at most, so Brownlow tasked me with keeping tabs on him.'

'Okay so what's so urgent that you need to talk to them?'

'I took everything I could off Aldridge's phone and gave it back to him but I have it tracked. He got himself a speeding ticket last night doing thirty-eight in a thirty.'

'And you want to interrupt the meeting to tell them he's been done for speeding?'

'No, Roz.' She removed two A4 sized photographs from a folder and handed them over. 'This is Aldridge being snapped by the speed camera.' Sure enough the picture showed the balding Dr Aldridge at the wheel of his car at 7.15pm. 'I took a punt and pulled in footage from other cameras in the area. This is taken from a CCTV camera located at a breaker's yard fifteen minutes later.' A second photo showed Aldridge getting out of his car at the side of the road.

Kray shook her head. 'This is all very interesting but I still don't get it.'

'He didn't take his phone with him. Now why would he make this journey without his mobile? He could have been meeting up with the killer. I need to let DI Brownlow know because I think the next step is to pick Aldridge up and question him.'

'Where was this taken?' Kray held up the photograph taken at the side of the road.

'Brindley Place.'

An incendiary device went off in Kray's head.

'This is excellent work, come with me,' Kray said picking her coat off the back of the chair.

'Are we going to see the DCI?'

'No we're going to pick up Aldridge.'

'This is police harassment!' Aldridge said as he parked himself in the same chair he had vacated the day before. His solicitor sat beside him and unpacked her notebook and pen. She was in her early forties, dressed in a smart suit and wearing an expression that said *why the fuck am I here again?* The name on her visitor's badge read 'Ms Nicki White'.

Aldridge continued his rant. 'And how come I'm talking to you? It was some other clown yesterday, rabbiting on about my whereabouts like his life depended on it. Do I have to remind you people that I have been the victim of a vicious blackmail? No wait a minute, I know the answer to that, and the answer is yes! But none of you are interested in that?' White placed her hand on his arm. It seemed to do the trick, he calmed down.

'I need to ask you a few questions on a different matter. You are not under caution,' said Kray.

'Does that mean I can walk out now?' Aldridge stood up and headed for the door.

'It does but it would not look good, Harry, so I suggest you take a seat.'

Aldridge looked at his solicitor who nodded her head. He slumped down into his chair.

'I am going to show you a series of photographs, Harry, and I want you to tell me what you were doing.'

'Photographs? I don't understand?'

'Last night at 7.15pm you were caught by a speed camera on Parkinson Road.'

'Oh shit, that's three more points.' Aldridge flung himself back waving his arms in the air.

'DI Kray, have you brought my client into the station for questioning because he has a speeding violation?' White asked.

Kray scowled back. 'No.' She slid a second picture to Aldridge. 'This is time-stamped fifteen minutes later at Brindley Place. You are seen here getting out of your car, Harry. Where were you going?'

'Nowhere, I was out for a walk. This has been a stressful time you know?'

'Why did you leave you mobile phone at home, Harry?'

'Don't know, I must have forgotten it.'

'Okay, so let me get this straight. You are under stress because of the investigation, I get that. So to ease the pressure you don't take a walk along the Promenade, or go to the park. No, you choose to unwind by paying a visit to the Crown Estate. A place where the crime rate is twelve times the national average, where muggings and petty theft are commonplace and, if you believe the local media, drug dens occupy more tenancy space than residents. Are you seriously telling me this is how you choose to alleviate your stress? And you go there without your mobile phone. Come on, Harry you'll have to do better than that.'

'I told you I forgot it.'

'Yes you did, Harry, now why don't you tell me what you were doing on the Crown Estate?'

'Nothing, I was taking a walk.'

'No one takes constitutional on the Crown Estate, not unless they have SAS backup.'

'My client has answered your questions, DI Kray and I see no reason for you to detain him further,' White chipped in, getting up from her seat and closing her notebook.

Kray looked her straight in the eye.

Maybe this will change your mind, Ms White.

'Richard Moore died of a drug overdose yesterday around 8.30pm.' Kray placed her third and final photograph on the table. 'I was the attending officer and couldn't work out where I had seen him before. Then I remembered, the last time I saw him he was handing you drugs and you were giving him money. Richie Moore is the dealer featured in the blackmail photograph, isn't he, Harry? I could not for the life of me recall where I had seen him before, and then when I learned that you were in the vicinity when he died, the penny dropped.'

Ms White sat down and leaned into Harry.

'You are not obliged to say anything,' she whispered in his ear.

'Now do you want to tell me what you were doing on the Crown Estate yesterday at 8pm?' Kray asked sliding the photograph in front of Aldridge.

'What the fuck is this?' He pushed the picture of Moore lying on a mortuary slab back across the desk.

'Are you denying this is the same man that I saw in the blackmail picture? I can go get it to jog your memory, if it would help?'

'This is bullshit! You arrest me for handling stolen goods and completely ignore the fact that I have been blackmailed. I'm a victim too in all of this and I've had bugger-all support from you. You fuckers are hanging me out to dry – like it was me who administered the Suprane to those poor women. You think I was stealing the Suprane to pass on to Moore who in turn gave it to the killer.'

'Steady.' White put her hand on Harry's arm. He yanked it away.

'Don't fucking steady me.'

'Did you go and see Richie Moore?'

'You think I've been making up the blackmail story.' Kray was now out of her depth, this was the new line of inquiry coming from Brownlow. 'Well I'm telling you it was fucking real. And it was Moore who was behind it.'

'Are you saying it was Moore who blackmailed you?'

'Who else could it have been? I've been telling you people that but no one wants to know. He knew I was an addict, he knew I could lay my hands on the Suprane, so he blackmailed me.'

'Do you have any proof, Harry?'

'No, but who else could it have been? It was Moore all right.'

White was turning an attractive shade of pink, scribbling furiously in her notebook.

'Harry, I have to advise you—' she said clearing her throat.

'Oh fuck off, you're as bad as them. I've lost my job, my reputation and probably my home all because you lot refused to believe I was being blackmailed. I had things under control with my habit, then Moore decides to turn the screw and I'm fucked. It's gone, it's all gone.'

'Harry I can't believe that—' Kray got no further.

'Believe what you want. Moore had me over a barrel and he knew it. Well he doesn't now.'

Nicki White exploded in a cloud of protestations and denials.

Kray ignored her. 'Harry did you kill Richie Moore?'

'Richie Moore was slowly killing himself anyway, I just helped him along.'

'What did you do, Harry?'

'When I arrived he was about to shoot up so I said I'd join him. I bunged him twenty quid and cut myself some fresh gear from the pile. I pretended to do mine but put the whole lot into Richie. He had it coming for what he did to me. He took everything. I got nothing now.'

'Harry Aldridge, I am arresting you for the murder of—'

The door burst wide open and the large bulk of ACC Quade bustled into the room, closely followed by the PC with a ginger bob and DCI Jackson.

'Kray! My office now!'

Interview terminated, fourteen thirty-seven.

Chapter 54

Kray wheeled her trolley around the supermarket, her phone pinned to her ear.

'Hi, Mum, how are you doing …?' She paused for the stock response, then continued, 'Yes I'm fine thanks, I got off shift early today.'

She reached the checkout with three bars of chocolate, a loaf of bread and four bottles of wine. The woman behind the till scowled at her for being on the phone.

'Yes I'm eating well, you don't have to worry … no I don't need anything … look I have to go, Mum, I'm at the supermarket … I'll give you a bell later. Okay?' Kray hung up and shook her head.

The look on the checkout woman's face said it all, *'So you're eating well then?'.*

Kray caught her disapproving glare.

'Do you want a bag?' she asked.

I'm not going to stuff it in my fucking pockets, now am I? Kray returned the stare.

'Yes please, that would be good,' Kray replied, placing the items onto the belt.

The checkout lady picked up the first bottle and dinked it through. She gave Kray a sideways glance. *What would your mother say?*

'Would you like help with your packing?' she asked with a plastic smile.

Kray stopped, holding a bar of chocolate in mid-air. *Do you think I'm fucking useless?*

'No, I'm fine thanks.' Kray put the items into the bag, a process that was punctuated with more sideways glances. Back in the car her head was filled with the checkout lady. *I'm not going back there again. Cheeky bitch.*

The traffic was light and she made good time. Before long she was in her kitchen peeling the foil wrapper off the chocolate and cracking open the first bottle. The wine tasted good, like it was capable of washing away the day. Which was precisely what Kray had in mind. She could not work out who had been more furious, Quade or Jackson, each one trying to outdo one another as to who could shout the loudest or listen the least. The day had not ended well.

Kray gathered up the bottle, the chocolate and her fast emptying glass, and headed upstairs to the bathroom. She stripped off and ran a deep, hot bath with so many bubbles she could barely see the wine bottle sitting on the wooden ledge. She sank into the suds and slurped her wine.

Kray mulled over the shouting match that had taken place in Quade's office. Despite churning the discussion over and over in her head, it still remained unclear if she had been put on garden leave, had been suspended from duty or was on the sick. She was sure all three had been mentioned at some point or another. But either way she was not in work and was not expected to return for a while. That much was made clear.

Quade had taken the lead, piling into her about not being able to leave the case alone and for stepping on their toes. She disregarded Kray's account of why she was interviewing Aldridge and told her she had engineered herself a way to get back into the investigation. The fact that Kray was about to arrest Aldridge for murder didn't seem to matter. What mattered was that she had been told to leave well alone and had disobeyed a direct order. Jackson had spent the whole time reiterating what the ACC was saying but in a louder voice, as if that made it sound like they were his own words. Both of them steadfastly refused to believe that Kray was acting as part of her own investigation. They kept reinforcing the point that she had been told to back off, and here she was sticking her nose in where it didn't belong. It was around about that time when Kray told them both to 'go fuck yourselves' and mutterings of 'suspension' were being mentioned.

The wine level in the bottle was past the label and the chocolate had disappeared within minutes. She was exhausted. Not enough sleep, coupled with being emotionally shredded, was beginning to take its toll. She poured herself another glass.

'Fuck 'em,' she told herself, raising her glass above the bubbles. 'Let them get on with it. Wacko will be on the sick soon enough the way he's going, and that will leave Mrs Blobby and Brownbag to track down the murderer. Fucking marvellous.' She raised her glass, her eyelids felt like ton weights as she finished off the bottle. Minutes later she was asleep, dreaming of being in her kitchen, with the sun pouring through the open windows, and Joe fixing dinner while they drank cold beer.

There was a loud thump on the front door. Kray woke with a start and dropped the glass into the water. The bubbles were gone and the water was cold.

'Shit,' she said as she hauled herself over the rim of the bath and into her bath robe. Another two thumps echoed from her hallway.

'Alright, I'm coming,' she shouted, padding her wet feet down the stairs to the front door. She opened it to find Tavener holding a bottle of wine in one hand and a bunch of flowers in the other.

'I have no fucking idea what I'm gonna do with those.' She nodded at the bouquet. 'But you can bring that with you.' She went back up the stairs calling behind her, 'Come in and make yourself at home. I'll be down in a minute.' She went to her bedroom, threw on a baggy top and jeans and headed back downstairs to find him in the kitchen opening and closing cupboard doors.

'Had a tough day?' he said.

'Yeah something like that.'

'I heard. In fact, everyone heard.'

'They're in the end cupboard.'

He opened it to find an array of glasses. He picked two off the shelf and poured wine into both. 'What happened?' He handed her one.

'I'm not exactly sure.' Kray propped herself against the worktop. 'I think I might have been rude to them.'

'You think? It's the talk of the station. Those walls are thin you know?'

Kray sniggered into her glass. 'Not sure they had to be that thin.'

'No, that's true, I could hear you from the car park.' They both paused to take a sip. 'Aldridge has been charged with the murder of Richie Moore.'

'Fucking hell.' Kray shook her head looking down at the floor.

'I reckon they were so desperate to be seen to make progress they took your collar and claimed it as their own.'

'Wacko and Mrs Blobby will be fighting over who will give the next press conference. My money is on the wider one.'

Tavener laughed.

'Did you really tell them to go fuck themselves?'

'Yeah, I think I might have done.'

He laughed again. 'So, are you suspended?'

'I don't know.' Kray took a mouthful of wine. 'I really don't know.'

'Did they take your pass and warrant card?'

'Nope I still have them.'

'Then you're not suspended. However, I'm not sure what the correct HR term is, but I reckon you're fucked.'

'Yes, I reckon you're right.'

There was an audible buzzing. Tavener fished his phone from his pocket.

'Bollocks, I gotta go. There's an all-hands briefing in thirty minutes. I wanted to come round to see you were okay.'

'No rest for the wicked.'

'With those guys running the show it's more like no rest for the one-legged man in an arse kicking competition.'

Tavener put his wine on the worktop and made his way through to the hallway.

'Thanks for the wine and, err, the flowers.' Kray followed him out.

'Let me know if there is anything I can do.'

'I will thanks, but I'm fine.'

'I'm pretty useful you know.'

'Yes I'm sure you are.'

'I could set your clock on the mantelpiece to the correct time if you'd like?'

Chapter 55

Sampson is grumpy. I have the silver rod holding his head to the table while his body winds itself around my arm. I slide my hand along and clamp my index finger and thumb either side of his jaw bone with my first finger pressing on top of his head. The rod comes away and I have him.

I lift him up and stare into his lidless eyes. His tongue flicks out. He wants to be fed but more than that, he wants to sink his fangs into my flesh and inject me with enough venom to kill a horse.

One day I will have you, one day.

I pick up the glass with the latex membrane stretched over the top. I offer it up to him and he opens his mouth. The glass rubs against the underside of his jaw and his enormous fangs hinge forward.

You are a big boy, Sampson.

I pull the glass away and wave it in front of his face. His coils tighten around me as he strains against my grip. I bring the glass within reach again to rub it against his mouth, he opens wide and fakes a strike. I pull it away. I touch the rim against the underside of his jaw and he lunges at it. One fang penetrates the rubber while the other spills yellow liquid on the outside of the glass.

'Fucking behave,' I say to him, holding on tight.

The next strike, both fangs bite through the membrane and a gush of venom hits the bottom of the glass. I disengage him and he goes in for another. Thick yellow liquid coats the side as he bites down against the rim. I massage his venom glands. After several smaller strikes, he's done.

I lower his tail into the cabinet and rest his head against the side. I pull my hand away and withdraw my arm. Sampson curls himself up, waiting for his treat.

I dangle the mouse by the tail and lay it onto the sand at the other end of the tank. It darts around exploring its new surroundings. I can see its nose, held in the air, sniffing out any danger that might be lurking nearby. Sampson flicks his tongue out. I know what he's thinking: *Do I want to eat, or do I want to play?* He adopts the trademark S-shape and watches impassively as the mouse runs around, keeping tight into the corners of the glass. Sampson sways with his head poised in mid-air, measuring the distance. The mouse leaves the relative safety of the corner and ventures out. Sampson flexes his body and strikes, snatching the mouse clean off the bottom of the tank. He retreats into his usual coiled position and I watch two tiny legs kick as Sampson's jaws open and close to devour the rodent. Maybe the mouse had a cold, because he certainly didn't sniff out danger when he should have done.

I wonder if she has the ability to sniff out danger, or is she just another mouse?

There are times in the life of every man when he knows instinctively that he has done something wrong but has no idea what it is. That described Duncan Tavener to a tee as Kray booted him out of the house like he'd taken a crap on her coffee table. He returned to his car with the sound of the front door crashing shut behind him.

Back in his flat, watching sport on the TV with a beer, Tavener was considering his experience to be a life lesson. *Okay, so I won't take flowers again.*

Kray stared at her reflection in the dressing table mirror. Her eyes were bloodshot and raw from the constant dabbing of tissues. She had spent the last two hours watching the minute hand tick its way around the clock face, keeping perfect time. Perfect, that was, apart from the fact that the fucking thing was precisely one hour slow.

The sound of the clock ticking away played like a metronome in her head. With every increment an image exploded into her mind like a never-ending procession of flash cards. The faceless body of Madeline Eve, the screen shot of Lucy Frost raising her glass in the Purple Parrot, the look of terror on the face of Ania Sobotta at the Trafford Centre. A myriad of memories crowded in, suffocating the life out of her. And all the while the hands on the clock ticked away the time.

Kray was losing her sanity.

She picked up a make-up pad and applied a thin layer of cream. The soft cotton glided over her face removing the grime of the day. If only it was that easy to erase the thoughts torturing her soul. She reached her cheek and the expensive foundation slid away to reveal the red scar beneath. She stopped and ran her finger along its length. The thin ridge felt like a chasm cut deep into her face, ragged and uneven.

She could feel her skin pricking as a fly walked across the scar. The muscles in her face twitched. The sound of buzzing filled the room, the wings of a million flies beating out their droning tone. Another fly pitched on her face, followed by another. Soon her face crawled with the sensation of dancing insects.

The room spun on its axis and she felt sick. Her thoughts crashed together.

Rampton was told I set him up.

He attacked me because someone told him to.

All the while flies landed onto her face and neck. The buzzing got louder.

The phone box outside in the street.

Her favourite table at the Purple Parrot.

Walking hand in hand across Park View.

Her scars were on fire, burning into her flesh. She screwed her eyes shut as tears ran down her face. The buzzing was deafening. Her skin crawled.

The knife sticking out of Joe's neck.

The blood, there was so much blood.

Suddenly all was quiet. The flies were gone. The buzzing had stopped. She opened her eyes.

Ice-cold shivers racked through her body. Her reflection stared back - with her narrow face, high cheek bones and big brown eyes set slightly wide apart. The pieces tumbled together and fell into place.

The killer knows me. And I'm next.

Chapter 56

Kray picked her keys off the table and careered down the hallway to the front door. Her stomach was in knots, her vision bled in and out of focus. Her breathing was short and shallow. A tourniquet of panic wound around her chest.

She reached the downstairs toilet to pull her coat from the back of the door. A stream of Chardonnay and chocolate vomit hit the back of the porcelain as she spewed into the bowl. Her legs gave way and she clung onto the seat. She heaved again, but nothing came out.

She unwound toilet paper from the roll and wiped her mouth. She rocked back onto her heels and tugged her phone from her pocket. Who was she kidding? She was in no fit state to drive. She ordered a taxi.

After a few minutes her mobile beeped to announce her cab was waiting outside. Kray left the house and gave instructions to the driver. Sitting in the back she tried to clear her thoughts, tried to focus on the actions she had to take rather than the terrifying prospect running riot in her head. Her stomach churned as the car lurched through the empty streets. Eventually they pulled over and she handed the driver fifteen pounds.

She hurried through a double set of doors and took the stairs two at a time to the second floor. The place was deserted, the only light spilling into the office came from the street lighting outside, giving the rooms an eerie quality. Kray walked along the corridor with Quade's last remarks booming in her head '… and I do not expect to see you at the station, is that clear?' It was, but obviously not clear enough.

She reached her office and turned on her laptop, leaving the main light switched off. The blue screen illuminated the corner of the room as she began clicking away at the menus on the screen. Unlike last time she knew what she was looking for, or to be more precise, she knew what he looked like.

Kray scrutinised the mugshots flashing before her, scouring back through the years. She glanced at the digital clock at the bottom of the screen, it read 1.35am.

After a while she sat back in her chair to stare at the ceiling.

This is hopeless. Think, woman, think! I have to narrow down the search.

She went through the sequence of events in her head. Her focus had been on stalking through Rampton's latest stretch in jail, but when she thought about it again, that made no sense. If her worst fears were true it must have taken place before that. It had to have been before he attacked her.

Kray entered different dates into the search bar and flicked through the names, each one accompanied by a mugshot. Image after image spooled across the screen. Nothing.

Then bingo!

The face of a young man filled the screen. He had shared a cell with Rampton for four weeks while on remand. Kray looked into his eyes and a cold shudder ran through her. It had to be, nothing else had come remotely close. This was him. A flicker of recognition fired in her brain. *I've seen you before. How the hell ...?*

She clicked the print icon and the lights in the hallway outside flickered into life. She looked at her screen trying to work out what the hell had just happened, half expecting to see that she had hit a toolbar command saying, 'Switch the lights on'. She heard footsteps.

Kray closed up her laptop and ducked down below the desk. The footsteps were getting louder. She held her breath and watched a shadow pass across her doorway.

It must be Wacko, what the hell is he doing in here at this time? She heard the office door at the end of the corridor open and the sound of a light switch being pressed. It was time to get out of there.

Kray crept to the door and peered around the corner. It was definitely Jackson, she could hear him moving around in his office. Then the thought hit her. *I can't fucking go, the picture is on the printer!* Kray hurried to the incident room and creaked the door open. Across the office, against the wall, sat a bank of printers, she crouched down and scuttled over.

Where the hell is the printout?

She checked each of the document trays, but they were empty. *How the fuck?*

Then she saw the red flashing LED: it had run out of paper.

Kray cursed under her breath, gently levered opened the tray of the nearest printer and lifted out a wad of paper. She fed it into the machine with the blinking LED and pressed reset. The machine whirred and spat the printout into the tray at the back.

The printer next to her began spooling out paper.

Jackson must be printing something out too! Kray heard him coming down the hallway. *Shit!*

She grabbed her sheet of paper and ran into the corner of the room, disappearing under a desk just as the fluorescent lights came on. Her heart was thumping so hard in her chest she was sure he could hear it. She could sense him in the room but was too scared to take a peek.

After a while Kray heard the handle on the door and it all went dark. She crumpled onto the carpet and breathed deeply. From her crouched position she negotiated her way around the furniture and reached the door. She cracked it open to listen. Wacko could be heard talking to himself, like he was rehearsing a speech.

What the fuck is he saying? Kray's curiosity was burning a hole in her, but this was not the time or place to indulge her curiosity. She scurried down the hallway and out of the station. In her pocket was a balled-up sheet of paper.

She had no idea how he knew her or why he had shared a cell with Rampton. But she did know that his face was narrow, with high cheek bones and big eyes set slightly wide apart.

His name was Jason Strickland. He was going to kill her.

'Do I have a shit load of news for you.' Kray shivered as the wind cut through her jacket. She wrapped it tight around herself. Pale wisps of pink trailed across the sky as the sun woke up the clouds. Her feet were soaked from walking through the grass, wet from the morning dew. She stamped them on the ground.

'I got into a fight at work with Wacko and Mrs Blobby and came off worse. The fuckers wanted me gone so they could claim my arrest and get some good news in the papers. I can't blame them I suppose, because it's not me that has to stand up in front of the cameras spouting the usual drivel. No hang on, what am I saying, of course I can – fucking tossers. But anyway, that's not all …' Kray reached into her pocket and pulled out the ball of paper. She unwrapped it and flattened out the creases against her chest. 'I reckon this is him: Jason Strickland. I know it's mad, isn't it? I think this is the bastard that killed those people and there is no one I can tell. Here I am holding the mugshot of a serial killer and not a single soul will take me seriously. How frustrating is that?' Kray knelt down and put her hand onto the cold marble. 'Ha, but who am I trying to kid? I'm coming up with theories that are so fantastic even I'm struggling to get my head around them. So I can't really blame people for thinking I've gone bat-shit crazy. And the other bombshell is, I think Strickland convinced Rampton that I had set him up and persuaded him to attack me. Rampton failed and now he's coming after me. See, I told you I was losing it.'

She traced her finger around the lettering that spelled out Joe's name. She felt him close. His warm breath on the back of her neck. His arms holding her tight. The touch of his mouth on her cheek.

'I'm scared. What should I do?'

A gust of wind blew through her jacket and in an instant, he was gone. Kray screwed up the sheet of paper and replaced it in her pocket. The time for indulgence was over.

She knew exactly what she had to do.

Back home the first thing Kray did was eat toast. She needed to slow down her thought processes and eat something. This was never going to work if her blood sugars were at rock bottom and her head was in the shed. She couldn't remember the last time she ate food that hadn't been handed to her over a counter in a brown paper bag, and she was pretty sure chocolate and wine didn't count as a balanced diet. Kray was starving.

The bread popped out of the toaster and she layered on butter, she would have to give the jam a miss because of the mould. The first slice disappeared in minutes to be followed by another, washed down with strong black coffee. There was a loud knock at the door.

Kray opened up to see a white van parked outside her house.

'Bloody hell you boys don't mess about. I haven't long called.'

'That's us, lady. I have a job card here but why don't you talk me through what you want.'

Soon the house was filled with the sound of banging and drilling. Kray made more coffee and offered a cup to the man with a van.

'Christ!' he said taking a sip.

'Yeah sorry, I like it strong.'

'There's strong and then there's suicide strength. I'll be awake until the weekend drinking this.' Kray smiled at him, he was a welcome distraction. 'Are you sure you want these fitting as well?' he asked.

'Yup, front and back please. Not too high up, for obvious reasons.'

'Okay, you're the boss.' He beavered away for the hour and she watched as he put the finishing touches to the back door. 'That's your lot.'

'Thank you. They gave me a rough quote on the phone, do I pay you?'

'No, we will send you an invoice. Gone are the days when we were paid on completion of the job. Some unscrupulous tradesmen used to bump up the price and ask for it in cash. I'm sure you can guess the rest.'

'Okay, well thank you for coming out promptly.'

'These are for the front ...' he handed Kray a set of brand new keys, '... and back. Those dead bolts are going to be a little stiff to start but they will loosen up in time.'

Kray waved him off as the van pulled away. She went out to her car and came back with an assortment of plastic bags, but this was anything but her usual weekly shop. She emptied them into the middle of the lounge floor and sorted through her purchases. She picked up three of the items and went upstairs. In each of the bedrooms she left a hammer under the bed and on returning downstairs she deposited another in the cloakroom and one in the living room. She looked at the pickaxe handle laying on the lounge floor and wondered where to put it. She also wondered what made her buy it. She shook her head and walked into the hallway, she could figure that one out later.

Kray tested one of the bright shiny keys in the lock - it turned perfectly. Then she closed the front door, reached up and grasped the heavy dead bolt. It wouldn't budge. She gripped it with two hands and heaved it across. It slammed into place with a thud.

Kray nodded her head in approval.

Now try to get in, you fucker.

Chapter 57

Kray could see the house looming up on the right. It stood out like a sore thumb. A 1940s bay fronted, semi-detached property with a small front garden. While the other properties in the road could be described in much the same way, this one was noticeably different. Largely because it looked as though it had remained untouched since Thatcher disposed of it in the great council house sell-off. While other houses sported new windows, swanky front doors and paint jobs, this one had the appearance of requiring scaffolding to stop it falling down.

Kray passed the house and pulled over to the kerb on the opposite side of the road. She pressed the button in her armrest and the wing mirror swivelled out until the place was in view. The street was quiet but for a couple of young mums walking with prams and an older resident pottering in his garden. Nothing moved at number eighty-six Spring Bank Way - the last known address of Jason Strickland.

Kray settled back with her eyes firmly fixed on the mirror. In the passenger footwell was the last of her purchases — a small crowbar — bought at the third hardware shop of the morning because they had run out of hammers. It was for protection only, this was going to be a stake-out. Or at least that's what she kept telling herself over and over. It wasn't really working.

Kray looked at the clock on the dashboard, nothing had stirred for the past fifty minutes. She was getting itchy feet.

'Stay calm, stay focussed,' she said to herself. 'Let's get the lay of the land before diving in.'

The minutes ticked by. She turned on the radio and scanned the dial, all the commercial radio stations seemed to be synchronising their playlists to broadcast back-to-back adverts. She switched it off. Then Kray reached for the crowbar from the foot well and weighed it in her hand.

She turned on the radio again and listened to music this time, who would have thought of that? Music being played on a radio station? The song finished and another bout of ads kicked in.

Fuck it.

Kray shoved the crowbar up her sleeve and stepped out of the car. *Stake-out my arse.* She passed number eighty-six on her left and kept walking. There was no sign of an alarm box and the back garden butted up against the one behind. She reached the end of the road, turned, and retraced her steps. When she was level with the house she bent down to tie her shoelace. The house was still, it looked like no one was home. She darted up the path and skirted around the side to the back. All was quiet.

Kray reached the back door. It was timber-framed with frosted glass panels, to the right was the kitchen window. The frames were so rotten a child could stab their fingers through the wood. She peered over the window ledge; the room beyond was empty. She rapped on the window, it rattled. It was better to know if Strickland was at home and beat a hasty retreat, rather than bump into him in the house. No one came to the door.

Kray levered the edge of the crowbar between the doorframe and the door and pushed. The wood splintered and the lock jumped out of its recess, the back door creaked open. She entered the kitchen, closing the door behind her, and listened. Nothing. There were dirty dishes in the sink and a frying pan sat on the gas hob. She stepped on the peddle bin to reveal several ready meal trays and an empty milk carton. The kettle was cool to the touch.

Kray sniffed the air, it smelled like something had gone off. Then it dawned on her – the house smelled old. Like one of those frozen in time museums you can visit where they show how people lived in a bygone age.

She crossed into the hallway and eased open the living room door. Her knuckles were white from gripping the crowbar. This too was like stepping back to the early eighties, a big brown Draylon sofa and two arm chairs filled the room. A wooden coffee table that had long since lost its varnish dominated the centre of a threadbare rug. The wallpaper was patterned with raised orange flowers set against a cream background. The room smelled as if it hadn't had the windows open in thirty years. She scanned around and moved on.

The stairs creaked as the treads bore her weight, and the landing had a giant white paper ball for a lamp shade. She opened the door to the left: it was the bathroom, kitted out with a chunky, green avocado suite. Kray checked above the wash basin – there was one toothbrush. The next room was a bedroom with a single bed against the wall in the corner. It had the feel of not having been lived in, there was not an item out of place. She opened a drawer and found it full of neatly folded men's clothes. The bed was made up with sheets and blankets, it looked odd without a continental quilt. Kray was so fixated with the bedspread she almost missed it. On the wall above the bed hung a poster of a man smiling for the camera, holding a baseball bat. He wore a cap with an oversized peak, and above the peak was an emblem – a bird's head set in a blue circle.

A jolt went through Kray like she'd been shot. Her fingers curled tightly around the crowbar.

The next room along was another bedroom. This time with a double bed covered in a brightly coloured throw. This room did at least show signs of life. A large dressing table sat in the bay window with enough make-up and brushes to run a salon. She opened the wardrobe door to find a row of dresses and tops. Then a picture sitting on the bedside table caught her eye, and she picked it up. It showed a couple sitting in a bar posing for the camera. They were both tanned and smiling broadly.

Kray almost dropped it. Staring out of the picture was a woman with a thin face, high cheek bones and big eyes set a little too wide apart.

Fucking hell.

She had seen enough. Kray crept back down the stairs into the hallway, making her way to the kitchen, but stopped in her tracks. There was a door leading under the stairs. She opened it to find rows of coats and jackets hanging on rails, while others hung from hooks. She sifted through them, some were new but others looked old and worn. Kray put her hands into the pockets, they were empty. As one of the coats parted to one side Kray saw a heavy metal dead bolt with a padlock. She moved the coat further to reveal a door set into the wall at the back. The key was sticking out of the lock. Kray tucked the crowbar under her arm and turned it, the padlock sprung open with a click. She removed the hasp, slid back the bolt and the door swung towards her. She removed the coats from the back and opened it wide. A set of stairs ran from the cloakroom down into a cellar. She could see the first five steps and then no more as the blackness engulfed whatever was below. Kray reached around the doorframe groping for a light switch, there was nothing, just bare brickwork.

Kray heard a noise behind her.

Two fists struck her square in the back and she tumbled forwards into the abyss. Her hands flew out in front of her to break her fall, but she grasped at nothing. She hit the first few steps on the way down with a thud, then there was half a second of silence, followed by a sickening splat as she landed on the concrete floor below.

I knew there was a good reason why I never replaced that handrail.

Chapter 58

Kray felt like she was floating down a lazy river, bobbing gently on the waves while meandering her way through a sea of loveliness. Warm and woozy. Her consciousness rose to the surface only to bob back down into the darkness. She flicked open her eyes, all she saw was the colour grey. She slipped back under.

She came back again and was aware of an acrid taste in her mouth and her tongue was stuck to the roof of her mouth. Her eyes opened and she realised the grey that filled her vision was a concrete floor. She was lying on her side with her head on the ground.

Kray fought to stay conscious. The room spun and she felt sick. Her head hurt and she was fast becoming aware of a sharp pain in her right leg. In fact, she was fast becoming aware that she was in agony.

Kray tried to sit up but couldn't move her arms or legs, they were stretched out in front of her. She rocked from side to side, levered herself onto one elbow and finally righted herself. She was sitting on the floor, bent forward at the waist with her legs stretched out in front of her. Her wrists and ankles were bound together with four thick black cable ties that were secured to an eyebolt set into the floor. Her right arm felt like it had been ripped from its socket while a bloody mat of hair stuck to the side of her head. Her stomach heaved and she vomited down her front.

'That could be concussion,' a voice said from the other side of the room. Kray looked around trying to locate the sound. The pain in her leg was unbearable. A figure came into view, dressed in a floral slip with long black hair that framed her face. 'You took a bump to the head and fell heavily onto your side. It's gonna hurt like a bastard.'

Kray shuffled herself forwards towards the eyebolt and bent her legs to take the strain off her muscles. She looked up and tried to focus on the face. She could hear the words clearly but the figure in front of her was blurred.

'You had a nasty fall down the stairs. I keep meaning to replace the banisters but you know how it is. I just can't seem to find the time.' The voice was soft and melodic. Kray screwed up her eyes and shook her head. The fog was clearing.

'Who are you?' she croaked.

'I'm surprised you need to ask that. You tracked me down, broke into my house and fell into my basement. You must know who I am …' The figure knelt down and smiled. The wig and make-up were professionally done but the face was unmistakeable. Kray felt a knot of panic twist at her guts when she realised she was staring at Strickland.

'Well this is a turn up,' he said getting to his feet. 'Here am I concocting all sorts of elaborate plans on how best to deal with you and … hey presto … you show up at my house. What an absolute delight.' Strickland strutted around the room, the hem of his dress making a swishing sound as he moved. 'You see there is an advantage to being pathologically paranoid. I know every car that parks in our road so when you turned up, it rang alarm bells. Then I see you get out and walk in the direction of my house, well there was only going to be one outcome. You were going to break in with the intention of arresting me, or whatever you had in mind.'

Kray looked down to see that blood had seeped through the knee of her jeans. The right side of her body throbbed in time with the pain in her head. Strickland stepped forward and placed a bottle of water and a packet of biscuits on the floor at her feet.

'You need to drink water and you're bound to be hungry.'

Kray didn't move. 'The police will be here soon, they know my movements, so when I fail to report in they'll be smashing down your door.'

'I'm not sure they will, you know. I'm not sure they are looking for you at all. They haven't up to now anyway.'

'They're on their way and then we will put you away for a long time.'

'How long do you think you've been here?'

Kray didn't answer.

'Go on. Take a guess, how long do you think you've been here?'

Again she said nothing.

'You have already been here for a day and a half and I haven't had Mr Plod bashing down my door to find you. You see the fall down the stairs rendered you unconscious, but it was the application of a strong sedative that ensured you stayed that way. At least until I was ready.'

Kray looked down at her wrist, her watch was gone. She looked at her jeans pocket expecting to see the outline of her phone: that, too, was gone. She had no idea of the time or what day it was. Her head spun with the thought that she had been out cold for that length of time. No wonder she felt like shit.

'Anyway, to finish my story,' he continued, 'I see you get out of your car and walk to my house. It's obvious what you had in mind, so as you crept in the back door, I crept out the front. It was important that you had the run of the place so the penny would drop. I put the key in the padlock, I knew you would find it and wouldn't be able to resist taking a peek. Then all that was required was a little shove. You are so predictable Roz, honestly, I mean mix it up a little.' Strickland laughed and flounced off to the other side of the room.

All of a sudden Kray felt a rabid thirst grab her by the throat and a hollow emptiness in the pit of her stomach. She struggled against the plastic restraints tying her to the floor.

'Do you like my handiwork? It's called a Hilti bolt. It took me ages to fit, but I think it will do the job nicely, don't you? I was drilling and hammering away, and you slept like a baby through the whole performance. You've caused me some major planning issues but I think I've got things straight.'

'Why did you kill Lucy and Madeline? Why murder the two men? And what does it all have to do with me?'

'Questions, questions. I don't have time for that now. I need to pop out for a while. You have water and food, I suggest you make the most of them. I'll be an hour or so, then I'll be back to see you.'

'You won't get away with this.'

'Oh, but I think you'll find I already am.' He switched off the light and walked up the stairs. Kray heard the door at the top slam shut and the bolt sliding across.

Alone in the basement she became aware of a yellow glow coming from a glass tank in the far corner and red and green LED lights shining in the other. She could hear the low hum of the freezers but the rest of the room was silent. She was ravenous. She shuffled forward and could just reach the bottle with her finger tips, she toppled it over towards herself and grasped the cap. She had enough movement in her hands to twist it off.

How the fuck am I going to drink that? She strained her neck, forcing her head down. Her stomach muscles hurt as they crunched together. The top of the upright bottle touched her lips and she squeezed the plastic sides. Water welled up into her mouth and onto the floor. Kray squeezed until the water would rise no more then turned her attention to the biscuits. She clawed at the packaging with her finger nails, eventually splitting open the wrapping. Biscuits spilled onto the floor. Kray lunged forward and picked one up. She doubled herself over but it was no use, she wasn't flexible enough to grip it with her teeth. She jerked her hand and tossed the remaining biscuits onto the floor, then rolled onto her side. She shuffled her body around in an arc until the food was in reach, then with her head on the floor she scooped it into her mouth with her tongue. She repeated the process as much as she could. It was arduous work and her body ached like hell, but it was worth it.

Stay calm, stay calm and think. Someone will notice me missing and come looking.

After she had eaten everything she could reach, she scanned the room. There were three freezers over to the left and an odd-looking glass tank with an orange glow in the far corner. Propped against one wall was a bank of tools along with a workbench on casters. Try as she might, there was no way she could pull her hands or feet free from the cable ties: the sharp plastic dug into her skin every time she moved. There were no windows just brick and plaster walls with strip lights in the ceiling. Kray frantically searched for anything that would give her an edge, something that would give her that slight element of surprise when Strickland returned. But there was nothing. Her back ached, her legs ached, her neck ached - everything ached.

Kray lost track of time. The bolt at the top of the stairs slid across. She jumped, forcing herself to be fully alert. She heard the sound of high heels on the wooden steps and looked up but could see nothing. Then the room was flooded with bright light. Kray had to blink her eyes to shield them from the glare.

'I've had to reschedule,' the soft voice said. 'Now you are here, my plans and preparations have gone out the window.' Kray squinted, allowing her eyes to become accustomed to the bright light. Strickland was standing directly in front of her. Tears blurred her vision, she rubbed her eyes against her shoulder. 'But I've made a few adjustments and I think things will work out just fine.'

Kray's eyes cleared and she stared at him in horror. He was wearing a shimmering dress of emerald green, with a fitted bodice and a pencil skirt. She felt her head was about to explode.

That's, that's my dress. He's wearing my fucking dress!

Strickland walked towards her. It was like looking into a full-length mirror.

Kray froze as her own face gazed down at her.

'Fucking weird, isn't it?' he said in a deep, resonating voice. The hair, the eyes, the mouth, it was her. Kray was staring at herself.

'Don't I look pretty?' Strickland returned to the soft melodic tones, flicking a stand of hair away from his face. 'Now I'm going out and I will see you when I get back.' The hair on the back of

Kray's neck and arms stood to attention as she watched herself turn and walk back to the stairs.

'Now be good. Oh, and don't bother yelling for help because believe me, no one can hear you. I've tried.' The room went dark and she heard the sound of high heels on wood. The door at the top banged shut and the bolt banged into position.

Chapter 59

I'm on parade.

The taxi cruises to a stop and I pay the driver.

'Keep the change,' I say, giving him my most dazzling smile. I get zero reaction from the cabbie. Roz is attractive in her own way but she is not a Madeline or a Lucy. I very much doubt I'm going to be beating them off with a stick this evening.

The bouncers open the door and step aside, allowing me to pass. There has to be a ten-inch gap between me and the tattooed guy working the door, obviously he doesn't feel the need to squash his body against mine as I enter. The bar is mostly empty. I order a large dry white wine which arrives in the usual glass bucket. I pay the young man behind the bar but he's too busy checking out the dolly birds at the other side of the room to even notice me. My favourite table is free. I saunter over and slide up onto the stool.

The place is quiet, not full of the usual pissed-up parties. It looks a little sad. I sip my wine as a rowdy group of men fall through the door.

'You're okay so long as you behave yourselves, lads,' the bouncer tells them as they troop past him. *Now this is more like it.*

I raise my glass and gaze into the camera in the corner. *Cheers.* I wonder who will eventually see this and freak out. My skin tingles. I glance over to the crowd who have just walked in. A couple of them are looking over. I bat my eyelashes and look away. I take a glug and drain half the glass, the wine tastes so good. One of the men walks straight up to me.

'You on your own, love?'

'Looks like it.' I smile.

'Only I couldn't see another drink on the table so I figured you might be. Or maybe you're waiting for someone?' He turns his head in the direction of his mates and smiles. He has perfect white teeth. He's older than the others, maybe mid-thirties, and in good shape.

'You always so observant?'

'Most of the time, especially where a pretty woman is involved.'

I blush at the compliment, this is turning out better than I thought. He is ruggedly handsome with short cropped hair, wearing a tight-fitting T-shirt. His hands have the appearance of someone who does manual labour, strong and hard. The third finger on his left hand is naked.

'I think your friends want you.' I nod my head in the direction of the six manic faces smiling back.

'They are fine without me for a while. What's your name?'

'You can call me Roz.' I pick up my glass and drain it down in one. He's not slow to pick up the signal.

'Can I buy you a drink?'

'Yes, that would be good, thanks.' His face lights up like he's just had a treble come up on the dogs. 'I need to go outside to make a call. It's noisy in here.'

'They do make a racket when they're out.' He gestures to his friends who have lost interest in smiling in our direction. 'Dry white wine, am I right?'

'Thank you.' He turns and walks to the bar, his mates jeer as he approaches.

I remove a tissue from my pocket and wipe down the glass. Then I slide from the stool, gather up my bag and walk to the door. He watches me as I leave. I stand on the edge of the pavement and hold my hand aloft. The taxi breaks hard and swings around in the road. I step into the vehicle.

'The Alexander Hotel please.' The cab speeds away.

I sit back into the seat and smile, mulling over the ruggedly handsome man waiting at the table for me to come back. I chuckle to myself as I think of him wondering what the hell he was going to do with a large glass of dry white wine. His mates were going to take the piss out of him something chronic. It would have been too easy to select him, and anyway that's not the plan. I might have DI Roz Kray tied up in my basement, which is a shocking development, but I'm not going to abandon months of planning altogether.

The cabbie pulls up and I hand over five pounds. I step out and a man in a pantomime costume of top hat and tails opens a massive glass door for me to enter. The hotel is pretty basic but has delusions way above its three AA-star rating. I hang a left past reception into the bar. It's all chrome and glass with a massive silver ice bucket sat on a central stand with the necks of Champagne bottles standing proud. At the far end there is a sign discretely placed at the entrance to a second bar. I offer my ticket to the woman at the door and she hands me something in return. I walk in.

In stark contrast, this bar is more like a state room with wooden panelling around the walls and cut-glass light fittings adorning the ceiling. The place is full of smartly dressed men and equally glamorous women. My shimmering dress of emerald green was wasted in the Purple Parrot, but I fit in perfectly here. I am a week earlier than planned, but the unexpected visit of a certain DI forced me to change the day.

I order a wine at the bar, and it arrives in a delicately ornate glass - no fish bowls to be had here. There was a time when the Alexander had a growing reputation as a pickup joint, then a bright spark worked out they could make a good living out of it. The man next to me introduces himself.

'Hi, I'm Chris Dodd, with a double D.' He winks and points to his name badge pinned to his lapel. He has slicked back hair and wears his forty-odd years well. His eyes crease around the edges when he smiles. But when he does, all I can see is a sleazy twat who's only here for one thing. I like him already.

'Oh hi, I'm Roz.' I offer my hand and he takes it in a wet fish handshake. 'I haven't …' I hold up my badge, pointing my name in his direction. 'I didn't want to put holes in my dress.'

He laughs. 'I can understand that. It's a pretty dress.'

'Thank you.'

'Do you live—' He's interrupted by an elegant woman striking her glass with a silver tea spoon.

'If I could have your attention please, ladies and gentlemen. Welcome to the Hotel Alexander and welcome to our Matchmaker event. My name is Rachel, I will be your host for this evening and I'm sure you're going to have a fantastic time tonight.'

Dodd smiles and touches my arm.

He's perfect.

'Let me explain how this evening is going to work. Each of you gorgeous women have been allocated a table number and you *stunning* looking men ...' The theatrical Rachel emphasised the word stunning and wiped a hand across her brow, the women whooping in appreciation. 'As I was saying, you *stunning* looking men have a schedule of names, you will sit with each lady in turn according to your list. You have five minutes to find out as much about one another as you can, then when I blow my whistle ...' Rachel blew it just in case no fucker knew what a whistle sounded like, 'the men will move around to the next lovely lady. I'm sorry but tonight you men do all the work, am I right, ladies?' The women whooped again.

'No change there then,' Dodd piped up, prompting murmured appreciation from the blokes.

What a wanker. He is absolutely perfect.

'Thank you for that.' Rachel was positively gushing. 'You both score each other out of ten and at the end of the night we will collect your papers and match you up depending on your preferences. We will contact you tomorrow with the outcome and then the rest is up to you. Is everybody clear?'

There was a general nodding of heads.

'Of course, if during the evening you should feel that mutual spark of attraction ... well you don't have to wait for us to contact you, if you know what I mean.' Rachel dipped at the knees to emphasise the sauciness of the comment. 'Now, do you all want to get to know each other?' She looked like she was about to die from over acting. The group mumbled their approval. 'So, if everyone has a drink, we will make a start.' Rachel flounced off waving her arms in the air like she was casting a spell.

Fucking hell I bet she's hard work. I take up my spot at table fifteen.

I feel a hand on my shoulder; it's Dodd. 'See you in a little while.'

'Yes you will, Chris, yes you will.'

Chapter 60

Kray's head was dropping like a nodding dog on the back shelf of a car. The sedative was still in her system and waves of exhaustion washed over her. She fought to stay awake but she was losing the battle. She had to stay alert, she had to think her way out of this, but her head was foggy and her body ached. Her wrists were streaked red raw from tugging and grating them against the plastic ties. It was no good, they were locked firm around the eye bolt.

She felt woozy and lowered herself over onto her side. Maybe if she just closed her eyes for a second, just enough to clear her mind. Then she could ... The drug took hold once more and Kray was asleep in seconds.

Strickland's face filled her dreams, it was a face she knew, from way back. She remembered it was a warm night in August, she could recall it vividly because nights like that are so few and far between. There was a house party that had spilled onto the road. The station had taken a deluge of calls from residents complaining of noise and anti-social behaviour. Bottles were being smashed on the road and there were accounts of drug taking. It was all hands on deck.

Kray was in the area working on another case and went along in support. Brownlow was there too. He was barking orders and strutting around like an SS officer on steroids. In her dream Kray could see herself arriving at the property. Two police cars were blocking the road with their lights flashing - it was all kicking off. There were men and women running away, while others stood their ground to yell at the police. She entered the house and could see a young man sitting passively in the corner with his arms folded across his chest. People were being corralled into the living room while the police conducted a search of the premises.

Kray could see herself pushing open the door to the downstairs bathroom to find a ball of coke, neatly wrapped in cling film, floating in the toilet. She fished it out and held it in her hand. She was about to hand it over to the officer in charge when the passive lad caught sight of her and went berserk. He flew into a rage, screaming at her from across the room, something about being an evil bitch. She could see his face contorted and spitting insults.

It was Strickland.

Tavener was flicking through the private tabs on the Boston Magic website. He was not a happy copper. They had worked on this before and had gleaned as much intel from the site as they could. The results were properly documented but for some reason it had to be done again. The investigation was treading water and going nowhere. It was another late shift for everyone. Quade had made it clear that they all had to make their apologies to their families because they weren't going to see much of them until this was over.

The other reason his frustration was boiling over was because he hadn't heard from Kray since he saw her at her house. He had called her mobile several times and had dropped by her place with another bottle of wine. But there was no one home and her phone was switched off. He didn't know what he'd done wrong but it looked like it was serious shit.

Brownlow marched into the incident room. 'Right, listen up, I want someone to go and calm down the manager of the Purple Parrot. Ever since his place was implicated in the Gorgon killings he's been like Jodrell Bank looking out for single white females drinking on their own. It would appear he's had another one and is completely flipping out. He's talking about involving the press because we're not interested. So who—'

'I'm on it.' Tavener closed his laptop and slung on his jacket. Even a trip out to the Purple Parrot was better than this.

The whistle sounded to signify the end of the dating round and the guy opposite leaned back in his chair. He was a nice enough chap, whose wife had left him for a younger model and was now ready to find love again. It was a sad story, far too sad for it to be him. I scored him a nine.

No sooner than the chair was vacant Chris Dodd was sat in it, leaning forwards with his elbows on the table. 'Well, how have you got on?'

'Okay I suppose. How about you?'

'Okay, there a few interesting women here but I'm not really sure. Do you know what I mean?'

'I do, Chris, but I reckon things are about to get a lot more interesting from here on in.' I smiled and sipped my wine maintaining eye contact.

'Me too.'

'Right is everyone ready?' asked Rachel. She blew her whistle. 'Off we go!'

Fuck she's annoying.

'So, tell me about Roz?' Chris was fast off the mark.

'I'm thirty-five, widowed, I own my own home, have a responsible job and I'm fed up of fucking waiting.'

Dodd's eyes widened, I can only presume his other speed dates had taken a different tack with their opening line.

'Oh eh ...' He was lost for words. 'Waiting for what?'

'A man.'

'A man,' he repeated. His face was an absolute picture.

'Yes, a man.'

'A man for what? A man in your life? Or a man to do your garden? What?'

'Do I have to draw you a diagram, Chris?'

His mouth gaped open. Then he swallowed hard.

'Oh, I see.'

'The other men here are okay but that's not what I'm after. I'm not interested in an evening where we waste time having cocktails followed by a starter. I want to dive straight into the main course. You know what I mean, Chris?'

'I do, I do indeed.' He was regaining his cocky composure by the second. 'I like diving straight into the main course as well. Cocktails and starters are overrated.' He slides his hand across the table and touches his little finger against mine.

'So, what do we do next, Chris Dodd, with a double D?' I rub my foot against his under the table.

'I don't know, what do you suggest?'

'How about we stop fucking about scoring each other out of ten and we go to a place where we can fuck about for real.'

'That sounds like a plan. I'll buy a bottle of wine to take with us.'

I get up and place my name badge on the table.

'Where are you going?'

'To get a taxi.'

'But she's not blown the whistle yet.'

'Go on Chris, live dangerously.' I slink out of the bar avoiding eye contact with anyone. I can see Rachel make a move towards me as I head for the exit. Dodd scurries along behind. If only women realised how easy this game was to play. I mean, blokes would fuck a ring doughnut if you laid it on a plate for them.

Tavener pushed his way through the knot of people drinking at the bar. He asked to see the manager, but before the woman could answer he felt a tug on his jacket.

'Where the hell have you lot been?' This guy had a nose for coppers. 'I called ages ago. She's gone now.'

'Okay sir, is there somewhere we can go to talk?' The man beetled off through the crowd and Tavener followed. They went through a door, and up a flight of stairs to a scruffy office with papers strewn over the floor. 'Come in and excuse the mess, it's month end.'

Tavener suspected the room was likely to be in the same state whatever the day.

'You called the station, sir, and reported a woman behaving suspiciously?'

'I did. Ever since you guys tipped us off about those poor women we've been on the lookout. I can't afford to get a bad reputation around here, we need all the trade we can pack in and if people start staying away, the brewery will kick my arse.'

'What did you see?'

'She was sat at that table, the one you lot are always on about. She was on her own, then a bloke came up to speak to her and she left. He was pretty pissed off, he'd bought her a drink or something.'

'Do you have her on your CCTV?'

'Yes that's why I brought you up here.' He pointed to the fourteen-inch monitor bolted to the wall in the corner, with the screen split into four. 'It's the one at the top left.' He picked up a remote control and wound the footage backwards. Tavener sat patiently watching the footage, the manager cursed under his breath. 'This just goes to show how long ago I called you,' he said. Tavener smiled an apology.

'There, there she is. I'm telling you she was acting weird.'

Tavener squinted at the screen, the image was flickering and the resolution was poor.

'Let me.' He took the remote and jabbed at the buttons. The film moved backwards and forwards in time. Then he hit pause. His stomach fell through the floor.

The drive back to the station was a blur. He spoke to the team who run the imaging suite and told them to clear their workload. He had something important to process, something vital to the investigation.

They did as they were told, they had the memory stick and it was all systems go. Then, thirty minutes later it was all systems stop. Tavener had run headlong into a brick wall called DI Brownlow.

'So what? So what if Roz is having a drink in a pub? I fail to see why we should jump around.' Brownlow was delighted that Tavener had managed to diffuse the pub manager but was less than impressed with what he had brought back with him.

The freeze frame on the screen showed Kray sat at a high table looking into the CCTV camera with a glass of wine in her hand. She had a look on her face that said *Cheers.*

'You of all people should know she can get a little intense about things. She was probably retracing Gorgon's steps to see if her famous 'coppers' intuition' whispered anything in her ear.' Tavener bristled at the slight. 'Have you tried to call her?'

'Yeah a number of times and I've been to her place but she's not there.'

'Maybe she's taking the opportunity to slide off the grid for a while. I wouldn't worry about it if I were you, she can be hot headed when she wants to be.'

'But I am worried, this is not like her.'

'Okay let's take a step back. You think this is Gorgon impersonating Roz, right?'

'Yes that's a possibility.'

'Let's step through what we know. We know he selected women from their pictures on the Boston website. Is Roz featured on that site?'

'No, she isn't. But you have to admit she has the same facial characteristics as Madeline and Lucy.'

'Yes, and in Roz's case those characteristics are ten years older than the other victims – at least! She doesn't fit the profile. The other thing we know is Gorgon calls the victim's place of work to report them as sick. Have we had a call about Roz?'

Tavener shook his head, admitting defeat.

'No, you're barking up the wrong tree, Duncan.' Brownlow pointed at the screen. 'This is Roz having a glass of wine in a bar, trying to put the past week behind her.'

'But if she was going to do that, this is the last place she'd go.'

'How do you mean?'

'I got the distinct impression from her that she wouldn't be seen dead drinking in the Purple Parrot.' Tavener regretted his choice of words as soon as they left his mouth.

Chapter 61

I step out onto the pavement and pay the driver through the open window.

'Are you alright, mate?' the cabbie asks, swivelling around and resting his forearm on the back of the seat. Dodd is rolling about in the back trying to get out of the car. I reach inside to take his arm and haul him towards the door.

'He's fine, just a little too much to drink that's all. Come on, babe, let's get you home.' I try to make light of the situation.

The driver shakes his head. 'If I'd have known he was that pissed-up, love, I would not have picked you up.'

'I know, I'm sorry. He doesn't travel well in the back of cars either. It's a combination of too much drink and the journey home.' I grab hold of his arm and yank him through the passenger door, heaving him onto his feet. My arm wraps tightly around his waist to keep him upright. 'Thank you, bye!' I close the door and we stagger down the road. I can see the driver watching us – he's not buying it. I stop, rummage through my bag and bring out a set of keys. The front gate creaks open and we stand in the porch. The cabbie pulls away.

Fuck that was close.

I march Dodd back down the path and onto the road. I gave the taxi driver a false address as a sensible precaution which I am now fast regretting. My house is three streets away and with Dodd turning into a dead weight, this was going to be a challenge.

'Ish this weres you live?' he asks, waving his arm in the air.

'No, Chris, my house is a little walk away. Come on, won't be far.'

'Yous live ins a nice area.' He struggles to put one foot in front of the other.

'Come on Chris, let's get you back then we can have some fun.'

'Ooo yesh, I really want to have fun.' He makes a grab at my breast but misses and pulls the both of us into a hedge.

Fuck, this guy's tolerance is low, either that or I've seriously miscalculated.

I wanted to avoid getting him back to my place without something inside him but I may have overdone it. I persuaded him it would be a good idea to have a couple of drinks to get to know each other properly before jumping in a taxi. At the time, with most of his blood leaving his head to swell his cock, he would have agreed to anything. That gave me ample opportunity to slip a generous helping of Rohypnol into his drink to help him along. I planned to finish the job when he was safely back at my house. But at this rate he's not going to make it. Dodd is fading fast and we still have about two hundred yards to go.

We weave our way across the junction to my street. He's stopped talking now and has his head down. That's a bad sign, soon it will be lights out for Mr Dodd.

'Here we go Chris, a little bit further.' My house comes into view just as his legs give way and he lands on his knees. I stumble forwards. 'Fuck, get up you useless prick,' I snarl at him.

'Was, was is you say? Are we here yet?'

'Not far now.' I hook my arm under his and heave him to his feet.

'Oh, ish nice round here isn't it?'

'Yes it's lovely.' I pull him down the road.

'I thinks I knowsh this place.' He straightens up to look around. 'I've been here before.'

'That's good, Chris. When was that?'

'A fews years back now.' Dodd was definitely rallying. I seize the opportunity and hurry him to my door. 'Yesh it was defineshly here.'

I prop him up in the porch as I unlock the front door. He lunges at me and plants a slobbering kiss on my mouth. I shove him into the hallway.

His hands are all over me. He's made a fucking remarkable recovery for a man who fifteen minutes ago couldn't negotiate his way out of the back of a cab. His hand presses against my thigh, forcing my dress up. I grasp his hand, halting its advance.

'Another drink Chris, how do you fancy another drink?'

'Thas would be fugging great.' He laughs. 'Lead on.'

He smacks my arse as he follows me into the kitchen. Maybe a little more additive is in order.

Kray jerked herself from her sleep. There was a noise. She heard it above the humming of the freezers. It was coming from upstairs, it sounded like a door slamming shut. She struggled onto her elbow and sat up. She had no idea how long she had been out.

The sound of voices drifted down the stairs. She strained to hear. There were two voices. Kray could hear a man and a woman talking and laughing. She raised her head and yelled at the top of her voice.

'Help! Help me. I'm down here!' Her voice resonated off the walls. 'Help! Help me!'

Kray continued to scream her lungs out until her throat hurt. No one came. She could hear occasional movement coming from upstairs and caught the sound of distant voices, but most of the time it was quiet. After a while there was nothing. The semi-gloom wrapped itself around her and the hours passed.

Her body spasmed as cramps took hold of her muscles. She shifted position and slumped onto her side. The concrete floor felt cold against her cheek. Waves of exhaustion swept over her. She had to keep awake, she was desperate to remain alert. But her eyes closed and she drifted into a fitful sleep.

In her dreams Strickland was there again, his snarling face spewing insults at her from across the lounge. He was on his feet coming at her. A uniformed officer stepped in and grabbed him.

They fought. Strickland was trying to free himself from the officer's grasp, desperate to get to Kray. She could see herself standing in the doorway watching this cocky bastard spit his vile vitriol her way. *What the fuck have I ever done to you?*

The officer was at the end of his tether and wrestled him into an arm lock.

'Right that's it, you're under arrest,' he said, marching him across the lounge towards her. Kray waited until he was close, then—.

Kray was ripped from her dream by the sound of a body slamming into the concrete floor beside her.

Chapter 62

'Fucking hell!' yelled Kray as she tried to claw herself away from the shattered body lying face up on the concrete floor. The ties held her in place, cutting into her flesh. 'What the f—'

'This is Christopher Dodd, with a double D,' a voice called down the stairs. 'He's going to be staying with us for a while. Why don't you two get to know each other. I'll be down in a little while to make the formal introductions.' Strickland slammed the door and slid the bolt into place.

Kray blinked her eyes against the orange gloom. The man next to her wasn't moving. A dark halo of red seeped from beneath his head and spread out on the floor. She tried to catch her breath and stop shaking. After several minutes she was back in control. Her headache had gone and her mind was clear. Kray stared down at the man wondering if he was dead or alive. She noticed his chest rising and falling with shallow breaths, but the expanding circle around his head told her he wouldn't last long.

A wave of panic gripped her. Kray leaned forward and grasped her left hand with her right. She squeezed with all her might and pulled. The plastic cuffs slid across her skin as she mashed her hand through the loop. Then it was stuck. She clenched her teeth, crushed her left hand again and tugged for all she was worth. Pain shot up her arm as the sharp edges gouged into her skin. The harder she squeezed, and the more she pulled, the further the plastic tie slipped over her hand. Then with a huge yank she freed it from the tie. Her hand was on fire, she looked down to see flaps of skin hanging off.

Kray leaned over to Dodd and pulled him closer, patting down his pockets. Nothing. They were empty. Strickland had stripped him of his possessions before launching him down the stairs. She pulled his jacket aside and began to unbuckle his belt. She tried to pull it through the loops on his trousers, but it wouldn't budge. She tugged again but Dodd just rolled towards her. The fucking belt was too tight. She grasped the metal spigot on the buckle, working it back and forth, but it held firm. She couldn't break it off. Then she saw it, glinting against the yellow glow coming from the tank. In his lapel, Dodd was wearing a decorative pin.

Kray flipped over his collar and fumbled with the button at the back, she squeezed the wings together and it came free. She fiddled with the pin and pulled it from the material. The full damage to her hand was plain to see, a bloody mess of the flapping skin and exposed flesh.

She twisted the cable tie so the clasp was facing upwards and drove the sharp end of the pin into the locking mechanism. Her hands trembled as she felt around, trying to locate the gap between the interlocking teeth. She found it and rammed the pin home. The ratchet disengaged and she felt the tension give way. The black plastic cuff loosened around her wrist.

Before Kray could pull her right hand free she heard the bolt slide across and a shaft of light entered the basement. She pushed the belt back through the buckle to at least give it the appearance of being done up. The sound of high heels clip-clopping on the steps echoed above her. She covered her left wrist with her right hand to hide the fact the tie was no longer in place.

'How are we getting on?' Strickland asked. He reached the bottom step and flicked on the light. He was carrying a handbag in one hand and something else in the other. Kray screwed her eyes tight shut to protect her vision. 'Oh dear, Chris doesn't look well does he? Is he dead?' Kray slowly opened her eyes staring at the floor. 'I said is he dead, DI Kray?'

'I don't know,' she answered, looking up. Strickland was dressed in her shimmering green outfit, his hair and make-up a perfect match for her own face. He made his way over to Dodd, knelt down and put two fingers on his neck. 'Looks like he's still with us, but I fear not for much longer.'

'Why me and why him?'

'Ah yes, your burning questions.' He retrieved an old dining chair from the corner and set it down in front of Kray. 'I suppose given what's going to happen, there is no harm in you knowing. That's why I brought these.' He held out a photograph for Kray to look at. 'You will have seen this one while you were snooping around upstairs. It shows my mother and father on holiday. It's lovely don't you think?' Kray nodded her head. 'What it does not show is that my father was an abusive fuckwit who used me as a punch bag. But however much of a sadistic bastard he was, it was nothing compared to her.' His long fingernail pointed at his mother. 'She tortured me physically and mentally from the time I was able to understand what was going on, right up until the time I killed her. Take a look, take a close look.' He held the photograph at arm's length. Kray had one eye on the picture and the other fixed on Strickland.

'I see it,' she said.

'Look closer Roz, take particular note of the facial features. That's what the face of pure evil looks like. To the outside world my mother was a saint, especially being married to my father. But in reality, she was a malevolent bitch capable of anything. And only I could see it. I was the only one able to recognise that look – the look of pure evil. Do you know that look continues today? Vicious women wreaking their own particular brand of evil on the world and no one, not a single person, can see it but me.'

'So you take it upon yourself to kill them, for the benefit of the rest of the world?'

'Yes, but not just that. I want the world to see what these bitches are capable of, I want everyone to wake-up and see them for what they are.'

'You impersonate them and commit terrible crimes in their name, so people can see what they are truly like.'

'Got it in one, Detective Inspector. I do like working with bright people.'

'But you selected the other women from the Boston Magic website. I'm not a member of that site.'

'No, you're not.' Strickland removed a newspaper cutting from its protective cellophane wrapping and placed it on the floor in front of Kray. She peered at the picture. The headline at the top read: 'A Full House for Operation Clean Sweep'. Next to the write-up was a picture of the team, taken on the steps of the police station.

'I don't get it, I wasn't part of Clean Sweep,' she said.

'Look again.'

Kray examined the photo. On the second row, smiling at the camera, she saw her own face. Tiny triggers of memory fired off in her head.

How the fuck can that be? Then she remembered.

The force wanted to publicise its success in taking down a major drug ring in the heart of Blackpool. But the Chief had one eye on the publicity and the other on how his force was portrayed.

'Brownlow, I want more women in the shot,' barked the Chief. 'All I can see are white middle-aged men, get it sorted.' So that's what Brownlow did and why Kray ended up in the news article when she had nothing to do with the bust.

'I still don't get it?' she asked looking up into his eyes.

'No, you don't get it, but Carl Rampton did.'

Chapter 63

The very mention of his name made Kray's scars ignite, her skin burnt, she flinched.

'You see, Rampton was sent down as part of that operation and as a memento of the hatred he felt for everyone involved, he kept this article. Every night he would take it from its hiding place and swear and curse at it. That man needed revenge, he needed someone to hate. So, I gave it to him. You possess the same features of evil, Roz, and you have to die. I spotted you in the picture and convinced Rampton that you had planted evidence which got him put away. He was like putty in my hands. He wanted a target, I gave him you. When he came out he sliced you up but failed to finish the job. So that got me thinking that I should do a proper job and, while I'm at it, what about the other witches of Satan? They deserve to die as well.'

A memory went off in Kray's head like a cannon.

'By the way,' Strickland continued. 'Did you enjoy your trip to the Trafford Centre? I wanted to take my time, I wanted to be sure you were otherwise engaged and I wasn't going to be disturbed when I picked out this lovely dress. The look on that Polish woman's face was an absolute picture. I hope you appreciate the trouble I took to fuck with your head – were you late for work? It made me laugh thinking of you staring at that clock, wondering how the hell it had lost an hour. And did you enjoy finding the bodies in the dark? I thought that would add a little extra drama.'

But Kray wasn't listening. Her mind had catapulted back to the house party. It was a warm night in August, Strickland was there, he went crazy when he clapped eyes on her. He fought with a copper and was led out of the lounge. Kray stepped in front of the officer and … *Fuck!*

She was reeling, struggling to hold herself together. The final piece of this horrific jigsaw fell into place. Kray felt her stomach heave, she was going to throw up.

It was me, it was down to me after all.

Kray snapped out of her daydream to see Strickland standing by the freezers.

'To chill her blood, how so divine,

Walk in her shoes, her face is mine.'

He opened the door to reveal the black mannequin heads with chicken skin textured faces stretched across them. It took a few seconds for Kray to process what she was seeing.

'This is Madeline,' he said pointing to the top head, 'and this is Lucy. Aren't they beautiful? Say hello, girls. I hope you enjoyed discovering their bodies in the dark? I thought turning the electricity off at the mains would add to the drama.'

Kray stared at the frozen faces, her mouth gaped open. Tears streaked down her face.

'With evil dripping from your pores,

The next face I need to take … is yours.'

Kray stopped breathing, she tore her gaze away from the hacked flesh and saw the empty black frosted head sitting on the bottom shelf.

'That's right, DI Kray. The last one is for you.'

Kray shook as waves of fear washed through her. A ball of vomit hit the back of her mouth. It splashed onto the floor.

'But first we need to complete the ritual. Chris Dodd, with a double D, has to die.' Strickland walked across to the shadow board and ran his hands over the tools. 'Which one do you think, Roz?'

Kray didn't know where to look. Her head snapped between the dissected skin staring at her with black frosted eyes from the confines of the freezer and Strickland selecting his weapon of choice. He had the nonchalant air of a man selecting a golf club.

'I've done the lump hammer and the screwdriver already, umm, how about this?' He lifted a wood chisel from the board and weighed it in his hands. 'It doesn't matter that events are happening in a different sequence. Normally your face would be with the others by now, and then we would have the pleasure of despatching dear old Chris. I say *we* because of course to the outside world it would be you watching the life die from his eyes. But with you turning up unannounced, my plans had to be amended. I can live with that.'

Kray shuddered as she watched a version of herself toy with the chisel.

Strickland walked to where Kray was sitting and held out the tool. 'What do you think?'

'Don't.'

'Oh, but I have to.'

He knelt beside the stricken figure lying on the floor and tilted Dodd's head from side to side. 'Which jugular vein do you prefer, right or left?'

'Don't kill him.'

'I don't mind changing my plan, but I'm not going to ditch it altogether.'

'Let me do it.'

'What?' Strickland stopped in his tracks. 'Why would you want to do that?'

'I kill him and you let me go.'

'I ask again, why would you want to do that?'

'Because then people would see how evil I am for real. It would not be pretend, it would be a true representation of what you have known all along.'

He scraped the underside of his chin with the cutting edge of the chisel. 'That's an interesting proposal, DI Kray.'

'You want people to see evil, I will give them evil.'

'But then I would have to let you live and I *so* want to complete my set.' Strickland motioned towards the naked head at the bottom of the freezer.

'What do you want the most, another trophy or … for the whole country to finally take notice? Just imagine that, Jason, your moment of triumph at last. People would finally see the truth of what you have known all along. You would be proved right.' Kray shuffled forwards keeping her left wrist covered. 'Just think about that.'

'That is an attractive proposition.' Strickland came in close and stared Kray in the face, brandishing the weapon. 'But to do that I would need to release you. How do I know you wouldn't use this chisel on me?'

'How could I? You release one of my hands, I am still anchored to the floor. People turned a blind eye to the terrible truth for all those years and now you have the chance to be finally proved right. You were right all along. That has got to feel good, Jason. That has to be worth deviating from your plan.'

'I can see how that would work.' He got up and rummaged around in the handbag, returning with a mobile phone. 'You kill him and I record it, that way everyone can see what a cruel, sadistic bitch you are.'

'You would be proved right Jason, just think how that would feel.'

'I like this. I like this a lot.'

'Give me the chisel Jason, and I will take this innocent man's life to save my own.'

'This is good.' Strickland moved forward with the tool outstretched.

Kray struggled against the ties. 'You will have to release one of my hands, Jason. I can't kill him if my hands are bound.'

Strickland gazed into Kray's eyes and his face hardened. 'You must think I was fucking born yesterday. You evil bitch!' He grasped the chisel with both hands and raised it above his head.

Chapter 64

Kray lunged forward and smashed her fist into Strickland's throat with every ounce of strength she had left. The blow sent the chisel spinning into the air and he staggered backwards clutching his shattered larynx. Kray felt a searing pain in her hand as the pin impaled itself into her palm. She ripped her right hand free from the loosened tie, dug the metal pin out of her hand and stabbed it into the cable tie looped around her ankle. The point wouldn't locate properly between the teeth.

Strickland lurched around choking and coughing. His eyes bulged from their sockets as he tried to suck air into his lungs. He toppled back and fell hard against the shadow board.

Kray forced the pin between the plastic teeth and the tie sprung open. She tore her right foot free and jabbed the point into the final lock.

The shadow board came away from the wall in slow motion, tipping forwards under the weight of the tools. It fell against the tank, shattering the glass. Strickland was kneeling on the floor with his head bent forward, clutching at his throat. His face was turning purple.

Kray fumbled around trying to open the last of the ties. The fucking thing wouldn't budge.

The flat copper coloured head of Sampson glided through the gap in the broken glass. As Kray noticed the snake for the first time, her jaw dropped open. Sampson lowered himself to the ground, his tongue darting out, tasting the strange new molecules in the air.

The pin was stuck in the mechanism, Kray's fingers clawed at it but couldn't dig it out.

Sampson dropped to the floor and headed straight for Kray. She froze. Her eyes flicked between watching Strickland regaining his breath and the snake advancing towards her.

Kray could hear her heart pounding in her chest. The snake was only feet away. She tensed her body and kept absolutely still. The snake glided over her captive leg, over the back of her hand and back onto the floor. He paused when he encountered Dodd lying on the floor but he wasn't interested. He doubled back on himself.

Strickland was on his feet. Kray could hear a gurgled rasping sound as he tried to suck air into his lungs. He saw the broken glass and freaked out. Sampson was heading his way. He stumbled across the room to reach his snake rod and calliper. The snake wound itself into a coil, adopting his terrifying S-shape. Strickland crashed around looking for his tools.

Sampson struck.

His deadly fangs sunk into Strickland's thigh and he let out a scream. He tried to grab the snake, but Sampson disengaged and struck again, latching onto his arm. Strickland whirled around trying to shake him off but the fangs held tight, sinking deep into his flesh. Then as fast as it had happened Sampson let go and slithered off into the corner.

Kray jolted herself into action. She yanked the pin from the lock and rammed it back in, this time the ratchet disengaged. She was free.

Strickland collapsed on the floor holding his leg. Kray leapt to her feet and launched herself at him, punching and kicking for all she was worth. He was in shock and couldn't comprehend what was happening. Kray kicked him twice in the head and landed him a heavy blow full to the face. Strickland keeled over and went limp.

Kray backed away to the other side of the room and looked under the tank to see Sampson coiled up in the corner, watching the proceedings.

So that's what one looks like. She unfurled Dodd's belt from his trousers then placed her fingers on his neck. He was gone.

Kray dragged Strickland across to the other side of the room and rolled him onto his front. He was groaning and regaining consciousness. She wound the belt tight around his wrists and secured them behind his back. She slumped to the floor, exhausted.

Strickland flicked open his eyes. His cheekbone was swelling and turning black. He rolled over onto his back.

'I need a hospital,' he croaked through broken lips. 'I've been bitten.'

Kray observed him from a safe distance.

'He doesn't like you, does he?' she said.

'Call 999, tell them I've been injected with the venom from—'

'A Russell's Viper,' Kray interrupted.

'How do you ...'

'I just do.'

Kray leaned over and kicked the freezer door shut.

'Please, I need anti-venom. I can feel the bites starting to burn, I don't have long.'

Kray wasn't listening. She was remembering being angry, walking down the Promenade. Joe was in the car yelling for her to stop. She could see the blade as it sliced through her clothes, tearing through her flesh. Then Rampton was in mid-air being propelled backwards by Joe. They landed on the pavement with a splat. The knife was sticking out of Joe. The blood ... there was so much blood. Then she saw the house party, Strickland was being manhandled out of the room. She stepped in front of them and ...

'Kray!' Strickland shouted, forcing himself into a sitting position. 'Listen to me, you have to call 999, you cannot leave me to die from a snake bite. You are a police officer, remember that. First and foremost, do your duty.'

Kray snapped out of her thoughts. 'You're right. I can't leave you to die from a snake bite.' She got to her feet, picked up the chisel and plunged it into his neck.

Chapter 65

'Self-defence. The internal investigation came back with a verdict of self-defence. Mind you, this was against a man who kept the faces of two dead women in his freezer, had a dead man in his basement and a venomous snake in a fish tank. I didn't need to pull off an Oscar winning performance to convince them, the decision kind of made itself. I did have to untie his hands before they arrived though – would have been a bit of a giveaway.'

The morning sun felt cool and she stamped her feet on the ground to dislodge the grass that had stuck to her shoes. She took the top off a bottle of water and poured it into the vase of freshly cut roses. She was putting on a brave face. This was her first visit since her encounter with Strickland. Kray was trying to hold it together.

'I'm still suspended from duty. It's been five weeks now but that doesn't matter, I could do with the time off to be honest.' She crouched down to arrange the flowers and took a cloth from her bag to wipe the grime from the stone. Tears ran down her cheeks.

She dug into her pocket and brought out the pin from Dodd's lapel. 'I brought you a present, this saved my life. A man I never knew gifted this to me. It saved me.' She placed the pin on the headstone. It burned yellow in the sunshine.

She could put it off no longer.

'I have to tell you something and you're not going to like it. I didn't kill Strickland out of vengeance. I should have done, but I didn't. After all, he was the one who convinced Rampton I was the devil incarnate and you died trying to save me. I think you would understand me killing him to avenge your death, but I didn't. I killed him out of guilt.' She began to sob, her shoulders rocked back and forth. She steadied herself by gripping the stone with both hands.

'You died because of me. You died because of a moment of madness. I attended a house party, it had got out of hand and loads of coppers were there. I found a ball of heroin in the toilet and fished it out. There was this guy screaming at me, calling me an evil bitch and going crazy. Turns out it was Strickland. An officer bundled him out when it looked like he was going to turn violent. He was a nasty piece of work and kept screaming at me. I lost my cool. When he was being frogmarched out of the house I stepped into his path and crashed into him. And … and …' The words dried in the back of her mouth. 'I slipped the drugs into his jacket pocket.'

She leaned forward and rested her forehead against the marble.

'Can you fucking believe it? I shoved them in his pocket! I did it to teach the little bastard a lesson, that's all. He was charged with possession with the intention to supply and ended up in prison with Rampton. He was there on remand and got off with it before it went to trial. It was all for nothing!

'The only reason Rampton was locked up with Strickland was because of me. The reason you are dead is because of me.'

Kray crumpled against the headstone, sobbing. She struggled to catch her breath. The recurring dream sequence that had relentlessly played in her mind over the past month pounded in her head.

It was always the same.

Joe was cooking a meal in their kitchen. It felt like summer. They were warm and the sun spilled through the window splashing sunlight across the worktops. The BBQ was on and he was putting the finishing touches to a salad. He had that rolling chopping action going on, the one that shreds the vegetables really thin. They were both drinking beer.

Joe looked across at her. 'We can have dinner whenever you're ready, Roz. I have all the time in the world to cook dinner. When you're ready, Roz, when you're ready.'

Roz drew the chef's knife from her bag. It glinted in the sun. 'I'm ready now.'

The blade felt cold against her wrist. The sharp edge scored her skin.

'I want to see you but not in my dreams, I want to touch you but not in my thoughts. I've had enough of just being me, when all the best times I've ever had in my fucked-up life have been about us.'

She dragged the blade across her skin. Beads of blood broke the surface.

'It's fucking hard, you know, being one half of a jigsaw to find that the best part is missing. The part that makes everything else right. When it's gone, nothing makes sense. I'm not sure I can live with myself, knowing what I know.'

She rocked the blade backwards and forwards. More blood broke through her skin.

'What am I supposed to do!' She tore her gaze away from the rivulets of blood tracking down her wrist. The pin was glowing gold in the sun.

'You gave me this, didn't you?' Kray picked up the pin, spinning it between her fingers. 'You sent that man to me. You made Strickland select him out of the hundreds of men that evening. You wanted me to live.' She held the pin in one hand and the chef's knife in the other. 'If I choose one you can cook for me for ever, if I choose the other - who knows? Help me choose. Help me ...'

The sun was as overhead as it gets in a holiday resort on the west coast of England. Kray walked down the hill feeling the warmth against her back. The knife was tucked away in her bag. The brass pin lay on top of the headstone. Her feet were covered in wet grass cuttings, and for the first time ever, it didn't seem to matter.

Acknowledgements

I want to thank all those who have made this book possible – My family Karen, Gemma, Holly and Maureen for their encouragement and endless patience. To my fantastic proofreaders Nicki, Jackie, Simon, Caroline and Sharon who didn't hold back with their comments and feedback. I'm a lucky boy to have them in my corner.

I would also like to thank my wider circle of family and friends for their fantastic support and endless supply of helpful suggestions. Not all of which are suitable to repeat here.